THE
First

Six Weeks
OF
School

2ND EDITION

From Responsive Classroom®

ISBN: 978-1-892989-81-9
Library of Congress Control Number: 2014958331

Cover and book design by Helen Merena
Photographs © Alice Projansky and Jeff Woodward. All rights reserved.

Center for Responsive Schools, Inc.
85 Avenue A, P.O. Box 718
Turners Falls, MA 01376-0718

800-360-6332
www.responsiveclassroom.org

Fourth printing 2017

PUBLISHER'S ACKNOWLEDGMENTS

Although this book contains the collective wisdom of countless educators who have collaborated over thirty-plus years to develop and continually refine the *Responsive Classroom* approach to teaching, three individuals deserve special recognition: Roxann Kriete, Paula Denton, and Mike Anderson.

Roxann Kriete and **Paula Denton** wrote the first edition of this book. They gathered the many pieces and strands of advice about start-of-year foundation setting that *Responsive Classroom* program developers had formulated to date, broke them down into specific steps for each of the first six weeks of school, and articulated everything in clear, engaging language that spoke to all teachers. The book went on to become one of the most respected publications in the education world, selling 200,000 copies since its debut in 2000 and changing the lives of a generation of teachers and students.

Mike Anderson, who has over twenty years of experience teaching children and adults as an elementary school teacher, *Responsive Classroom* consultant, and *Responsive Classroom* program developer, crafted the second edition of this well-loved book. His charge was to build upon the success of the first edition by bringing in the latest articulations of *Responsive Classroom* practices and fresh examples of these practices being used in today's classrooms.

In fulfilling this challenge, Mike brought his decades of teaching and consulting experience to bear. He combined his own insights with those of many *Responsive Classroom* colleagues. The result is a book filled with practical strategies that are both time-tested and up-to-date, at once familiar and fresh, preserving the best of the original edition while ushering in important new features. Mike has created a new edition that will transform another generation of teachers and students.

To Roxann Kriete, Paula Denton, and Mike Anderson, Center for Responsive Schools is deeply grateful.

Center for Responsive Schools would also like to express appreciation to the following people for their involvement in the creation of this book: Jim Brissette, Sarah Fillion, Mary Beth Forton, Courtney Fox, Babs Freeman-Loftis, Suzy Ghosh, Trisha Hall, Cathy Hess, Julia Luteran, Lynn Majewski, Caitie Meehan, Helen Merena, Elizabeth Nash, Kerry O'Grady, Diana Pelletier, Carolyn Rottman, Jill Samuels, Marc Swygert, Cory Wade, Margaret Berry Wilson, and Alice Yang.

CONTENTS

The Promise of a New Year

There's something fresh and exciting about a new school year—a sense of boundless optimism and crisp new beginnings. And every year, the first six weeks present us with a wonderful opportunity to help students transition smoothly back into school routines and start to connect with each other. It's an ideal time to begin showing them that school is a safe place, that they're important members of the classroom and school communities, and that they can look forward to an engaging, challenging, and fun year of learning.

Now let's leap ahead from those early weeks of school to a cold January afternoon and peek inside a classroom. Ms. Lopez's third grade room is warm and cozy. Except for a minor bump here and there, the day has gone smoothly. Students have been immersed in their learning and enjoying being at school together. For the last forty-five minutes, they've been working industriously on various projects. In one corner, four students are huddled on the floor creating a mural of key scenes from the book they've read together. Nearby, another small group is reviewing science books, noting topics they'd like to research.

Other students are scattered around the room, some writing poems, others finishing math assignments. Ms. Lopez sits at a table working on math with a few students at a time. Every five to ten minutes, she calls a small group over for a short check-in and some coaching on the fractions unit they're working on as a class.

Although this mid-year school day may seem too good to be true, for this class it's actually the norm rather than the exception. We might conclude that Ms. Lopez doesn't have to work hard at teaching, that she's one of those rare intuitive educators with a powerful and entirely natural ability to teach well. In truth, she does not consider herself a gifted teacher. She remembers all too well her first few years in the classroom, when she struggled with basic classroom management and questioned whether she could stay in the profession.

Over the years, though, she's worked to develop a skill set—a collection of ideas and practices—that she begins using during the first days of each school year to create a solid foundation for her students' learning. Had we looked into her classroom then, we'd have seen her using that skill set to establish classroom routines, set expectations, nurture positive relationships, and develop a sense of shared purpose. On that foundation (and using the same skill set), she then builds a learning environment that's safe, joyful, and rigorous, one where all students, regardless of their strengths and challenges, can thrive.

The Responsive Classroom® *Approach*

In the following chapters, you'll find guidance to help you do that critical early foundation-building. You'll learn practical ways to teach children essential skills, incorporate fun activities into their learning, structure the day, teach discipline, build academic engagement, and more. These suggestions can work in any school setting and with any curriculum, and all are based on the *Responsive Classroom* approach to teaching.

Responsive Classroom is an evidence-based way of teaching that offers practical strategies for bringing together social-emotional and academic learning throughout the day. The approach is associated with greater teacher effectiveness, higher student achievement, and improved school climate. Since 1981, the *Responsive Classroom* approach has provided teachers like Ms. Lopez with the resources to develop skills in four areas of teaching:

- Offering engaging academics

- Building a positive community

- Effectively managing the classroom

- Matching instruction to students' developmental strengths and needs

The strategies and ideas in this book will help you hone your skills in each of these four key areas—no matter your level of familiarity with *Responsive Classroom* ideas and practices.

Goals for the First Six Weeks

As you guide each year's class through the early weeks of school, four overarching goals are to: 1) create a climate of warmth, inclusion, and safety; 2) teach classroom routines and behavior expectations; 3) help students get to know and care for the classroom and school environment; and 4) establish expectations for academic work. Here's a bit more information about each of the goals.

1. ***Create a climate of warmth, inclusion, and safety.*** To build the trust essential for learning, students need to know one another (and us) and develop a sense of belonging and significance in the classroom. Students also need to know that we will set reasonable boundaries for behavior, and exercise vigilance and sound judgment to ensure that everyone is included and safe.

2. ***Teach classroom routines and behavior expectations.*** For students to do well from the start, a sense of order and predictability in daily school life is critical. It enables them to relax, focus their energy on learning, and feel competent. During the first few weeks, we identify global expectations for the year: students will take care of themselves, each other, and their classroom and school.

3. ***Help students get to know and care for the classroom and school environment.*** To feel a sense of ownership of the school and classroom, students must have some time to become familiar and comfortable with them. We carefully teach children the appropriate and creative use of materials, develop guidelines about sharing resources, and teach children how to take care of their school environment.

4. *Establish expectations for academic work.* We want to generate excitement and enthusiasm for the curriculum students will engage in this year. Starting on the first day of school, we teach active participation and focused effort, thoughtful conversation, cooperation, and collaboration. We pay attention to the process as well as the products of students' learning and hold high expectations in both areas.

Although the first six weeks of school are a distinct, critical time for meeting these four goals, there's nothing exact or magical about the number six. Sometimes a class accomplishes the goals in less time; sometimes it takes a bit longer. In general, though, the six-week timeframe makes sense for most teachers and students. Meeting these goals through effective and joyful teaching, no matter the grade or curriculum you teach, is what this book is all about.

Getting the Most From This Book

This book divides the first six weeks of school into five time periods: the first day of school, the rest of week one; week two; week three; and weeks four through six. For each grade range (K–2, 3–4, 5–6), each time period leads off with a concise list of teaching goals and an overview of key experiences it's important for all students at all grade levels to have during that time period. In week one, for example, a central goal is for all students to explore key academic supplies such as books and science equipment.

After reading the goals and overview for the time period, you'll be ready to dive into the strategies that will help you accomplish the goals for your grade range. Use the color coding to quickly find the grade ranges you want: gray for all grades; blue for K–2; orange for 3–4; and teal for 5–6.

The strategies are organized as follows:

- ***Sample Schedules*** provide ideas for balancing academics with social-emotional learning and active times with quiet ones. You can use these schedules as is or adapt them to fit students' needs and any school or district requirements.

- ***The Flow of the Day*** offers key routines and tips for Morning Meeting, recess, lunch, quiet time, closing circle, and more.

- **Teaching Academics** helps you set up rigorous and engaging academics to meet your students' needs and abilities.

- **Teaching Discipline** shows you how to establish rules and expectations for students and teach them positive behavior.

In addition, check the appendices for the following helpful information:

- **Key Practices**—brief explanations of the *Responsive Classroom* practices discussed throughout the book.

- **Activities**—descriptions of the energizers and the Morning Meeting and closing circle activities mentioned in the book, as well as ideas for interactive learning structures.

- **Read-Alouds**—sources of favorite read-alouds that work especially well during the early weeks of school.

- **Special Situations**—tips on having a guest (substitute) teacher, welcoming a new student, and preparing for indoor recess and field trips.

I hope this book will help you make this a highly fruitful time of year. Think of your efforts during the first six weeks of school as a worthwhile investment—one that will pay off richly all year long!

First Day of School

Goals for All Grades

This chapter provides a range of ideas and tips to serve as starting points as you plan for what is arguably the most important day of school. Regardless of the grade level you teach, these key first-day goals benefit all students. On the first day of school, our goal is for every student to:

- ***Feel a sense of belonging and significance throughout the day,*** understanding that they matter and have an important place in the newly forming learning community. They'll feel safe and enjoy their first day.

- ***Start to learn classmate's names*** and begin to connect with each other. Building social connections on the first day is the first step in ensuring that students feel included in the community.

- ***Learn and practice a few key routines*** needed for a successful first day of school—and for every day that follows.

- ***Experience a sense of excitement and competence about the academic work and learning ahead.*** Starting the first day of school with engaging academics helps students stay motivated all year long.

Overview for All Grades

When I prepare for the start of school, I review my class list and picture students walking through the door that first morning. Arranging tables, bookcases, and supply bins helps me envision students working on science projects, doing math activities, painting, practicing a class play, and having peer literacy conferences. Even taking plastic covers off computers and wiping shelves builds my sense of anticipation.

Along with my enthusiasm, there's anxiety mixed in as well. There's so much to do that it can feel overwhelming. So as the start of school nears, I'm always reminding myself to keep things simple and focus on what's most important:

"I've learned that people will forget what you said, people will forget what you did, but people will never forget how you made them feel."

— MAYA ANGELOU

9

All the effort we put into this day will indeed make a difference, helping children to feel safe and welcomed. And when they get home and talk about their first day with parents and other caring adults, it will be *how they felt* on this day that will shape their stories and go a long way toward ensuring their success in school this year. Did they feel that their teacher already knows them a bit? Did they enjoy talking with classmates? Were lunch and recess fun? Did they feel engaged with their learning?

Preparing for the First Day

During the summer, I have to overcome my tendency to overdo it and plan out the entire school year. So a few days before the start of school, I give myself permission to focus just on preparing for the first day.

Setting Up the Classroom

Given how excited I am about all we'll be doing together in the coming year, it's tempting to cover the walls with posters of ancient pyramids, writing workshop protocols, number lines, and grammar tips, and to pack shelves with interlocking cubes, dice, cards, games, magnifying glasses, and paints. But it's important to remember that all this isn't needed on the first day. In fact, a classroom that already looks in full swing on day one can be disorienting. A room that's tidy and inviting, with open wall space and shelves, can feel more welcoming to students.

Furniture—To set the stage for collaborative work, consider arranging tables (or clusters of desks) so students can sit in small groups. To relieve anxiety about seating on the first day, I designate seats. I also set out table-tent cards, giving each table a color name, to provide a quick way to call up students and to group and regroup them as needed ("Mia, John, Alex, and Denesia—head to the yellow table").

Then at each table I set out crayons and colored pencils for the students' first activity: decorating name tags. Since I haven't yet introduced students to crayons or colored pencils, we use ones left over from last year. Once we've explored these materials more thoroughly, I'll add new ones to the community supply bins.

A circle area—A space where students can join in one circle makes for a safe gathering spot for class discussions, mini-lessons, and activities—where all voices are heard, all people are valued, and everyone can see and be seen. Many teachers have the class sit in a circle on the floor; others arrange chairs in a circle. Whichever way you choose, students and adults in the circle should be able to see one another easily.

Since you'll use the circle for many purposes, keep it open in the middle but have a chart stand or whiteboard accessible for writing messages and listing ideas. In small classrooms, you may have to move furniture each time you need to create a meeting space, so one of the first class routines to practice together will be moving desks and chairs safely.

Classroom supplies—Consider keeping supplies out of reach or clearly marked as off limits until students need to use them and can explore them together, either through Guided Discovery or Interactive Modeling (see Appendix A). For example, I take materials that won't be used until later in the year, such as base ten blocks and microscopes and tuck them away in a closet or supply cabinet to keep them out of sight.

Materials that will be used early and often—but not right away—I keep in bins or on shelves. I use signs to let students know these are for use soon and to build a sense of expectancy: "Coming Attraction!" "Opening Soon!" "Under Construction!"

Classroom walls—Walls covered with all sorts of displays can lead students to feel overwhelmed, but bare walls and boards look too bleak. One way to strike a balance—displaying just enough to pique students' curiosity—is to keep most wall space or bulletin boards blank, but give them bold titles and attractive frames. The framed, open spaces serve as a sign that we'll build our classroom displays together.

Getting to Know Your Students

When teachers know their students, students sense it and feel more connected with school and more motivated to learn. Even before the first day of school, you can start getting to know your incoming students. Here are a few ideas:

- *Check in with last year's teachers*—In addition to insights into academics, they may also be able to give you a heads-up about other strengths and challenges students may have.

- *Review student records*—Report cards, test scores, reading levels, and even attendance records can give you insight into many aspects of students' school histories.

> **Bulletin Board Title Ideas for the First Day**
>
> ➤ Hopes and Dreams for the Year
>
> ➤ Birthday Chart (for grades K–2)
>
> ➤ Favorite Books and Authors (for Grades 3–4)
>
> ➤ All About Us
>
> ➤ Word Wall (include a few words to start)

- **Talk to other school personnel**—If you have a student with profound academic, social, or emotional needs, a counselor, administrator, or special education teacher will likely contact you before school starts. Or you can touch base with them for an update on the child's current needs.

- **Review developmental characteristics of the ages you teach**—Reviewing common child development characteristics can be especially helpful if you're teaching a new grade. For example, knowing that seven- and nine-year-olds tend to be anxious might sway you to use more structured activities in second and fourth grades. Knowing that six-, eight-, and ten-year-olds tend to like working in groups might lead you to use small groups more in first, third, and fifth grades.

Communicating With Parents*

Connecting with parents toward the end of the summer helps prime the relationship for a fruitful year of collaboration. With about two weeks to go before school starts, I send a friendly letter home to parents (see example at right) to introduce myself, generate a sense of warmth and trust, and share a few tips for helping their child get ready for the first day of school.

*Note: In this book, for ease of reading, the term "parent" is used to represent all the caregivers involved in a child's life.

Here are some other ways to start building connections with parents:

- Have an informal open house before the first day.

- Call or email parents.

- Create a website with news about what's happening in the classroom and school, and include contact information.

When we forge effective lines of communication with parents and make the effort to get to know them, we become more effective teachers for their children. We can more easily share information with them and they're more likely to do the same with us. And the more we know about our students, the better we can support their growth and meet their needs.

Greetings, Parents!

I hope you're as excited as I am about the start of school. We are going to have a great year together!

First, let me introduce myself. My name is Mike Anderson, and I have been teaching at Hilltop School for five years. I have a passion for writing and science and also love to read stories aloud. Outside of school, I'm an avid gardener, love to hike, and am a huge Red Sox fan. I live in Durham with my wife, Heather, our children, Ethan and Carly, and our dog, Olive.

Here are a few ideas for helping your child get ready for the first day of school.

➤ Ask your child to think about something from their summer to share with the class.

➤ Talk with your child about some learning goals and hopes for this year. What do they want to learn? What do they hope fourth grade will be like?

➤ Starting about a week before school, help your child get back on a school schedule so they'll be well rested and have a great start to the year!

I'll be in school putting the finishing touches on our classroom on Tuesday afternoon, August 26, from 4:00–6:00 p.m. If you and your child would like to check out our classroom, please stop by then. If you're not able to, I look forward to seeing you on the first day of school—August 28.

Have a great last two weeks of summer!

Mr. Anderson

8:15 **Arrival:** Greet students at door, decorate name tags

8:30 **Teach chime signal** (play Freeze Game)

8:40 **Morning Meeting**

- Greeting: Teacher greets each student around the circle
- Sharing: Invite each student to name a favorite animal
- Group Activity: Sing "Peanut Butter, Grape Jelly" together
- Morning Message: Teacher reads first, then everyone reads

9:00 **Tour the school**

- Interactive Modeling: Lining up, walking in halls, bathroom procedures
- Visit cafeteria

9:45 **Snack**

10:00 **Outside time** or energizer inside

- Walk boundaries of playground
- Teach "circle up" procedure
- Practice circling up by racing the clock

10:20 **Special** (music, art, PE, library, or technology)

11:00 **Math**

- Explore counters
- Energizer: Skip Counting

11:40 **Recess**

- Teach Freeze Tag
- Practice circling up

12:00 **Lunch** (help with logistics, sit as a class)

12:30 **Quiet time**

- Choices: Drawing or using counters

12:45 **Read-aloud:** *The Bugliest Bug*

- Teach "turn and talk"

1:15 **Writing**

- Interactive Modeling: Getting materials, putting materials away
- Explore pencils and writing journals
- Write/draw: One thing I like to do

1:45 **Reading**

- Teach "book shopping"
- Activity: Everyone picks 3 books for book bags
- Independent reading: 5–10 minutes
- Practice "turn and talk" about reading

2:15 **Outside time** or energizer inside

- Play Freeze Tag (outside) or Skip Counting (inside)

2:30 **Set up first dismissal**

- Pass out notes/forms for home
- Pack backpacks
- Check on bus numbers/walkers
- Brief cleanup

2:50 **Closing circle**

- Sharing: One thing I liked about school today

3:00 **Dismissal**

- Walk students to buses/exit

Kindergarten, First & Second Grades

Young students walk through the door showing a variety of first-day-of-school emotions. Some cling nervously to a parent's hand, even hiding their faces. Others bound through the door, bouncing up and down. For most, the first day of school is both exciting and a little intimidating. Our focus today is on making sure these young students have a smooth transition from summer to school and feel welcomed, safe, and excited about learning.

Flow of the Day

Beginning the First Day

Settling In With Name Tags

After you greet children and help them find their seats, giving them something concrete to do is a great way to settle nerves—and decorating name tags is a tried-and-true first task. Be sure to have premade blank tags and crayons at the ready plus some paper for drawing in case anyone finishes early.

Signal for Quiet Attention

Once the initial hubbub settles a bit, you can use the simple, step-by-step technique of Interactive Modeling (see Appendix A to learn more) to teach a routine that's essential for creating a calm, orderly classroom: responding when you give the signal for quiet attention. We want to teach students how to stop, get quiet, and look at us when we give the signal. Establishing this routine early in the day will help ensure that the rest of the day (and year) goes smoothly.

The Power of Name Tags

Name tags are, of course, a great way to help everyone learn each other's names. Plus, on the first day of school, having a name tag sends an important message to every student: "You belong here. You have a place in this class."

Many teachers use a calming chime as the signal. Other possibilities include a quiet bell or rainstick. To practice this routine, try the Freeze Game: While students color and chat, ring the chime and prompt students to see how quickly they can freeze. You can also use these practice times to create a positive tone and start building community: "Wow! Our class became quiet in seven seconds. We'll keep practicing this over the next few days and see if we can break our record." Then, later in the day, teach a visual signal for quiet attention such as a raised hand, which is especially useful in the cafeteria and hallways.

Morning Meeting

This first Morning Meeting lays the foundation for all those to come and helps children meet their needs for belonging, significance, and fun right from the start. Many students experience some first-day jitters, so it's usually best to save any explanations about Morning Meeting for day two. Today, simply say, "This morning and every morning, we're going to gather as a class to begin our day together."

Then call students to the circle one table at a time: "Hanin, Joshua, Ann, Sadia. Come find your spot in the circle" or "Blue Table, come to the circle." Names on seats or spots in the circle help ensure that everyone knows where to go and feels included.

Next, use a simple meeting structure like this:

- *Greeting*—Once everyone is seated, greet students one by one around the circle: "Good morning, Sara. Good morning, Enrique. Good morning, Ben. . . ." Because you'll do all the talking, this is a safe first greeting and reinforces the importance of learning names.

- *Sharing*—Lead a simple around-the-circle sharing about favorite animals: "Jasmine, what's your favorite animal? Devon, what's your favorite animal?" and so on.

- *Group activity*—After everyone has had a turn sharing, sing a lively song together, such as "Peanut Butter, Grape Jelly." (See Appendix B for song lyrics and directions to activities and learning structures mentioned in this chapter.)

- *Morning message*—To conclude the Morning Meeting, invite students to read a message you've written ahead of time on a chart or whiteboard (see sample message above). In kindergarten, you might just read the message aloud. In first or second grade, you might first read it aloud and then have the class read it chorally.

Try to keep Morning Meeting today and for the rest of this week relatively short, about ten to fifteen minutes. Students' wiggling bodies will be a sign that they're ready to move on to something new. To learn more about *Responsive Classroom* Morning Meeting, see Appendix .

Touring the School

Touring the school before recess and lunch can help young children feel more at home. Here are a few key stops to make:

- *School office*—Introduce students to the office staff and principal.

- *Nurse's office*—Meet the nurse and learn where to go for "hurts" such as scraped knees.

Sample Morning Message

August 28, 20--

Good morning!

Today is our first day of school.

I hope you have a great day!

Mrs. Ortiz

Morning Meeting Sharing Tip

Young students may be shy about speaking in front of a group. If this seems particularly true for the students you teach, consider skipping the sharing component of Morning Meeting for the first few days. Start to include sharing as students become more comfortable with "public" speaking.

- *Cafeteria*—Teach and practice basic lunchroom procedures such as lining up, getting trays and utensils, and throwing away trash.
- *Bathroom*—Show students where bathrooms are located; teach and practice routines such as flushing toilets, washing hands, and throwing away paper towels.

You can use Interactive Modeling to teach the routines for these areas.

Morning Snack

A regular snack time helps fuel students for learning and provides a break from more structured tasks. Starting today and throughout the first week, model and practice snack routines, such as how to get a snack, where to eat it, and how to clean up.

After snack, tour the playground for some fresh air and help students learn what to expect during recess. This is also a good opportunity to teach circling up on the playground: On your signal, students stop what they're doing and form a circle around you to listen for further instructions. As with the Freeze Game used for teaching the signal for quiet attention, you can turn this into a fun activity where children circle up as quickly as possible when they hear or see the signal.

Middle of the First Day

Recess

Just as young children tend to be both excited and anxious about the first day of school, they're also likely to have mixed feelings about recess. Teaching students basic expectations and routines goes a long way toward making recess go smoothly.

Some teachers stay with students during their first recess to help make sure it's fun and inclusive. Later in the year, students won't need this much support, but on the first day, I think it's crucial for establishing expectations.

A simple game to play with young children is Freeze Tag. Because you taught circling up earlier, call out "Circle up!" before you play to give students more practice with this routine. (Remember to reinforce their efforts: "You circled up quickly. It took only twelve seconds!") Once children are in a circle around you, teach them the expectations for being the tagger and then serve as the tagger for the first round. Afterward, circle students up again and have them focus on how you've been tagging: "How have I been gentle and safe as I've tagged you?" Students may notice that "You didn't hit hard," "You just tapped me," and "You only used one hand." Again, reinforce their efforts: "You noticed a lot. Keep noticing how I'm tagging as we play again. That way, you'll be ready to tag safely when it's your turn to be a tagger."

Lunch

Heading into the cafeteria after recess, remind students to line up the same way you practiced during your school tour. To help ensure that no one worries about who they're sitting with, assign seats for lunch. You may also want to give students a suggestion for what to talk about during lunch and a reminder to be sure to eat their lunch—something first-day excitement may cause them to forget!

Even if other adults supervise lunch, consider staying with your class for some or all of it. You'll have another chance to bond with students, establish expectations for lunchroom behavior, and learn more about students as you observe them in a different setting.

Quiet Time

After the stimulation of recess and lunch, ten to fifteen minutes of quiet time can help students reset and have a smoother transition to the afternoon's learning. Begin today to set the expectation that during quiet time children will choose an activity to do alone and stick to that activity for the duration of this time. Give them just two or three choices of what to do during this time, ideally all choices stemming from activities done earlier in the day. For example, students could color with crayons (used for decorating name tags) or explore with counters (introduced during math time).

Students need time and practice to build stamina for quiet, independent concentration, so circulate around the room and give them frequent, friendly reminders to help them stay focused on their choice. This first quiet time lets you see how long students can maintain their focus and evaluate what routines you may need to adjust or teach. To help students build stamina, you might also try breaking up quiet time into smaller chunks, having children maintain quiet attention for just two or three minutes at a time and then reflecting on how that went. To learn more about quiet time, see Appendix A.

Ending the First Day

Dismissal Logistics

Building in some extra time for end-of-day routines can help avoid a chaotic rush to the door and enable everyone to finish today on a high note. If students need to take papers or forms home, you might do a quick check before gathering them for the closing circle to make sure everything is stowed in a take-home folder and packed in students' backpacks.

You can also use this time to introduce the expectations for taking care of the classroom by having students look around the room and find one or two things they can pick up or straighten. Then, to ensure that every student gets on the right bus, attach a small sticky note with bus numbers to shirts or backpacks and walk them to their buses when the bell rings.

Closing Circle

Just as you and your students met in a circle for Morning Meeting, meet again in a circle to conclude the day. Students will likely be wiggly and tired, so avoid talking too much about how closing circles work. Simply gather in the circle area and invite students to share one thing they enjoyed about school today. Then finish with another round of "Peanut Butter, Grape Jelly." With this closing circle, the day ends on a positive note and reminds everyone they're part of a community in which each person is valued. To learn more about closing circle, see Appendix A.

Teaching Academics

Right from the start, we want to establish a positive tone for learning, getting students excited about school and feeling confident about themselves as learners. All year long, they'll help one another learn, and this spirit of collaboration can be established today.

Materials

We need to guide young students, who are new to many classroom materials, in exploring even the most basic supplies, such as math counters and pencils, and the most fundamental knowledge, such as where on the page to start writing or how to get a book off the shelf and put it in a reading bag. A little time invested now will help children use materials more effectively and save time throughout the year.

It's also important for each child to have easy access to basic supplies. If they don't, grabbing will likely ensue, setting a negative tone for the day. When children first decorate name tags, for example, set out paper cups with a few crayons for each child to use. Later, after you've taught students how to share table supplies, they can place their crayons in a community bin, symbolizing that in this classroom, collaboration and sharing are the norm.

Academic Routines

On this first day, introduce just a few simple routines that you can build on over the coming days and weeks. For example:

- Sitting in a circle and being ready to listen

- Raising a hand to ask a question or add an idea

- Turning and talking (partner chat)

Use Interactive Modeling to show students exactly how to carry out these routines and to give them immediate practice.

Academic Activities for Early Success

When students experience academic success early on, they're much more motivated to learn going forward. To set students up for success today, choose learning activities that enable all students to participate fully, regardless of their academic skills, and keep activities short, varied, and lively. For example:

- *Math*—After children explore counters, use an energizer, a whole-group activity that gets students moving while continuing their learning. Skip Counting is a simple and fun choice for an energizer on the first day. First and second graders can skip-count by twos to twenty, alternately sitting and standing with each number. Kindergartners can simply count to ten by ones, alternately sitting and standing. You can also use this activity to reinforce students' collaborative work and math thinking: "Did you notice how well we counted together? Now that you have the pattern down, are you ready to challenge yourselves and count all the way to thirty?"

- *Reading*—Before starting a read-aloud, model how to share an idea with a partner and how to listen to a partner's idea. Then pause periodically while you read to ask open-ended questions and have students practice sharing ideas with partners. If you're reading *The Bugliest Bug*, for example, you might ask: "What do you think the spiders will do next?" "If you could be any bug on this page, which would you choose, and why?" A simple partner chat deepens students' engagement with the text and fosters inclusiveness.

- *Writing*—In the circle area, guide students in brainstorming things they like to do and chart their ideas. Then, after students explore pencils and writing journals, have everyone pick one idea and write or draw about it for a few minutes. Finish with a partner chat: "Turn to your partners and tell them about what you wrote or drew."

From time to time, while students partner chat or work together on a task, step back and observe how they do. You might notice, for example, that many children aren't looking at their partners while sharing and make a note to practice that skill later this week.

Building Excitement for Learning

From day one, we want students to begin thinking of themselves as capable learners. We can use envisioning teacher language to cultivate this self-image—for example, by calling students "readers," "writers," "mathematicians," "scientists," and "teammates." We can also explicitly name the skills students are learning and project a tone of confidence that they'll be successful this year. For example:

Situation	Envisioning Language
Introducing counters in math	"Mathematicians use lots of tools to learn about math. Today, we're going to explore some tools that will help us count."
Introducing "turn and talk" for reading	"Readers can learn more from books by talking with others about what they read. Today, we're going to practice this key skill."
Introducing writing journals	"Many writers keep writing journals. Today, you'll get your own writing journal. We'll use our journals for all sorts of writing this year."

When setting a tone of excitement, avoid using terms that imply judgment such as "fast readers" or "great writers." We want all students to identify themselves as readers, writers, mathematicians, scientists, and teammates, all of whom are working to learn and grow.

Reinforcing Students' Efforts

When we let students know specifically what they're doing well, we help build their self-confidence. Here are some examples of reinforcing language to use on the first day:

Reinforcing Language
"I noticed that you place the math counters back in the bin very carefully. That's really taking care of our math supplies."
"As you came to the rug for our read-aloud, I saw you walking quietly. That helps everyone get ready to listen."
"We just read for five straight minutes. That's quite an accomplishment for the first day of school!"

If you're reinforcing the positive behavior of just one student, it's best to do so privately (simply stand close and speak quietly) to prevent embarrassment for the student or a sense of competition among classmates.

Teaching Discipline

In many ways, the teaching of discipline is embedded in everything we do as teachers. Everything discussed in this chapter—how we greet children, facilitate recess, teach academics, and more—impacts the climate of our classroom. Here are some steps for building a well-managed, positive community and teaching positive behavior right from the start.

Using Teacher Language to Create a Positive Tone

To create a classroom climate that's inclusive, safe, joyful, and purposeful, our language should reflect those values. For example:

Situation	Positive Teacher Language
As children first arrive	"Hi, Amira! I'm excited you're here today! Let me help you find your table group."
When modeling lining up	"Everyone, watch how I line up safely and respectfully."
As the class walks in the halls	"First graders, I notice how quietly you're moving through the halls. That's going to help students in the other classes focus on their work."

Notice how in these examples the teacher names the expectation, lets children know she saw them meeting the expectation, focuses on behavior (not children's character), and frames everything in the affirmative. A respectful tone of voice, open body posture, and friendly facial expression also help convey the message that school is a safe and welcoming place.

Routines for Positive Discipline

In addition to the signal for quiet attention (see page 16), model and practice other basic routines that will foster a safe and orderly environment. As you set up routines, you'll naturally embed the values of respect, kindness, inclusion, and safety that will inform the creation of classroom rules in the weeks to come.

Redirecting

If Kayla grabs a book from Marc, and Marc shrugs and gets another one, it may be tempting to ignore Kayla's misbehavior. However, by ignoring this small misbehavior, we would be condoning it. Marc and Kayla (and others nearby) might then assume it's okay to grab things. Instead, we want students to learn from day one that we're there to take care of them and make sure that everyone is acting kindly. So instead of saying nothing, we might calmly give a redirection: "Kayla, give the book back to Marc. If you want to borrow a book, ask first."

Here are some ways you might respond when children go off track with their behavior on the first day of school, using redirecting language in a matter-of-fact, respectful tone:

Off-Track Behavior	Redirecting Language
Billy takes the crayon Maria is using.	"Billy, give Maria her crayon. Use your own set right now."
Many students are not paying attention when you're giving directions.	"First graders, turn your bodies and your eyes toward me while I give directions."
Oscar shoves another student during Freeze Tag.	"Oscar, we use only gentle touches in this class. Come stand by me." When it's time for him to re-enter the game: "Remember to use gentle touches."

To learn more about the *Responsive Classroom* approach to teacher language and discipline, see Appendix A.

Useful Routines to Teach for Positive Discipline

➤ Responding to signals for quiet attention

➤ Bathroom procedures

➤ Carrying a chair safely

➤ Lining up and walking in the hallway

➤ Circling up outside and lunch procedures

➤ Raising a hand to ask a question

LAST THOUGHT
K-2

Whether the day goes totally smoothly or has a few bumps, remember to maintain a warm, calm, positive tone. By getting your young students off to a great start, you're making a much bigger difference than you could ever imagine!

8:15 **Arrival:** Greet students at door; make name tags; teach signal for quiet attention

8:30 **Morning Meeting**

- Greeting: Students introduce themselves
- Sharing: Invite each student to name a favorite food
- Group Activity: Who Remembers?
- Morning Message: Read to class; then read together chorally

8:45 **Interactive Modeling:** Transition from circle to desks

8:55 **Math**

- Explore math book
- Work with pattern blocks (20 minutes)
- Interactive Modeling: Storing math book in cubby
- Energizer: Skip Counting

9:45 **Tour the school** (inside)

- Interactive Modeling: Lining up, walking in halls
- Visit cafeteria; teach procedures

10:15 **Snack**

10:30 **Tour the playground**

- Teach and practice circling up
- Tour the playground
- Teach Category Tag
- Reflect on how tagging was safe

10:50 **Reading**

- Open up fiction section of library
- Interactive Modeling: Picking a "just right" book
- Book shopping (students choose books)
- Silent reading (15 minutes)

11:40 **Recess** (play Category Tag)

12:00 **Lunch** (sit with table groups)

12:30 **Quiet time**

- Choices: Read or use pattern blocks

12:45 **Read-aloud:** *Tales of a Fourth Grade Nothing*

1:05 **Energizer:** "Hello, My Name Is Joe" chant

1:10 **Special** (music, art, library, PE, or technology)

1:55 **Writing**

- Introduce writing journals
- Brainstorm: Things we did this summer
- Explore crayons, colored pencils, markers
- Personalize journal covers

2:40 **Cleanup and logistics**

- Confirm bus numbers
- Pass out any forms
- Pack up

2:50 **Closing circle**

- Around-the-circle sharing: One thing I enjoyed about today
- Homework: Think about learning goals or "hopes and dreams"

3:00 **Dismissal**

Third & Fourth Grades

For third and fourth graders who enter the class full of excitement and anxiety, we want to be at the door to greet each one: "Good morning, Janeya! Welcome to third grade!" "You're Thomas? Glad to meet you, Thomas." "Hello, Yessenia. I'm glad you're here!" As we greet students, show them where to put their backpacks, and help them find their seats, we're creating a welcoming and caring tone first thing on this all-important day.

Flow of the Day

Beginning the First Day

Making Name Tags

For an initial task, creating name tags gives each student something concrete to do, a chance to survey the room, and time to settle in. Wearing name tags also sends the message that names are important and every student is valued. For the first week or so, I have students wear name tags to help everyone learn—and remember to use—each other's names.

Signal for Quiet Attention

Once everyone has settled in a bit, I teach how to respond to a hand signal for quiet attention, using a simple, step-by-step technique called Interactive Modeling (see Appendix A to learn more). I start by saying, "When I raise my hand, it's everyone's job to stop whatever you're doing. Then turn and face me, ready to listen. I'm going to show you what that should look like." Next, I turn to a student (a volunteer I've prepared in advance) and say, "Alicia, I'm going to pretend to be working. You pretend to be the teacher. After a few seconds, raise your hand. Everyone, watch what I do when I see her signal."

After the modeling, we all practice together a few times. I tell them they can also raise their hands and help spread the signal around the room, but I don't make doing so mandatory. Then, throughout the morning, we do some quick, playful practices with the hand signal. Sometimes, I'll even time how fast students can respond, but I intentionally don't demand immediate silence. Students need a few seconds to finish what they're doing before they're able to fully focus on me.

Morning Meeting

To help bring the class together from the start, hold a Morning Meeting today. This first meeting should be simple and last no more than fifteen to twenty minutes. I save an explanation about the purpose of Morning Meeting for day two because children are excited about *doing* school today, rather than hearing about it.

The goal for our first meeting is simply for students to start using each other's names, make some personal connections, and feel safe and included. Here's a sample meeting plan:

- **Combined greeting and sharing**—Students go around the circle and introduce themselves by stating their name and a favorite food: "Hi, my name is Oden. I like pepperoni pizza." Model this before asking students to do it.

- **Group activity**—Play a few rounds of Who Remembers? about students' favorite foods: "Who remembers people who liked pizza? Who remembers people who liked sweet things?" (See Appendix B for directions to the activities, learning structures, and songs mentioned in this chapter.)

- **Morning message**—Keep this first message brief. See the example at right.

If time is tight on the first day, simplify the Morning Meeting even more by having students just say their names and then either playing three rounds of Just Like Me or going right to the morning message; introduce sharing later in the week. To learn more about *Responsive Classroom* Morning Meeting, see Appendix A.

> **Sample Morning Message**
>
> August 28, 20——
>
> Happy First Day of School!
>
> I hope you're as excited as I am for the first day of school! Think about some things you did this summer that you would like to share.
>
> Have a great first day!
>
> Mr. Kirke

Touring the School

Even if third and fourth graders are familiar with the school, a quick tour on the first day is reassuring. Plus, any new students can begin to learn their way around, and everyone gets a movement break. You can point out where bathrooms and water fountains are and teach some basic routines, such as lining up and cafeteria procedures. If you tour the playground, you could also practice circling up and teach a simple game such as Category Tag so that during recess students will have more time to actually play.

Middle of the First Day

Recess

Recess can be stressful for students, especially on the first day. To ensure that it goes smoothly today, provide some structure and join students if you can. Practice circling up for a minute or two. Then play a simple game such as Category Tag. Even if you didn't teach this game earlier in the morning, students can learn the rules quickly, start playing right away, and add categories of their own. On this first day, you may want to be "It" so you can demonstrate safe tagging and keep the tone of recess playful and inclusive.

Lunch

I always assign table groups for lunch on the first day. Although some students may grump a bit, many will be secretly relieved not to have to sit alone or jockey for a seat. Float from table to table, if possible, chatting with students and checking that conversations are respectful and include everyone.

Quiet Time

As a calming bridge to the afternoon, quiet time lets students unwind from recess and lunch and prepare for the afternoon's learning. Before students leave the classroom, tell them that when they return, they're going to have fifteen minutes to do a quiet activity on their own. Explain that once they choose an activity, you expect them to stick with it for the duration.

Give students two simple choices of things to do during quiet time today. For example, they may read a book they chose during reading or use the pattern blocks they explored during math. To learn more about quiet time, see Appendix A.

> **Quiet Time Tip**
>
> During quiet time, circulate to observe students and help them settle in with their choice. For children who struggle to stay engaged with their choice, give gentle reminders that this time is for quiet, focused concentration.

Ending the First Day

Dismissal Logistics

Planning a little extra time to get ready for dismissal is a good idea on this first day. Students will likely be both tired and excited, and they'll appreciate having an opportunity to double-check what they're doing after school and where they're going. Before your closing circle or end-of-day meeting, take care of any last-minute details so students can stay calm and positive.

In the coming days, you can teach students the routines for cleaning up the classroom. Today, to start building a sense of shared ownership of the physical space, simply have everyone pitch in to help pick up. You might say: "We're about to have our closing circle. Everyone, to help keep our room neat, find one thing you can straighten up before you go to the circle area."

Closing Circle

Because the first day can feel like such a whirlwind, try to end in a calm, purposeful way. A closing circle helps students end the first day on a positive note and feel energized about their learning.

As a way to prepare for tomorrow's activity about learning goals (or what many teachers call "hopes and dreams"), you might begin by asking students to spend a few minutes tonight thinking about what they want to learn and do in school this year. Then facilitate an around-the-circle reflection on a topic that's inclusive and positive. For example: "What's one thing you enjoyed about our first day of school?" or "What's something you're looking forward to tomorrow?" To learn more about closing circle, see Appendix A.

Teaching Academics

As we begin teaching our content areas today, we want to set a positive tone for learning and lay the groundwork for students to develop into confident learners. A primary goal for today (and for this entire first week) is to teach students how to work together in the classroom and be successful as individuals and as a group.

Materials

Introducing too many supplies at once can be overwhelming to children, so choose carefully for the first day: What will children need for the first few days of school? You can use Interactive Modeling to introduce supplies intended to be used in one straightforward way, such as glue sticks and pencil sharpeners. This will enable you to show students exactly how to use the materials and get some practice doing so under your watchful eye.

For example, before we glue a word list in our writing notebooks, I quickly model how to use glue sticks, ask students what they noticed, and invite them to practice while I coach and reinforce their positive efforts: "You're applying the glue carefully so that your work looks neat and our tables are clean." Whenever I model supplies with third and fourth graders, I try to keep the session lively and brief and tie it to the work we're doing in the moment.

Another useful technique, Guided Discovery (see Appendix A to learn more), can help children explore supplies that are more open-ended or complex in their uses. Although third and fourth graders have used colored pencils and markers before, a guided exploration can help them discover new ways of using them, such as using markers for graphing and colored pencils as editing tools.

These guided explorations can also help students build enthusiasm for resources they'll use all year long. For example, when introducing students to their math books, I have them explore the books with partners like this:

- Partners preview the book and use yellow sticky notes to tag three pages that have content they learned something about last year.

- They use blue sticky notes to tag three pages with content they're excited to learn this year.

- They use pink sticky notes to tag three helpful resources or tips in the book.

- To conclude, partners share one item they tagged with the whole class.

The chart at right provides more suggestions for using Interactive Modeling or Guided Discovery today.

Academic Routines

Because students will likely be excited, anxious, or both on the first day, focus on only the most essential (and straightforward) routines that they need for success today. For example:

- Using and putting away basic supplies (pencils, markers, paper) and learning materials (math book, reading bag, writing journal)

First Day of School Materials

Interactive Modeling Ideas:

➤ Pencils and sharpener

➤ Reading bag/bins

➤ Scissors

➤ Markers (especially putting caps on them!)

➤ Glue sticks, staplers

Guided Discovery Ideas:

➤ Drawing supplies (crayons, colored pencils, markers)

➤ Student textbook(s)

➤ Math manipulatives (pattern blocks or base ten blocks)

- Book shopping (picking "just right" independent reading books)
- Raising a hand respectfully to get the teacher's attention

Interactive Modeling is a great way to teach these procedures.

Using Envisioning Language

A key goal for this first day is to inspire students to picture themselves as successful learners and their new classroom as a fun, safe, exciting place where everyone gets to learn. The words we use can have a powerful and lasting impact on students, building their self-confidence and supporting their social, emotional, and cognitive growth. Some sample envisioning language:

Situation	Envisioning Language
During Morning Meeting	"We're going to be a strong learning community this year, the kind of group that works hard and plays hard. We're going to have a great year together!"
Before opening up the classroom library	"This year, you're going to get a chance to read lots of different books and stories. You'll be amazed at how much you'll grow and learn as readers."
During math or writing	"Later in the year, we're going to do some fun and challenging projects as a class. Start thinking about some projects we might want to try."

Engaging, Purposeful Learning

We want students to be excited about coming to school each day, and this anticipation can start on the first day. Some ways to help that happen:

- After exploring math books, consider a playful activity such as Skip Counting. Students can count by twos, threes, and fives, alternately sitting and standing each time they call out a number. This type of activity fully involves students, gets them moving, and provides practice in math.

- To open up the classroom library, doing an activity such as Just Like Me gets students sharing in active and interactive ways what they like to read. Possible categories might be "I like books about sports," "I like to read suspenseful books," and "I like to reread my favorite books."

This blending of lightheartedness, social connection, and academics is vital to the life of the classroom. Right from the start, we're working and playing together, helping to make learning a joyful, engaging, and purposeful process.

Reinforcing Students' Efforts

For students to gain a sense of competence from day one, they need to know what they're doing well. So we want to step back often to observe and then name the positive efforts we see, by the class as a whole and by individual students. For example:

Situation	Reinforcing Language
As the class explores pattern blocks	To the whole class: "I see lots of students using the pattern blocks in different ways. Some are making patterns, some are creating fractions, and others are building structures. As a class, we're thinking of many ways to use this math tool."
As a student picks out books during reading time	Privately, so as not to embarrass the student or foster competition in the class: "Maricela, I notice that you've chosen three very different books. Reading a variety of books will help you get different perspectives on many topics."

Teaching Discipline

Although third and fourth graders tend to have a lot of enthusiasm for learning, like all children they can also lose focus, get frustrated, or act unkindly. Establishing a positive classroom climate and teaching positive behavior will go a long way toward helping them be productive and caring all year long.

Using Teacher Language to Create a Positive Tone

From the moment students enter the room and throughout the day, our tone of voice, facial expressions, and body posture (all part of our teacher language) should convey an atmosphere of warmth, caring, and safety. This is an important first step in establishing expectations for positive behavior.

Whereas reinforcing language helps students build on their positive efforts, reminding language helps them stay on track. Some samples of these two types of teacher language:

Situation	Reinforcing and Reminding Language
As students arrive	**Reinforcing:** "Luisa, I saw you help out Maggie with her backpack. That was kind."
During math	**Reinforcing:** "Manuel, you look ready for our math activity. Your eyes are on me and your hands are still."
Before a transition	**Reminding:** "Class, we're about to transition from the circle area to table groups. What were some of our ideas for how we can move safely and respectfully?"

Routines for Positive Discipline

Explicitly modeling and practicing key routines brings predictability and efficiency to the day. In the morning, we taught how to respond to a hand signal for quiet attention. This afternoon, we'll use a soft chime, bell, or rainstick to teach students how to respond to an auditory signal in situations where they might not see a hand signal. Interactive Modeling is a great way to teach the auditory signal and other routines such as:

- Bathroom procedures
- Filling out lunch tickets
- Lining up to exit the classroom
- Moving chairs safely
- Transitioning from circle area to seats and from seats to circle area
- Walking quietly in hallways

These routines could also be modeled anytime during the first week, depending on your school's schedule and other logistical considerations.

The language we use when teaching these routines should clearly convey expectations for how our classroom community will look, sound, and feel. For example:

- *Before exiting the classroom:* "When we walk in the halls, we want to be respectful of other classrooms. What are some ideas for how we can show respect for others as we move through our school?"

- *Before modeling a routine:* "We'll be moving chairs a lot, so we need to make sure we do that safely. Notice how I carry this chair."

- *Before leaving the cafeteria:* "When we get up from our tables at lunch, it may get a little crowded. How can we take care of each other then?"

Nipping Misbehaviors in the Bud

As much as we hope that the first day of school will be free of off-track behaviors, we want to be ready to step in and redirect any incidents in the moment. Ignoring even small misbehaviors can erode your efforts to create a safe, caring learning environment. Here are a few examples of some off-track behaviors you might see on the first day, with ideas for how you might respond by using redirecting language in a matter-of-fact, respectful tone:

Off-Track Behavior	Redirecting Language
Jonah cuts in front of the line for lunch.	"Jonah, go to the back of the line."
The class gets too silly during an activity.	Stop the activity and say, "It looks like you're not in control of yourselves. I'm stopping the game for now. We'll try again later."
Lisa says to Maria, "You don't know that's a trapezoid? That's stupid."	"Lisa, we only use kind words in our classroom."

To learn more about the *Responsive Classroom* approach to teacher language and discipline, see Appendix A.

LAST THOUGHT

3-4

As we teach essential routines, help students begin to connect with each other, and engage them in their early academics, we're starting to build a community of learners. This is the essential work of day one.

Fifth & Sixth Grades

Although many upper elementary students are eager to see friends and dive right into new academic work today, others may be nervous about who's in their class and uncertain whether they're ready for new challenges. As soon as they walk into the room, we want all students—regardless of any first-day jitters—to feel safe, welcomed, and hopeful.

8:15 **Arrival:** Students complete personal survey and learn the signal for quiet attention

8:30 **Morning Meeting**

- Greeting: Welcome students
- Sharing: Students introduce themselves
- Group activity: Just Like Me
- Morning message: Read together

8:45 **Teach transitions**

- Moving from circle area to seats

9:00 **Wall space introduction**

- Introduce art supplies
- Personalize name plates
- Think of other artifacts

9:20 **Math**

- Explore math book
- Practice academic conversations
- Math activity: Pica Fermé Nada

10:15 **Snack**

- Model cleanup routine

10:30 **Outside time** (or tour the school)

- Teach and practice circling up (before going out)
- Tour the playground
- Teach Captain's Coming

10:50 **Reading**

- Introduce classroom library (open fiction section)
- Model choosing books from different genres
- Book shopping
- Independent reading (20–30 minutes)

11:50 **Recess** (play Captain's Coming or other game)

12:10 **Lunch**

- Sit with table groups
- Conversation topic: Uncommon Commonalities

12:35 **Quiet time**

- Choices: Read or personalize wall space

12:45 **Read-aloud:** *The Mysterious Benedict Society*

- Practice academic conversations with partners

1:00 **Energizer:** Just Like Me

1:05 **Writing**

- Introduce writing journals
- Brainstorm: "I know a lot about…"
- Practice academic conversations: "I might write about…"

1:50 **Special** (music, art, library, PE, or technology)

2:35 **Cleanup and logistics**

- Confirm bus numbers
- Pass out any forms
- Pack up

2:45 **Closing circle**

- Class reflection/homework: One thing I enjoyed about the first day of school
- Preview of tomorrow's learning

3:00 **Dismissal**

Flow of the Day

Beginning the First Day

Name Tags

Wearing name tags during the first few days of school helps every-one learn names and get into the habit of using them respectfully. So I invite students to personalize premade name tags or create their own, which gets them focused on a specific task soon after arriving and helps ease any first-day anxiety.

Personal Surveys

After name tags, I invite students to complete a brief personal sur-vey (see example at right), which serves several important func-tions. It gives students another manageable task to settle in with and lets them know that who they are as individuals matters. And I use the completed surveys in our first Morning Meeting to help us learn more about one another (see next page).

Signal for Quiet Attention

Introduce this routine early in the day and briefly explain why it's important. For exam-ple: "I'm going to use a hand signal to respectfully get everyone's attention without rais-ing my voice. I'll play the role of a student talking with my partner while Tanya takes the role of the teacher. When Tanya raises her hand, watch how I respond." Arrange with the student ahead of time to do this modeling with you.

After the modeling, check that students noticed how quickly you finished what you were saying and doing before turning your attention to Tanya, the teacher in this example. (You may also want to point out that doing so within ten seconds or so is a reasonable initial goal.) Explain that they may also raise their hands to help spread the signal. Later in the day, teach an auditory signal using a chime, soft bell, or other soothing sound for times when students aren't likely to see your raised hand.

First Day of School Survey

➤ What are three of your favorite books?

➤ What are some things you like to do on the weekend?

➤ What are two important things you learned last year?

➤ What is your favorite subject in school?

➤ If you could meet any famous person, who would it be?

➤ Who are some important people in your life?

➤ What are some things you hope to learn this year?

Morning Meeting

Morning Meeting is a structure that can help fifth and sixth graders settle into a new classroom, learn each other's names, and start to develop a positive sense of community. It can also help you introduce key skills that students will use throughout the day, give students chances to practice those skills, and build interest and enthusiasm for academic content.

To ensure that this first meeting feels low-risk to students, I plan it very purposefully. For example, I preassign seats in the meeting area and model how we'll form a circle, using a quick, step-by-step technique called Interactive Modeling (see Appendix A to learn more). As you review the Morning Meeting plan below, notice how it helps students develop a sense of belonging, significance, and fun early on the first day.

- *Greeting*—Students take turns introducing themselves by stating their names: "Good morning. My name is Lara." Model this greeting first, showing how to use a clear, confident speaking voice.

- *Sharing and group activity*—Play a few rounds of Just Like Me, using categories drawn from the personal surveys students did earlier. Make sure everyone is included in some of the categories you name. (See Appendix B for directions to the activities, learning structures, and songs mentioned in this chapter.)

- *Morning message*—Keep this first message short and sweet. See example at right.

> **Sample Morning Message**
>
> Welcome to Fifth Grade!
>
> Good morning, everyone. I'm very excited for us to begin our year together!
>
> What are some things that you like to do or are interested in learning?
>
> Mr. Anderson

Understanding the purpose of Morning Meeting will help older students stay invested and get the most from these important daily gatherings. So to conclude your first meeting, you might give a brief overview: "Our Morning Meetings will help us get ready for our work together each day. We'll practice some key skills in fun ways, build our classroom community, and make sure we get our day off to a productive start." To learn more about *Responsive Classroom* Morning Meeting, see Appendix A.

Middle of the First Day

Recess

Many fifth and sixth graders find recess stressful on the first day, especially if it's unstructured. Our goal during the first six weeks of school is to ensure that everyone feels safe and included—and one way we can do that is by making sure that this time is structured and supervised. By doing so, we'll set students up for success later in the year, when they'll have more independence at recess.

One way for everyone to have a great start with recess and build positive community at the same time is to play a whole-class game. I like to lead this game myself so I can make sure that all students feel safe and included. I tend to stick with Captain's Coming because it's simple to teach and play—and doesn't require picking teams, waiting to take turns, or getting tagged out, all of which can lead to an overly competitive tone and exclusion.

> **Structured Recess Tip**
>
> Because they're preteens, some students may give you a little push-back about having a structured recess. If so, emphasize why you're setting recess up this way and the importance of being active together in fun, safe ways now and all year long.

Lunch

If the lunchtime routines and expectations aren't clear from the beginning, and if the cafeteria isn't well supervised, students may feel hurried or say and do unkind things. As with recess, there are simple, concrete steps we can take to ensure that lunch is enjoyable for all students.

From day one, we can make sure that everyone has someone to sit and chat with while they eat lunch. Consider assigning tables to take the pressure off finding seats and help everyone feel included. Because students may not know each other that well yet, you could also place conversation starters on each table. In addition, I also:

- Pair up a student new to the school with one who knows the routines.

- Check that students are eating. Sometimes they get distracted and ignore their food, which makes for a long afternoon.

> **Lunchtime Conversation Starters**
>
> ➤ What's something you like to do outside of school?
>
> ➤ If you could travel anywhere, where would you go?
>
> ➤ What's one superpower you wish you had?
>
> ➤ What book or movie do you highly recommend?

Quiet Time

After the stimulation of recess and lunch, ten to fifteen minutes of quiet time is a welcome respite—for students and teachers alike. Talk with students about the expectations for this time, especially the importance of choosing an activity to do alone and sticking with that activity. Circulate and check in with students during this time, coaching them as needed and reinforcing their efforts to stay focused.

On this first day, you'll also want to keep choices limited. For example, students might read quietly or work on a math puzzle. The calmness of the room can help everyone get back into a learning mindset for the afternoon. To learn more about quiet time, see Appendix A.

Ending the First Day

Dismissal Logistics

With about twenty to thirty minutes to go in the day, we start to get ready for dismissal. It's a good idea to give students more time the first few days so they can settle into the end-of-day routines, helping to close each day on a positive note.

Remember that just because students are in fifth or sixth grade doesn't mean that they'll know what they're supposed to do at the end of school. Some students may have notes from home that they forgot to pass in earlier; others may need reminders about new bus numbers or afterschool activities. You may want to check in with individual students to make sure they know where they're headed after school while the rest of the class packs up any papers and forms that need to go home.

Cleanup

Once we're all set with dismissal logistics, students spend a few minutes picking up the room before gathering together for our closing circle. Even a few minutes of taking care of stray papers or pencils on the floor helps to strengthen students' ownership of the classroom. A cooperative cleanup routine also tells students that this is *our* room and all students need to pitch in to take care of it.

Closing Circle

When introducing the closing circle, be brief. Emphasize the importance of joining together at the end of day to make connections, celebrate accomplishments, and reflect on learning, which all serve to further strengthen our community. As with other aspects of school, when fifth and sixth graders know the purpose for an activity, they'll more fully invest themselves in it.

For the first-day closing circle, invite students to look back over their day and think of one thing they enjoyed that they want to share with someone at home. Everyone then shares one idea around the circle—another way they get to know each other and make new connections. To build a sense of excitement for tomorrow's learning, close with a preview. To learn more about closing circle, see Appendix A.

Teaching Academics

Creating positive energy for school and learning is one of the most important things teachers can do on the first day of school. When students look at the day's schedule, core subjects such as math, reading, and writing should be prominently featured. Then, during our academic teaching today, we want to focus on these two key first-day goals:

1. Begin teaching students what will happen during the academic learning times this year.

2. Enable all students to feel competent and excited about school and learning.

Materials

At some point in my career, I learned not to assume that older students already knew how to use classroom materials. Instead, it's best to introduce supplies deliberately so that all students know what materials to use and how they're expected to use them in *this* classroom, *this* year. This sets a foundation for everyone to succeed and increases the likelihood that materials will be well cared for.

You can use Interactive Modeling to show students how to use and care for straightforward materials like pens, pencils, and scissors. Use another technique—Guided Discovery—to help students explore and unlock the potential of materials that are more complex or open-ended, such as textbooks or journals.

First Day of School Materials

Interactive Modeling Ideas:

➤ Pencils and sharpeners

➤ Reading bag/bins

➤ Scissors

➤ Glue sticks

➤ Staplers

Guided Discovery Ideas:

➤ Drawing supplies (crayons, colored pencils, markers)

➤ Textbooks

➤ Journals

➤ Sticky notes

To learn more about Interactive Modeling and Guided Discovery, see Appendix A.

Academic Routines

Ultimately, we want students to be able to work independently. Not only is it an important skill for them to have, but it also enables us to work with individuals and small groups. This independence begins with our explicit teaching of academic routines. Starting simply will keep students engaged and boost their confidence as learners, so consider teaching just a few essential routines that students will use today. You'll have opportunities to introduce, model, and reteach routines during the next few weeks.

Here are some procedures to teach on the first day. Interactive Modeling is an effective way to do this teaching.

- *Partner chats*—To have productive academic conversations, students need to master essential speaking and listening skills—how to ask purposeful questions, give feedback respectfully, listen attentively, and so on. Today, we focus on the basics: taking turns speaking and listening. Throughout the day, students solidify the basics by engaging in brief partner chats after our read-aloud and during math, writing, and other content areas.

- *Reading routines*—Today I open just one section of the classroom library and teach students how to choose books from a few different genres. Then they get a few minutes to do some "book shopping" on their own and time to read independently.

- *Writing routines*—We join in the circle area for our first writing lesson, and I introduce writing journals. I explain that many writers use journals to jot down ideas and write drafts. Together, we brainstorm some initial ideas for writing topics in response to the prompt "I know a lot about . . ." and write them in our journals in a section labeled "Ideas."

Making Academics Meaningful

We don't want to overload students with tough academic work on the first day of school. In fact, all of the academics we do during the first few days should enable all students to have some success. Yet we want students to see that they are doing real work in school right away—and understand that the work is interesting, enjoyable, and purposeful.

Here are some practical ways to achieve this balance:

- *In read-aloud*—Choose a book that's exciting and suspenseful but not overly serious, such as *The Mysterious Benedict Society*. There will be time for more challenging books later in the year, once students feel safe enough to discuss sensitive content and can respond respectfully to different points of view.

- *In math*—Invite students to explore the math book they'll be using this year and then do a playful activity, such as Pica Fermé Nada, that reinforces mathematical thinking but is not overly competitive.

- *In reading*—Guide students in choosing a few books that they find interesting and can read successfully now.

Using Envisioning Language

On this first day, I make sure to use envisioning language—statements that help paint a picture of great learning possibilities—to get students excited about the year ahead. For example:

Envisioning Language	
For writing	"Did you know that many famous authors keep writing journals to capture their ideas? Today, we'll begin setting up our own writing journals. As we start to personalize the covers, we'll be generating ideas for a variety of writing projects this year."
For math	"We'll be digging into some interesting and challenging math content this year. Today, we'll explore our math books to preview some of what we'll be learning."
For reading	"Did you know that there's one thing that people who are skilled at reading do that's more important than anything else? They read a ton! As you choose books today, look for books that you'll really enjoy—ones that you'll look forward to diving into."

Reinforcing Students' Efforts

Throughout this first day, students should hear positive, honest, and specific feedback when they make choices or exhibit behaviors that we want to encourage. To the class as a whole, we might say: "Everyone was able to concentrate for ten straight minutes during reading. That can be tough on the first day of school, but you did it!"

We also want to reinforce individual students' efforts—and do so in private. That's because singling out students in front of their peers can embarrass them, while other students may get upset that we overlooked their positive efforts. So after a math activity, for example, we might say privately to a student: "Jamal, you had a lot of ideas during that activity. You were really thinking hard."

Teaching Discipline

In the same way that we teach math, literacy, and other content, so too should we teach discipline. This yearlong work begins on the first day of school and flows through everything we do. Every time we model a routine, use an energizer, or teach a lesson, we're also teaching positive behavior.

Using Teacher Language to Set a Positive Tone

The words and tone we use on the first day can leave a lasting impression. I'll never forget my sixth grade teacher leading off our first science class with a lecture—about not stealing *his* equipment and why he locked *his* cupboards every day. I felt mistrusted and hurt. Over time, I grew to respect and enjoy this teacher, but I could never quite shake off the initial tone he set.

Children just entering adolescence are highly sensitive and will often unconsciously mirror the body language and tone of their teacher, which in turn can have a huge negative or positive impact on how students treat each other. My approach on the first day of school—one that I'll continue to use all year long—reflects my belief that all children want to and can be productive members of our classroom community.

I often use reinforcing language to help students recognize and build on their positive efforts. Sometimes I'll use reminding language to help them remember for themselves how to stay on track. Consider how the following examples of teacher language convey faith in students:

Setting a Positive Tone	
Reinforcing Language	"Xeniyah, at lunch I saw that you chose to sit with a couple of students who are new to our school. I bet that helped them feel more comfortable on their first day with us. Were you remembering a time when you were the 'new kid'?"
Reinforcing Language	"Wow, that was fun! What did we do as a class that allowed our energizer to stay lively but not get out of control?"
Reminding Language	"Okay, everyone, it's time to get ready for lunch. Who remembers one of our ideas for lining up so it's calm and orderly?"

Notice how in each of these examples the teacher names the expectation, invites students' ideas, and assumes positive intentions, all the while using friendly words and tones.

Helping Students Get to Know Each Other

Feeling known is crucial to children's sense of belonging, which is foundational for their learning positive behavior. Knowing each other also allows students to collaborate in fruitful and friendly ways. One way to help students feel known is to assign seats, partners, and groups on the first day of school (and for the next few weeks). By mixing and remixing students, you establish two key expectations: We get to know everyone, and we all work together.

On the first day, we can have students begin work on a brief, tangible project that enables them to share their interests and favorites and start making connections with their classmates. For example, students can share their favorite books, songs, movies, and TV shows through:

- Digital slide shows
- Posters
- Personal displays on a class bulletin board or wall space using drawings, lists, or paragraphs

In addition to helping students learn about one another, a brief project gives us an opportunity to observe students, informally assess skills, and introduce supplies.

Routines for Positive Discipline

On day one, focus on just a few classroom routines that are essential for students' success. Here are a few routines to teach today:

- Auditory signal for quiet attention, such as a chime or other soothing sound (teach this after teaching the hand signal for quiet attention at the start of the day)

- Transitioning to and from the circle area
- Lunch sign-up
- Bathroom sign-out
- Walking in hallways

Interactive Modeling is an effective way to teach these and other routines.

Be Ready to Redirect

Whether because of nerves, high energy, or social jockeying, students may say or do things on their first day back in school that aren't okay. Right from the start, it's our job to convey that no act of unkindness—not even a small one—is acceptable. We can do this by giving students a firm, yet respectful and calm, redirection at the first sign of off-track behavior. For example:

Off-Track Behavior	Redirecting Language
Richard tosses his trash and it lands on the floor, but he doesn't pick it up.	"Richard, you missed the trash can. Go clean up your trash."
Two boys playfully jostle each other into the lockers when walking through the hall.	"Micah and John—physical play is not allowed in the halls. Go back and walk safely."
Jenna calls attention to Sara's outfit, snickering with a friend.	"Jenna, respectful comments only. We need to be kind to work together successfully this year."

To learn more about the *Responsive Classroom* approach to teacher language and discipline, see Appendix A.

The first day of school passes so quickly that we often lose sight of all that we accomplished. Focus on the gift you gave to your students today—a sense of calm, purpose, and joy. The positive tone you set on this first day will have a lasting impact on how students feel as they leave school today—and on how they feel when they return to school tomorrow and every day that follows.

Week One

Goals for Week One

During the first week of school, we continue the foundation building we began on day one to help every child be successful academically, socially, and emotionally. This week, we want every student to:

- *Experience a collaborative and inclusive learning environment* in which they can successfully do inspiring academic work.

- *Make personal connections* by working with a variety of classmates and learning and practicing each other's names.

- *Practice essential academic routines* (such as silent reading and sustained writing) and daily routines (transitions, lunch, recess, bathroom, and so on).

- *Explore some key academic supplies* (books, math manipulatives, writing supplies).

- *Generate learning goals* (or "hopes and dreams") for the year and see their work proudly displayed.

- *Brainstorm a list of possible classroom rules* in Grades 3–4 (students in grades K–2 will do this in week three).

Overview for All Grades

Mr. Bass's students bounce down the hall, waving and smiling excitedly. Even Angelica, who was so reserved on the first day of school, is beaming as she calls out, "Hi, Mr. Bass!" Most students return for the second day of school feeling more confident and knowing what to expect.

Teachers often worry that *now* is the time to move quickly into challenging academic work. After all, we'll soon have to administer reading assessments, follow curriculum pacing guides, prepare students for standardized tests, and so much more.

But diving right into challenging schoolwork may disrupt the sense of trust and safety that we established on the first day, and that sense of trust and safety is so important if students are to succeed academically. So rather than choose between academics and community, we can begin academic work through community building and build community through that academic work.

After all, our ultimate goal is to build a collaborative classroom, where children can develop social-emotional competencies *and* master rigorous academic content and skills. Teachers who devote time during the first six weeks of school to balancing community building, effective management, and engaging academics find that this approach pays off in greater learning throughout the rest of the year. So this week, we'll focus on setting goals, talking about rules, exploring materials, practicing routines, establishing clear expectations for behavior and effort, and building a climate of trust in which students can take the risks essential to learning.

We'll also continue our efforts to build a positive school-home partnership. We can do this by communicating with parents through a note sent home on Friday, a group email, or an update on the class webpage. And any daily interactions we have with parents, at arrival times or after-school pick-ups, are great opportunities to make quick connections. Reaching out and engaging them early in the school year lets parents know that we welcome, respect, and value them.

During week one, we're balancing children's academic, social, and emotional needs in everything we do with them. By week's end, we'll have a better sense of our students as individuals and as a community as we keep moving forward on our learning journey.

Kindergarten, First & Second Grades

Young children will approach this first week with great enthusiasm, especially if the days are broken up into bite-sized pieces that alternate between energizing and calming: A period of quiet reading might be followed by a lively song; the hubbub of recess and lunch can be followed by quiet time. To maintain a healthy balance this week, observe your students, gauge their energy level, and adjust your plans accordingly.

D A Y   2

8:15 Establish arrival routines and practice signals for quiet attention

8:35 Morning Meeting
- Greeting: Around-the-circle "Good morning"
- Sharing: Favorite Food
- Group activity: Sing "Peanut Butter, Grape Jelly"
- Morning message: Point to words as you read

8:55 Model/re-model Transition back to seats

9:00 Math Skip Counting energizer • Interactive Modeling: Taking turns with counters • Using counters to practice skip counting

9:40 Snack

10:00 Outside time or energizer • Review circling up and safe tagging • Play Freeze Tag

10:20 Special

11:00 Reading Introduce book bins • Explore books • Independent reading: 5–10 minutes • Around-the-circle sharing: One thing I liked about my book

11:45 Recess Practice and play Stuck in the Mud

12:05 Lunch

12:30 Quiet time Read, draw, or use counters

12:45 Read-aloud Practice simple partner chats

1:00 Energizer Just Like Me

1:10 Writing Write and draw about favorite foods • Partner chat: Favorite foods

1:45 Guided Discovery Introduce interlocking cubes • Add to math tools shelf and indoor recess options

2:20 Outside time or energizer

2:35 End-of-day logistics Pack backpacks • Check on bus numbers • Cleanup song • Transition to circle

2:50 Closing circle Share goals of closing circle • Around-the-circle sharing: Something fun from today

3:00 Dismissal

D A Y   3

8:15 Arrival routines and review/practice signals

8:35 Morning Meeting
- Greeting: Same as Day 2
- Sharing: Favorite game
- Group Activity: Sing "Black Socks"
- Morning message: Choral reading

8:55 Remind/re-model Transition back to seats

9:00 Math Teach Pop-Up Number • Introduce number line by using a human number line

9:45 Snack

10:00 Outside time or energizer • Practice and play Stuck in the Mud

10:20 Special

11:00 Reading Explore books • Independent reading: 5–10 minutes • Model/practice partner chats: One thing I liked about my book

11:45 Recess Play Stuck in the Mud

12:05 Lunch

12:30 Quiet time Read, draw, or use interlocking cubes

12:45 Read-aloud Practice simple partner chats

1:00 Energizer Just Like Me

1:10 Writing Introduce word wall • Model and practice Alphabet Aerobics • Write and draw about favorite games

1:50 Guided Discovery Introduce dominos • Add to math tools shelf and indoor recess options

2:25 Outside time or energizer

2:40 End-of-day logistics

2:50 Closing circle Partner chat: Something fun from today • Sing a song

3:00 Dismissal

D A Y 4

8:15 Arrival routines and review/practice signals

8:35 Morning Meeting
- Greeting: Same as Day 2
- Sharing: Favorite book/story
- Group Activity: Sing "We're All Back Together Again"
- Morning message: Choral reading

8:55 Remind/re-model Transition back to seats

9:00 Math Play Pop-Up Number • Practice with human number line • Try "one more and one less" problems

9:45 Snack

10:00 Outside time or energizer

10:20 Special

11:00 Reading Independent reading: 5–10 minutes • Partner chat

11:30 Establishing rules Brainstorm ideas: "Why do we come to school?"

11:45 Recess Play a previously taught tag game

12:05 Lunch

12:30 Quiet time Read, draw, or use dominos

12:45 Read-aloud Practice partner chats

1:00 Energizer Alphabet Aerobics

1:10 Writing Write and draw about favorite book/story • Partner chat

1:50 Guided Discovery Introduce scissors and glue • Preview learning goals (or "hopes and dreams") project

2:25 Outside time or energizer

2:40 End-of-day logistics

2:50 Closing circle Around-the-circle: One thing I'm looking forward to tomorrow • Sing a song

3:00 Dismissal

D A Y 5

8:15 Arrival routines and review/practice signals

8:35 Morning Meeting
- Greeting: Same as Day 2
- Sharing: Favorite piece of writing this week
- Group Activity: Sing a song learned this week
- Morning message: Choral reading

8:55 Remind/re-model Transition back to seats

9:00 Math Introduce hundreds chart on floor • Interactive Modeling: How to ask for help • Class challenge: Fill in chart with numbers

9:45 Snack

10:00 Outside time or energizer

10:20 Special

11:00 Reading Introduce new book bins • Independent reading: 10 minutes • Introduce teacher-student conferences

11:30 Establishing rules Reflect on "Why do we come to school?" ideas • Students start listing goals (or "hopes and dreams")

11:45 Recess Play a previously taught tag game

12:05 Lunch

12:30 Quiet time Read, draw, or use any math tool from shelf

12:45 Read-aloud Understanding character: "What do we know about _____?"

1:00 Energizer Alphabet Aerobics

1:10 Writing Pick one piece of writing from week • Make final draft • Post on bulletin board

2:00 Outside time or energizer

2:20 Fun read-aloud

2:40 End-of-day logistics

2:50 Closing circle Around-the-circle: One thing I enjoyed this week • Sing a song

3:00 Dismissal

Flow of the Day

Beginning the Day

Settling Into a Morning Routine

This week you can establish the usual routines for beginning the day. For example, children might hang up backpacks, get name tags, and read or draw. Then, once everyone is settled, the class gathers in the circle for Morning Meeting. Each day, help children ease into this same routine, and by week's end school will feel like a safe, predictable landing place. In the coming weeks, as students are ready, add extra steps to the morning routine, such as interacting with the morning message and doing morning jobs.

Morning Meeting Expectations

If you went right into Morning Meeting yesterday to calm first-day jitters, now you can back up and explain why we start each day with a Morning Meeting and set up some expectations. Because young students haven't yet developed listening stamina, they'll fidget if you talk too long, so keep explanations brief. Try sprinkling in little bits of explanation each day, gradually building up children's focus and understanding of Morning Meeting. For example:

> **Sample Morning Meeting Rules**
>
> ➤ Be friendly.
> ➤ Listen to others.
> ➤ Take turns.

- *Morning Meeting rules*—Post and refer to a simple set of rules in your circle area to help guide appropriate behavior during Morning Meeting.

- *Purpose*—You might simply say, "We're going to start each day with a Morning Meeting. These meetings will help us get to know each other and have fun together first thing every day."

- *Structure*—Young children find routines comforting. Let them know that Morning Meeting will follow a predictable pattern: "Each day, we'll meet in the circle. We'll greet each other, share news, do an activity, and read our morning message."

Morning Meeting Ideas

Repeating Morning Meeting activities helps build young students' confidence this first week. Use the same basic greeting, sharing, group activity, and morning message that you used on day one, making small adjustments as needed.

- *Greeting*—If on day one you used a basic "Good morning" greeting in which you greeted each student by name, on day two you might model how to pass a "Good morning" greeting around the circle, emphasizing key elements for students to practice (speaking audibly, using a friendly tone, looking at the person, and using names). This can become the greeting for the rest of week one. Remember to reinforce the class's use of these skills: "I noticed you all used a friendly voice when you greeted each other."

- *Sharing*—Likewise, if students shared about a favorite animal on the first day, have them share other favorites (a food, place to visit, book, or color), one each day for the rest of this week. Using an around-the-circle structure makes sharing comforting; varying topics keeps it fresh. Again, you'll want to name, model, and reinforce the key skills students should be practicing as they share.

- *Group activity*—On day two, you might sing "Peanut Butter, Grape Jelly" again. Then, on day three, use a different song or a chant to start building your class repertoire. Singing songs and learning chants are great week one activities because they're low-risk and their inclusiveness strengthens group cohesion. (See Appendix B for song lyrics and directions to activities and learning structures mentioned in this chapter.)

- *Morning message*—For kindergartners and first graders, who may not be reading independently, use a consistent morning message setup to begin developing fluency and comprehension. For second graders, vary your morning messages slightly each day.

Also this first week, review the morning message together in a consistent way. For example, read the message out loud first and then have the class read it together as you point to each word. A simple, engaging structure like this helps students practice critical literacy skills: listening, reading with fluency, speaking audibly, and working with print (reading from left to right and from top to bottom, recognizing spaces between words).

Grades K-1 Sample Message

August 30, 20—

Good Morning!

It's the second day of school.

I hope you have a great day!

Mr. Bass

Grade 2 Sample Message

August 30, 20—

Good Morning, Explorers!

Today will be another great day together!

Think about: What place do you like to visit?

Mrs. Sherman

Morning Snack

To help children begin settling into a predictable pattern, establish a consistent snack routine, such as get a snack, sit in their seat, eat, and clean up. You'll want to model and practice things like how to open snacks and clean up. Later in the year, you can add other elements to this time of day, such as choices of what to do when students finish eating. For now, keep snack simple so students can master the basic logistics.

Middle of the Day

Recess

On the first day of school, students had their initial experiences with recess. However, many will need help remembering where to go and what to do during this time. A few proactive reminders can help everyone be successful: "Who can remind us how we line up for recess?"

Leading a tag game during the first week can also ensure that all children have fun, are safe, and feel included at recess. If you introduced Freeze Tag on day one with you as the tagger, play this game again on day two. As students gain expertise, introduce variations (a student as tagger, multiple taggers, and so on). Introduce only simple recess games this first week so that students can focus on following the rules and playing well together. As they play, give any needed reminders—"Remember to tag gently with one hand"—and positive reinforcement—"Everyone is trying to unfreeze people who need help."

Lunch

Using assigned seats for lunch helps eliminate children's jockeying for seats next to best friends or rushing to get the "good" seats. Later in the year, once students are ready, transition to a more open-seating lunch. Because your presence will help establish a safe and relaxed tone, consider eating with students the first week. This will also give you more opportunities to build relationships with them. During lunch, you might also try to engage with children who are shy to help them feel more connected to you and to their classmates.

Whenever you see students being successful meeting lunchtime expectations, use reinforcing language to give positive feedback: "Lots of students are cleaning up their tables." "Look at how smoothly everyone is lining up. You know just what to do!"

Quiet Time

Early in the year, children will do better in quiet time if they're limited to two or three simple choices, such as reading, coloring, or using math counters. Limiting choices also helps students learn the routines of quiet time (especially staying in one spot and being quiet). For as long as it takes for children to develop the necessary stamina, continue your day one practice of breaking quiet time into smaller chunks, each followed by a brief reflection and refocusing.

The following table offers one suggestion for how to set up quiet time. As children become more capable of staying quietly focused, gradually increase quiet choice time and reduce reflection time, adjusting each based on children's needs and abilities.

Setting Up Quiet Time		
Day 2	Day 5	Rest of Year
• Settle in (1 minute) • Quiet choice time (2–3 minutes) • Reflection (1 minute) • Quiet choice time (2–3 minutes) • Reflection (1 minute) • Quiet choice time (2–3 minutes) • Reflection or energizer (1 minute)	• Settle in (1 minute) • Quiet choice time (5–6 minutes) • Reflection (1 minute) • Quiet choice time (5–6 minutes) • Reflection or energizer (1–2 minutes)	• Settle in (1 minute) • Quiet choice time (10–13 minutes) • Reflection or energizer (1–2 minutes)

Ending the Day

Dismissal Logistics

What needs to be taken care of at the end of each day? Your list may include cleaning the room, passing out notes for parents, packing backpacks, and making sure everyone knows where they're going after school, which is especially important when children have different destinations each day (an after-school program on Tuesday, a grandparent's home on Wednesday, and so on).

Consider making an anchor chart so students know what the end-of-day routine entails. To create a sense of predictability and allow enough time for students to enjoy a smooth end-of-day transition, practice these tasks as a class in the same order each day this week.

Closing Circle

In this first week, be sure to tell students the goals for closing circle: to reflect on and celebrate each day of learning together. As with Morning Meeting, when students know why they're joining together for closing circle, they'll approach it with more purpose and positive energy.

This week, keep the closing circle brief and simple. For example, sing a song that you've already introduced or have students share one thing they've enjoyed about the day. Remember to practice and reinforce the same essential speaking and listening skills that you're working on during Morning Meeting and throughout the day: listening to each other without interruption, looking at the audience, staying on topic, and speaking clearly.

Teaching Academics

During this first week, we establish the foundations for children to become confident, capable learners. We teach students how to share materials, ask for help, and efficiently complete other basic but essential academic tasks and routines.

Materials

If students are to accomplish the learning goals in this week's lesson plans, which materials are *essential* for them to use? This is another one of the balancing acts so important at this early point in the year. You do want to introduce materials that will build excitement about academic work, but you don't want to overwhelm students, so if they don't need a material this week, keep it safely tucked away.

Here are two techniques you can use to introduce materials to your students:

- *Interactive Modeling*—to teach the expectations for materials that should be used in a specific way, such as sharpening pencils without disturbing others.
- *Guided Discovery*—to enable children to investigate crayons, pattern blocks, glue sticks, and other materials that can be used in more open-ended ways.

See Appendix A to learn more about these two techniques.

By helping children learn how to use materials with creativity and care early, we teach them skills that will enable them to work safely, more independently, and with greater engagement all year long.

Academic Routines

On the first day of school, students got a taste of academic excitement and success. Now it's time to start teaching the routines that will support their best academic efforts throughout the year.

Though our inner teacher voice might be saying "Hurry! Hurry! Hurry!" remember that time spent teaching foundational academic routines now will mean that students can go much further with their learning as the year progresses. Here are some tips for teaching those routines:

- Just as you use Interactive Modeling to introduce materials that need to be used in a certain way, also use it to introduce academic routines that need to be done in a certain way, such as printing electronic files.

- Practice often and model again as needed. It takes a while for routines to become automatic, so be patient as students learn.

- Observe students carefully as they practice and offer reinforcement and reminders as needed.

- View mistakes as learning opportunities for students and coaching opportunities for you.

Useful Materials to Introduce in Week One

- ➤ Counters, cubes, dominos, blocks
- ➤ Crayons, markers, pencils, erasers
- ➤ Glue sticks, paper clips, stapler, tape
- ➤ Book bins, folders, sticky notes

Useful Academic Routines to Teach in Week One

- ➤ Appropriate voice volume
- ➤ Getting out/putting away materials
- ➤ Choosing a "just right" book
- ➤ Getting the teacher's attention (for example, staying in seat and raising hand quietly)
- ➤ Staying in one work spot

Academic Choice

When we give students practice making simple decisions, we help them learn how to make good choices about their learning. This week, give students basic choices about what they learn (for example, which book to read) or how they learn it ("You may choose to read in a chair or on the floor, whichever is more comfortable so you can focus on your reading").

To make good decisions, students need to know the purpose of their choice. Notice how the "where to read" prompt not only invites students to choose but also invites them to think about their decision, encouraging them to make a choice that will help them focus. On the next page is a simple Academic Choice lesson you can use or adapt to give students some early practice in making choices about their learning.

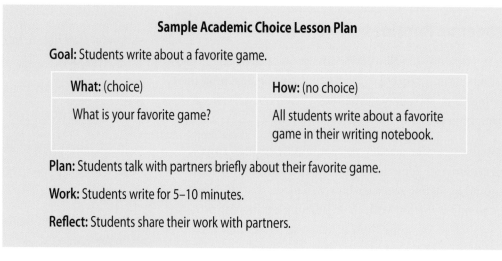

Sample Academic Choice Lesson Plan

Goal: Students write about a favorite game.

What: (choice)	**How:** (no choice)
What is your favorite game?	All students write about a favorite game in their writing notebook.

Plan: Students talk with partners briefly about their favorite game.

Work: Students write for 5–10 minutes.

Reflect: Students share their work with partners.

To learn more about Academic Choice, see Appendix A.

Teaching Collaboration

Throughout the year, students will work with partners, in small groups, and as a whole group. But successful collaboration is more complex than simply pairing children up and saying, "Work together." We have to teach students the skills needed to work collaboratively. Two key collaboration skills to teach this week:

- *Taking turns*—Let's say we want students to practice the math skill of skip-counting. Students could work in pairs, using the counters introduced on day one to create piles of two (or whatever multiples they're practicing). To be successful working with a partner means taking turns creating piles. With a student as your partner (having prepared him or her ahead of time), you can use Interactive Modeling to show how to do this. Then, give students time to practice with a partner, reinforcing their turn-taking skills and efforts at doing math: "I saw everyone taking turns with their partners. You were cooperating, and that helped you get your math work done."

- *Exchanging ideas with a partner*—Simple academic conversation structures such as partner chats engage students in their learning as they practice foundational speaking and listening skills. If children have been previewing books, for example, they can each talk with a partner about one thing they noticed. These first simple academic conversations will enable richer ones to flourish later in the year. Again, model the skills needed for talking with a partner (looking at the person, speaking clearly, staying on topic) and listening (looking at the person, keeping body calm, avoiding interrupting).

Notice that we can teach the same speaking and listening skills for academic work as for Morning Meeting and closing circle. For example, we might model how to speak with a friendly tone when passing a greeting at Morning Meeting and then reinforce that skill when children share ideas about writing topics with a partner.

Setting a Positive Tone for Learning

Here are a few ideas to help you continue building a positive learning culture during this first week:

- *Display student work*—Make it a goal to display at least two pieces of work from each student by the end of week one. To reinforce the value of the learning process, you might also invite students to display in-process work. For example, you might have students choose a math sheet or writing draft and use a piece of construction paper as backing to help make the overall display feel important. As students see their work covering the walls, they'll begin to feel a sense of pride in their efforts and a greater sense of belonging and significance in the classroom.

- *Preview upcoming content*—Throughout the day, preview some of the exciting learning that's on the way. For example, at the end of a math lesson you might say, "I saw everyone enjoying Pop-Up Number. Next week, we'll learn a new activity, Human Protractor, that's just as fun!" Or as students are writing you might mention, "We're off to a great start in writing this year. Pretty soon, we'll be ready to put together our first class book." By telling students about their upcoming learning, we create a sense of positive anticipation and help set the stage for future success.

Reinforcing Language

As we observe these young children this week and going forward, we want to notice and reinforce their progress and efforts. For example:

Reinforcing Language	
To the class:	"You're coming up with so many ideas for how we can use our cubes in math this year."
To a pair of students (privately):	"You took very good care of each other during your partner chat today. You each took turns speaking and really listening to your partner."
To an individual child (privately):	"Kritika, I noticed you stayed focused during independent reading today. You really seemed to be enjoying your book."

Notice the two examples where reinforcing feedback is given privately. Public recognition might make a student feel embarrassed or uncomfortable for being singled out, and other students may feel that we're trying to influence or manipulate them.

Teaching Discipline

On day one, we began teaching and modeling positive discipline—helping children understand and follow classroom routines, meet behavior expectations, and work well together. We continue that teaching throughout the week, while remembering to weave encouraging teacher language and playful activities into all that we do.

Building Relationships

At the beginning of every school year, getting to know each child is one of our primary goals. We make sure to observe every student (not just the ones who talk the most or command the most attention) and note something significant about him or her.

Helping students get to know each other is just as critical. For students to learn together, they must feel connected and safe enough to take the risks inherent to learning. One simple way to help students do this is by inviting them to share information about their families and their favorites at Morning Meeting. To extend this activity, create an All About Us bulletin board, which can also serve as inspiration for writing. Energizers such as A Warm Wind Blows and Just Like Me further strengthen students' connections with classmates while helping them recharge.

Routines for Positive Discipline

Continue teaching and practicing classroom routines with children this week, setting them up for success as they develop into responsible and independent learners. Throughout this week and beyond, we can use Interactive Modeling to teach new routines. We can also use our teacher language, especially reminding language (positive reminders to help students stay on track) and reinforcing language, as students practice previously taught routines.

This teaching doesn't need to be long or involved. For example, before students move chairs, you could say, "Who can remind us how to move a chair safely?" and then ask a volunteer to demonstrate.

Learning Goals

This week, we invite students to articulate their learning goals for the year—what some teachers call students' "hopes and dreams." We're getting to know our students better as learners and also laying the groundwork for next week, when the class will begin working together to establish classroom rules linked to their hopes and dreams.

You'll want to do this work with learning goals even if you're using pre-existing rules—perhaps ones developed by your team, grade level, or whole school—rather than creating new ones with students. Recognizing goals and then connecting them to rules, no matter where the rules come from, helps students see those rules as positive guidelines that create a safe, supportive classroom in which everyone can reach for their goals.

Here's one approach to helping these young students set learning goals:

- On the third or fourth day of school, prompt students to respond to this question: "Why do we come to school?" List students' ideas. If students offer a general idea such as "to learn," help them stretch their thinking: "What can we learn in school?"

- The next day, ask students to reflect on their list of reasons for coming to school. Then help them think about what they want to learn this year—some specific learning goals. For example: "Today, we're going to make another list. What are some of your hopes and dreams for the school year?" As an example, you might want to share some of your own hopes and dreams for the class: "This year, I hope that our classroom will be a place where all students find enjoyment and get to work at things that really matter to them."

- List students' ideas as they share. If students suggest ideas that seem unrealistic, coach them in rethinking. If Sebastian suggests that he wants to read all of the books in the school library, you might say, "It sounds like you want to do a lot of reading this year. Can I write that down as your goal?" Try to keep this brainstorming session short, perhaps five to ten minutes. Tell students that next week they'll come back to this list, add more ideas, and then choose one to illustrate and share. These goals will serve as a springboard for creating the classroom rules together.

<aside>
Learning Goals Discussion Tip

If you're a kindergarten or first grade teacher, you might want to wait until the second week of school to begin a discussion of students' learning goals. Young students often need more school experience before they can start thinking about what they want to learn and do in school.
</aside>

Responding to Misbehavior

We should expect young children to struggle at times with behavior as they adjust to school this week. Some may tire quickly and lose self-control. Others may simply forget the expectations for school. Whatever the reason, we want to step in promptly and help children get back on track by giving a simple, respectful, matter-of-fact redirection. For example:

Off-Track Behavior	Redirecting Language
After getting off the bus, Ruben races into school and down the hall.	"Ruben, stop. Walk the way we practiced."
Danielle uses a swear word.	"That word isn't okay here. Use a school-appropriate word."
At the end of the day, Jeremy rolls around on the floor.	"Jeremy, sit in this chair and wait for your bus to be called."

As you reflect on the first week of school, note all that you accomplished: learning names, helping students carry out routines more automatically, sparking their excitement about learning, and much, much more. Picture the progress individual students have made already, focusing on the small, incremental steps that are critical to their future success.

Third & Fourth Grades

Yesterday, our efforts focused on learning names, teaching essential routines, helping students' connect with one another, and boosting their feelings of trust and competence as learners. These same themes continue throughout this first week. Blending consistency and novelty will help students feel secure—"I know what to expect"—and get excited about their learning—"I can't wait to see what we'll do next!"

D A Y   2

8:15 Establish arrival routines and practice signals for quiet attention

8:35 Morning Meeting
- Greeting: Around-the-circle "Good morning"
- Sharing: After-school activity
- Group activity: Who Remembers?
- Morning message: After-school activity

8:55 Model/re-model Transition back to seats

9:00 Math Skip Counting energizer • Explore math book • Work with pattern blocks

9:45 Snack

10:00 Outside time or energizer • Review circling up and safe tagging • Play Category Tag

10:20 Reading Introduce reading stamina • Ideas for staying focused on reading • Reflection

11:00 Establishing rules Introduce learning goals (or "hopes and dreams") • Brainstorm ideas

11:20 Writing Introduce with energizer: A Warm Wind Blows • Journal topics (after-school activities) • Personalize journals

11:45 Recess Review/play Category Tag • Introduce tagger's choice

12:05 Lunch

12:30 Quiet time Reading, writing, pattern blocks

12:45 Read-aloud Practice partner chats

1:05 Special

1:50 Science Introduce science journals • Energizer: What's the Change?

2:35 End-of-day logistics Clean up, pack up, after-school destinations

2:50 Closing circle Around-the-circle: Something I'm looking forward to tomorrow • Homework: Think about learning goals for the year

3:00 Dismissal

D A Y   3

8:15 Establish arrival routines and review/practice signals

8:35 Morning Meeting
- Greeting: Around-the-circle "Good morning"
- Sharing: A place I'd like to visit
- Group Activity: A Warm Wind Blows
- Morning message: Goals for the year

8:55 Remind/re-model Transition back to seats

9:00 Math Guided Discovery: Dry-erase markers, boards • Energizer: High Low Up and Down

9:45 Snack

10:00 Outside time or energizer • Toilet Tag

10:20 Reading Review strategies tried yesterday • Book shopping

11:00 Establishing rules Brainstorm learning goals (or "hopes and dreams")

11:15 Writing Journal topics (place to visit) • Introduce writing stamina; writing (5 minutes) • Share one sentence with partner

11:45 Recess Teach new tag game: Fishy, Fishy, Cross My Ocean

12:05 Lunch

12:30 Quiet time Reading, writing, dry-erase boards

12:45 Read-aloud Partner chat

1:05 Special

1:50 Science Energizer: What's the Change? • Observation challenge

2:20 Homework Expectations • Introduce assignment books • Model and practice writing down assignments

2:40 End-of-day logistics

2:50 Closing circle Around-the-circle: What I enjoy about this class

3:00 Dismissal

DAY 4

8:15 Arrival routines and review/practice signals

8:35 Morning Meeting
- Greeting: Around-the-circle "Good morning" and handshake
- Sharing: A family member I like to spend time with
- Group activity: Sing "Ram Sam Sam"
- Morning message: Goals for the year

8:55 Remind/re-model Transition back to seats

9:00 Math Line and line segments • Introduce rulers: Model using as a straight edge

9:45 Snack

10:00 Outside time or energizer • Stuck in the Mud

10:20 Reading Keep working on stamina • Preview reading • Partner chat: One thing that happened in your book

11:00 Establishing rules Choose one goal (or "hope and dream")

11:15 Writing Sentences about goal • Model using stapler, glue, glue sticks • Illustrate goal

11:45 Recess Play a previously taught tag game

12:05 Lunch

12:30 Quiet time Reading, writing/illustrating goal, pattern blocks

12:45 Read-aloud Partner chats

1:05 Special

1:50 Science Observation challenge • Introduce hand lenses

2:20 Homework Practice math and writing homework • Passing in homework procedures

2:40 End-of-day logistics

2:50 Closing circle A Warm Wind Blows

3:00 Dismissal

DAY 5

8:15 Arrival routines and reflect on signals

8:30 Morning Meeting
- Greeting: Around-the-circle "Good morning" and handshake
- Sharing: What I like to do on weekends
- Group activity: Just Like Me
- Morning message: Think about rules

8:55 Remind/reflect Transition to seats

9:00 Math Line segments, rays • Model and practice measuring to nearest inch • Measure around the room

9:45 Snack

10:00 Outside time or energizer • Excuse Me, Please

10:20 Reading Build stamina; thinking as you read • Introduce sticky notes • Partner chat: Favorites

11:00 Establishing rules Reflect on goals (or "hopes and dreams") • Begin to brainstorm rules

11:20 Writing Journal topics (family member, weekend fun) • Writing (10 minutes) • Share one sentence with partner

11:45 Recess Play a previously taught tag game

12:05 Lunch

12:30 Quiet time Reading, writing, rulers

12:45 Read-aloud Introduce vocabulary words • Partner chat

1:05 Special

1:50 Science Skills of observation (brainstorming, journal) • Energizer: What's the Change?

2:35 End-of-day logistics

2:45 Closing circle Week in review • Play a favorite activity

3:00 Dismissal

Flow of the Day

Beginning the Day

Settling Into a Morning Routine

When arrival routines are relaxed and predictable, school becomes a safe landing spot for children. Each morning this week, just as on the first day, I like to be at the door, welcoming students into the classroom. I point out the day's schedule, posted in the same place every day, and use it to establish arrival routines so that students know what they have to do—store backpacks, get name tags (for the first week or so), read the morning message, and prepare for Morning Meeting. By the end of the week, most students will have our morning routine down pat.

Morning Meeting Expectations

On day one, to help students settle back into the rhythms of school, you dove right into a Morning Meeting without providing an overview. Today, take a minute to provide some context for this key daily routine. Here are a few points to highlight:

- Morning Meetings will help us get to know each other so we can work well together.

- Each day, we'll follow the same structure, but each meeting will be a little different, depending on what we're doing in school that day.

- Meetings will be fun and help us learn and practice skills we'll use throughout the day.

To let students know the expectations for Morning Meeting, some teachers also post a short list of rules in the meeting area (see example at right) and refer to these regularly.

*Sample Morning
Meeting Rules*

➤ Listen.

➤ Be friendly.

➤ Stay in control.

Morning Meeting Ideas

During this first week of school, Morning Meeting is a great time to blend predictability and novelty, both of which third and fourth graders relish. Try to stick with simple greetings and activities so students can master foundational skills, feel safe, and develop trust.

■ *Greeting*—We practice greeting others after setting clear expectations for using a respectful handshake, saying each other's names, and looking at each other. Each day, students need to hear what went well ("During today's greeting, I heard everybody say each other's names in a friendly way") and what they can do better ("When we greet each other tomorrow, let's challenge ourselves to use voices that can be heard across the circle"). This constant reflecting on how they did helps students gain a sense of competence and mastery.

■ *Sharing*—An around-the-circle sharing, where each student shares briefly about a given topic, is most effective this week. This sharing structure allows students to learn more about each other in a low-risk way. It also enables students to practice foundational speaking and listening skills such as using complete sentences, speaking audibly, and giving their full attention to the speaker.

> **Inclusive Sharing Topic Ideas for Week One**
>
> ➤ "After school, I like to _____."
>
> ➤ "If I could go anywhere, I'd like to visit _____."
>
> ➤ "A family member I like to spend time with is _____."
>
> ➤ "A pet I'd like to have is _____."

To help students build connections with each other, you may want to list their ideas as they share and display them. These ideas can serve as topics for writing workshops and inspire your choices of activities and energizers for the week.

■ *Group activity*—Third and fourth grade favorites such as Just Like Me and A Warm Wind Blows help students make positive connections with each other and move around a bit, which is especially important for children at this full-of-energy age. Simple, easy-to-learn songs such as "Ram Sam Sam" and "Black Socks" further build students' confidence and sense of class cohesion. And the activities and songs you teach during Morning Meeting can be used as energizers throughout the day, whenever students need a short break. (See Appendix B for song lyrics and directions to activities, energizers, and learning structures mentioned in this chapter.)

■ *Morning message*—Having a morning message for students to read when they arrive each day helps set a welcoming tone and piques their interest about the learning ahead. Messages that are short, with some simple interaction involving the text, are best this week. By using proper grammar, spelling, and punctuation, you're also subtly modeling and reinforcing writing skills.

Read the message together as a class to wind down the meeting and transition to the day's work. Reading the message in a consistent way each day this week—for example, chorally—gives everyone a chance to participate and helps students practice reading fluently.

Morning Break

This week, a designated snack time followed by a short movement break helps students maintain their energy and focus as they adjust to being in school all day.

- *Snack*—In the coming weeks, third and fourth graders will be ready to transition to a working snack, where they can eat when they need to (see page 131 for tips on managing this). This week, to keep things simpler for students, set a specific time just for snack. This will also allow you to teach everyone snack routines, such as cleaning up and repacking lunchboxes, that students will need to do independently throughout the year.

- *Movement break*—Facilitating a brief, whole-class outdoor game or indoor energizer gives students a chance to recharge for the rest of the morning. It also allows you to teach some games that students can play all year long while modeling and practicing expectations for safety, fair play, inclusion, and kindness.

Middle of the Day

Recess

Most likely, students will still need some support throughout week one. A recess option facilitated by an adult can be especially helpful for those students who struggle with this time of day. So even if you don't have recess duty, consider joining students and facilitating a simple game such as Freeze Tag that everyone can play.

To help all children be more successful at recess, model, re-model, and practice key skills such as taking turns and helping others if they fall. With purposeful teaching and supervision, recess can be safe and fun for all.

Lunch

For the rest of this week, just as on day one, assign lunch seats or tables. Early in the year, we want to do all we can to lessen students' stress over finding someone to sit with. We might explain our decision this way: "This week, I'm going to assign seats at lunch to make sure everyone has someone to sit with. Once we get our classroom rules set up, we'll plan how we can choose where to sit in ways that will make lunch inclusive and enjoyable for everyone."

Although you taught lunchtime routines on day one, children will likely need frequent reminders and re-modeling about these routines this week, especially if they need to follow any tricky procedures, such as for recycling or composting.

Quiet Time

In the same way that a consistent morning routine eases the transition from home to the classroom, a consistent quiet time provides students (and teachers) with a few peaceful moments that ease the transition from lunch back into learning.

Later in the year you may want to introduce more quiet time choices, but for now keep them limited so everyone gets used to the routine. To the reading and pattern block options of the first day, you could add writing and drawing. To further ensure a smooth transition from lunch, have students choose their quiet time option before they leave the room for recess.

Ending the Day

Dismissal Logistics

Typically, students' after-school schedules vary day to day. Setting aside a few extra minutes each day this week to prepare for dismissal will help everyone better manage this often confusing transition.

Also this week, begin establishing consistent end-of-day routines. Model and practice these over the course of the week, perhaps introducing one each day so as not to overwhelm students. Here are a few routines to consider:

- Stacking chairs
- Cleaning the room
- Packing backpacks
- Bringing coats and backpacks to a designated spot
- Transitioning to the closing circle area

Closing Circle

Just as you did on day one, reserve a few minutes at the end of each day this week to reflect on the day and bring it to a positive close. Students will likely still find an around-the-circle sharing of "One thing you enjoyed about today" or "Something you're looking forward to tomorrow" engaging and helpful in getting to know their classmates. On Friday, shift the focus slightly to reflect on the week as a whole, celebrating everyone's hard work and blossoming community.

Teaching Academics

The academic work begun on the first day continues this week. Our focus remains on teaching students what to do and how to do it while building a positive climate for learning. If we move too quickly into complex projects or challenging content, students may feel overwhelmed. But if we move too slowly, spending lots of time introducing materials and practicing routines but not getting into any real content, students may get bored. Either way, we risk their disengagement.

So this week we continue our balancing act. We purposefully introduce materials and set up key routines, dig into some rich content and build excitement for learning, and teach essential collaborative skills that will help students learn how to work together.

Materials

If third and fourth graders are to become self-directed learners, it's vital to teach them how to use materials independently. Although students may already have experience with the materials they're using this week, they still need to know the expectations for *this* class for *this* year. Just as you did for day one, consider what materials students will need to use during the lessons you're teaching this week. For example:

- Will students be making observations and recording their thinking in science notebooks? If so, materials to introduce might include hand lenses, colored pencils, science notebooks, rulers, and stopwatches or scales.

- Will they be working on geometry? Then they may need to learn how to use math journals, pattern blocks, and rulers or other measuring tools.

Tips for Introducing Materials

- ➤ Introduce materials just before students are going to use them so they can readily apply them to the lesson.

- ➤ Use Interactive Modeling or Guided Discovery to introduce materials (see Appendix A).

- ➤ Keep materials out of sight until you're ready to introduce them. This adds a sense of excitement and purpose to the learning process and ensures that students aren't tempted to use materials before they're officially introduced.

The key to success here is to teach about materials within academic lessons, not separate from them, so that students know how to apply the materials to their learning. For example, a science lesson in which students will closely observe small objects might begin with a Guided Discovery of hand lenses. Once students have explored lenses and how to care for them, the lesson continues with the teacher modeling how to make and record careful observations. Students then practice with small objects at their tables, recording their thinking in science journals (introduced the previous day).

Academic Routines

On day one, you began setting up the academic procedures of the room—picking a "just right" book, using a raised hand to gain the teacher's attention, putting supplies into cubbies. Now comes the work of establishing the daily rhythms of the room. What will each academic period look, sound, and feel like? What predictable routines will happen throughout the year? As with materials, it's best to do this teaching as part of your academic lessons.

Of course, each content area will have its own structure, so let's explore one as an example—a readers' workshop during the first week.

- *Day Two*—You might model and practice having students bring to the circle their reading bag with the books they need, along with pens, sticky notes, and other supplies. Then, you could do a mini-lesson on how to record an interesting part of a book on a sticky note.

- *Day Three*—Building on yesterday's lesson, you could have students practice finding a comfortable spot for reading and then reading independently for ten minutes while you circulate and help them stay focused. Students record interesting parts of their book on sticky notes (perhaps two or three today).

- *Day Four*—Again, students practice finding a good spot for reading and recording some thinking on sticky notes.

- *Day Five*—As a class, reflect on the procedures learned this week. Invite students to share what they think they're doing well as a class and what they want to improve on next week.

All academic routines take a while to become automatic. To help students stay on track, we'll need to model and model again, remind and redirect. We'll also want to reinforce students' progress: "Everyone stayed in their spots and read quietly. That's exactly how we want reading time to look and sound so everyone can be a successful reader this year."

Academic Choice

Academic Choice is a strategy for giving students some choice in what they learn, how they learn, or both. It helps build engagement in all content areas and provides a way to differentiate learning for all students. This week, we give students small choices that will lead to their being able to tackle rich, varied learning assignments later. Here are examples of simple choices we might offer students as they do their academic work this week:

- Using colored pencils or markers when illustrating learning goals (or what many teachers call "hopes and dreams") for the year (see page 83)
- Choosing five different objects around the room to measure in math
- Deciding which object to observe in science (a leaf, flower, or blade of grass)

Of course, teaching students how to make smart decisions involves more than just saying, "Here are your choices. Pick one!" We need to use language that prompts students to make good choices—ones based on their needs and interests as learners. Here are some examples of helpful teacher language.

Language That Helps Students Make Good Choices	
Before students choose:	• "Now that you've listed places you'd like to visit, choose one to write about. Look over your list. Which one seems most interesting—one that you could write about for five minutes today?"
	• "To practice using rulers, we're going to measure some objects to the nearest inch. Let's brainstorm some ideas for choosing objects that will help you become skilled at measuring with rulers."
After students choose and do the work:	• "You chose a place to write about today. What went well or what was challenging about the place you chose?"
	• "On a scale from one to five, where five is great and one is terrible, how well did you do with measuring today? What would you do differently tomorrow?"

To learn more about Academic Choice, see Appendix A.

Teaching Collaboration

Students' learning is richer when they collaborate—and collaboration is crucial to success in today's world. Throughout the year, students will need to collaborate with a partner and in small groups, but we can't expect them to work together successfully if we don't teach them the necessary skills, especially essential speaking and listening skills such as those listed in the box at right. So in week one, we begin that teaching by focusing on working with a partner. (In week three, we'll teach the skills for working with a small group.)

First, think about how each academic time provides opportunities for children to work with a partner and develop collaboration skills. For example, in Morning Meeting students might share about favorite hobbies. Then, during writing, they can write about those hobbies and share their writing with a partner to get feedback and help revising their work. In math and science, they can work with another partner and explore a learning tool, sharing ideas as they do so. During a read-aloud, students can discuss with a neighbor their responses to an open-ended question you pose: "What would you do next if you were Nick in *Frindle*, and why? Share with your partner."

Throughout these learning activities, students are exchanging ideas and building connections while developing foundational skills for collaborating. But for these experiences to take hold, we must explicitly model the skills first and then coach students as they apply the skills. We can do this effectively by using Interactive Modeling and by incorporating these skills into Morning Meeting and academic lessons.

Sharing and Displaying Work

In a supportive learning community, students feel comfortable sharing their work with others and learning from one another. This sense of confidence and trust enables them to take positive academic risks, which in turn leads to much deeper learning. Throughout this week, we can grow this kind of learning community by having students share their work in partnerships and then, at week's end, share illustrations of their learning goals for the year with the whole class.

Also, when students see their work displayed, they feel a greater sense of academic purpose, belonging, and significance. The idea is to display students' current work—both finished pieces (a math problem they completed) and in-process examples (an entry from their reading log or science journal)—and update displays regularly to keep them fresh.

Reinforcing Language

Throughout this week, step back from time to time and observe students' efforts. Then make it a point to reinforce the positives you see. For example:

Reinforcing Language	
To the class:	"We're doing well talking with partners. I heard many people restating what their partner said in their own words."
To a pair of students (privately):	"You listened to each other's ideas when you worked on those problems. You set a positive tone for working together."
To an individual student (privately):	"Andre, I heard you asking Keesha for help during science. That showed taking responsibility for your learning."

Homework

Setting students up for success with homework this week is time well spent. Consider beginning with a brief class discussion about homework. Explain what homework will look like during the year and why it's important for their learning: "We'll use homework this year as a way to get a little extra skills practice and for independent reading."

Ask students some questions to spark this discussion:

- "What time of day is best for you to do homework?"
- "Where's a quiet place for you to work?"
- "What can be challenging about homework?"

Throughout the week, model and practice routines, especially writing down assignments, packing papers neatly in backpacks, and passing in homework. For this week and next, help all children experience early success with homework by having them practice doing homework in class while you observe them. Seeing how long students take to complete these early assignments will also help you set realistic homework expectations.

Teaching Discipline

When children feel safe and know what's expected, they're better able to focus on learning and less likely to misbehave. Beginning on the first day, we worked to establish a predictable, positive climate, and we continue that effort for the rest of this week.

Building Relationships

During the first six weeks of school, helping students build positive relationships is a priority. It's something we can weave into the fabric of each day. For example:

- *Group students intentionally*—This ensures that students will interact with many different peers. At times, set up groups or partnerships randomly by drawing names from a hat or doing a card-matching activity. At other times, assign specific pairs or groups and observe how well students work together.

- *Choose activities that build connections*—Using activities such as A Warm Wind Blows and Just Like Me for energizers or Morning Meeting activities can help students discover commonalities. Each time students work in pairs, there's a chance for them to make new connections. You might even challenge students when working with new partners to find one thing they have in common.

- *Build student-teacher connections*—Chatting with students at recess or lunch and sharing school-appropriate stories about your own interests helps students get to know you, an important ingredient for building the trust necessary for great learning.

Routines for Positive Discipline

On the first day of school, we began the work of modeling and practicing classroom routines. We continue that work for the rest of this week. In addition to teaching new routines, such as how to ask for and give help during an activity or how to serve as line leader when walking in the halls, we also want to review and re-model routines from the first day.

Keep this review and re-modeling brief. For example, before the class moves chairs after Morning Meeting, you might say, "Yesterday we learned the safe way to move chairs. Who can show us how to do this?" Invite one volunteer to demonstrate and then have the rest of the class move their chairs. The more attention we give to helping students get these routines down during the first six weeks of school, the more autonomous they can be— and the more they can stay on track behaviorally.

Learning Goals

Helping students articulate their learning goals, or hopes and dreams, for the year is the first step in creating rules together. Perhaps Jaliyah wants to learn to multiply big numbers. Sam hopes to study a famous artist. Angela wants to make new friends. Later this week, the class will start creating classroom rules that guide behavior and support a safe learning environment, enabling everyone to reach for their goals.

Early in this week, we begin the process by helping students brainstorm possible goals in short sessions and spreading this brainstorming over the course of the week, giving them time to come up with lots of ideas. List their ideas and share your hopes and dreams for students for the school year as well. Mine is usually something like "I hope our class grows into a safe and strong learning community."

By the end of the week, have each student choose one goal to illustrate and share with the class. Then proudly display these on a bulletin board. You might want to have students use a worksheet like the one shown to help them come up with a goal that's achievable and meaningful.

As students work on their goals, encourage them to consider ones they truly care about and can realistically achieve in school this year. For example:

- *If students start with an idea they aren't that enthused about,* such as "I want to have better handwriting," push their thinking by asking, "Why is neat handwriting important to you?" If their rationale is "I don't know" or "My mom wants me to write neater," encourage them to focus on a goal that's more personally relevant. Perhaps a meaningful goal for this student is "To take the time I need to do careful work this year."

- *If students start with a goal that's clearly not realistic for this school year,* help them focus on one that is attainable. For example, if a student's goal is being a professional musician, help the student think instead about the skills needed to reach the long-term goal that they can focus on this year. For example, professional musicians need

Hopes and Dreams Planning Sheet

Name: _____ Date: _____

List what you really enjoyed doing in school last year: _____

_____

_____

List some challenges you worked on last year: _____

_____

What are some goals you have for this year? (List at least three.) _____

_____

Which goal would you especially like to work on this year? _____

_____

Draw a rough sketch to illustrate that goal:

stick-to-itiveness, and that's something all students can work on. A student might articulate this goal as "I want to work hard and keep trying, even when something is difficult for me."

Connecting Goals to Rules

By the end of the week, once students' goals are shared and posted, students are ready to think about how the class will need to function for everyone to reach their goals. We might say, "Take a look again at all the hopes and dreams we have. What are some rules that could help us work together so we can reach our goals?" After a brief discussion and some initial brainstorming, let students know that next week they'll do more brainstorming to create the class rules. (You'll read more about this step in the next chapter.)

Connecting rules to students' hopes and dreams for learning is important even if you'll be using rules developed by your team, grade level, or school rather than creating new ones with students. Making that connection helps students see the rules as positive guidelines that create a safe, supportive classroom in which everyone can meet their goals.

Responding to Misbehavior

No matter how well we teach positive behavior, students will still daydream, say or do unkind things, or lose self-control. We should expect students to make mistakes with behavior and know how to respond effectively when they do. One way to do this is by using redirecting language as soon as we notice students going off track. For example:

Off-Track Behavior	Redirecting Language
As students are practicing reading and staying in one spot, Brian gets up to get a new book.	"Stay in your reading spot, Brian. You can go book shopping later."
In the rush to line up for recess, Charmaine leaves her writing materials at her table.	"Charmaine, head back to your table and take care of your writing materials."
Rose pushes a student who cuts in front of her as the class lines up for dismissal and shouts, "No cuts, cheater!"	"Rose, come stand by me for dismissal. I know you're upset, but we only use kind words and touches in our classroom."

As the first week comes to an end, some students may tire and tend to make more mistakes as a result. For some, school requires an immense amount of self-control, and at times they may find it's just too hard to hold it all together. For others, testing limits is a way to see how we adults respond. For any misbehavior, prompt, matter-of-fact, respectful responses help every child know that you're there to keep everyone safe and secure—and on track for learning.

The first week is one of the most intense times of the school year. No matter how well it goes, you may be ready to collapse on the couch when you get home on Friday. Though you'll likely have planning to do, carve out some time over the weekend just to relax. You'll be much more rejuvenated for all the teaching and learning that will happen in the coming week.

Fifth & Sixth Grades

After the first day, most students will enter school with less visible anxiety as they make their way to class. However, even though students appear more relaxed and confident, we must remember that almost everything we'll do this week is still new to them. Even routines introduced on the first day will likely need to be modeled and practiced again. For the rest of this week we'll continue to focus on establishing key routines, building students' sense of excitement about academic work, and developing a positive class community.

DAY 2

8:15 Establish arrival routines

8:30 Review/practice signals for quiet attention

8:35 Morning Meeting
- Greeting: Pass Koosh ball "Good morning" around circle
- Combined sharing/group activity: A Warm Wind Blows
- Morning message: Thinking about learning goals (or "hopes and dreams")

8:55 Remind/re-model Transition back to seats

9:00 Math Multiplication facts with math partner • Introduce color tiles • Array challenge • Pica Fermé Nada

9:45 Snack

10:00 Outside time or energizer • Review circling up • Captain's Coming

10:20 Reading Model choosing a "just right" book • Introduce sticky notes • Independent reading (20 minutes)

11:00 Establishing rules Introduce learning goals • Brainstorm ideas • Students list their ideas

11:30 Writing Introduce writing an autobiographical sketch • List writing topics • Practice partner chats

12:00 Recess Captain's Coming

12:15 Lunch Uncommon Commonalities

12:40 Quiet time Reading, listing ideas for learning goals, using color tiles

12:55 Read-aloud Partner chat

1:10 Special

1:55 Social studies Introduce maps and atlases • Explore key features of maps and atlases

2:30 Introduce homework

2:40 End-of-day logistics Clean up, pack up, destinations

2:50 Closing circle Around-the-circle: Something I'm looking forward to tomorrow • Homework: Possible learning goals (for year)

3:00 Dismissal

DAY 3

8:15 Arrival routines

8:30 Review/practice signals

8:35 Morning Meeting
- Greeting: Pass Koosh ball "Good morning" around circle
- Sharing: Array card match
- Group activity: Sing "Peanut Butter, Grape Jelly"
- Morning message: More about learning goals

8:55 Remind/re-model Transition back to seats

9:00 Math Guided Discovery: Dry-erase markers, boards • Practice arrays on dry-erase boards

9:45 Snack

10:00 Outside time or energizer • Elves, Wizards, and Giants • Tagger's Choice

10:20 Reading Review choosing books; open nonfiction section • Independent reading (20–30 minutes) • Begin one-on-one conferencing

11:00 Establishing rules Choose a social and an academic learning goal • Introduce writing and drawing a goal (or "hope and dream") • Post first draft on wall space

11:30 Writing Review topic lists • Pick one topic and share with partner • Summarize sharing in journal

12:00 Recess Elves, Wizards, and Giants

12:15 Lunch Table groups

12:40 Quiet time Reading, writing, dry-erase board, book shopping

12:50 Read-aloud Partner chat

1:10 Special

1:55 Social studies Map scavenger hunt

2:20 Homework Introduce assignment books • Model and practice writing down an assignment

2:45 End-of-day logistics Clean room • Bring chairs to circle

2:50 Closing circle Around-the-circle: What I'm enjoying about this class

3:00 Dismissal

Week One Sample Schedule ■ Grades 5–6

DAY 4

8:15 Arrival routines

8:35 Morning Meeting
- Greeting: Greet neighbors with handshake
- Sharing: Array card match
- Group activity: Human Protractor
- Morning message: Introduce independent snacks

8:55 Math Multiplying powers of 10 • Practice multiplying with cards • Human Protractor

9:50 Outside time or energizer • Play a previously taught game

10:05 Reading Introduce and practice readers' workshop

11:00 Establishing rules Brainstorm rules • Continue work on goals (or "hopes and dreams")

11:30 Writing Share examples of autobiographical sketches • Share another topic with partner and write about it

12:00 Recess Elves, Wizards, and Giants

12:15 Lunch Table groups

12:40 Quiet time Reading, working on learning goals, using any opened supply

12:50 Read-aloud Partner chat

1:10 Special

1:55 Social studies Map the classroom • Two-day partner project

2:20 Homework practice Writing down an assignment • Completing an assignment • Handing in completed assignment

2:45 End-of-day logistics

2:50 Closing circle Human Protractor or Uncommon Commonalities

3:00 Dismissal

DAY 5

8:15 Arrival routines

8:30 Morning Meeting
- Greeting: Greet neighbors with handshake
- Sharing: Partner chat (something I like to do on weekends)
- Group activity: A Warm Wind Blows
- Morning message: Number collection

8:55 Math Finding factors • Array challenge • Class factor challenge with partners

9:50 Outside time or energizer • Play a previously taught game

10:05 Reading Review: What has gone well; what has been challenging? • Shop for books (10 minutes) • Independent reading (20–30 minutes)

11:00 Establishing rules Brainstorm rules and connect to learning goals • Complete and post goals (or "hopes and dreams")

11:30 Writing Introduce peer conferences • Practice peer conferences

12:00 Recess Play a previously taught tag game

12:15 Lunch Table groups

12:40 Quiet time Same as day 4

12:50 Read-aloud Partner chat

1:10 Special

1:55 Social studies Continue to map the classroom • Post maps

2:40 End-of-day logistics

2:50 Closing circle Week in review • Do an activity we've enjoyed • Preview next week

3:00 Dismissal

Flow of the Day

Beginning the Day

Settling Into a Morning Routine

With a day of school under their belts, fifth and sixth graders are ready to start learning the morning routines. (There are probably too many to teach all at once, so introduce a few at a time.) Make sure you're ready for students as soon as they enter the room this week, greeting them at the door, showing everyone where to turn in paperwork from home, reminding them to put on their name tags, and directing them to the circle to read the morning message.

Your positive and predictable presence first thing every morning this week will help school feel safe and establish an inviting tone that pays dividends all week—and all year—long.

Setting Up Morning Meeting

For the rest of this week, continue to emphasize the value of Morning Meeting. Fifth and sixth graders may need to hear this message multiple times to really understand it. And without this understanding, older students may sometimes feel a bit awkward about Morning Meeting.

So as you introduce a handshake greeting, you might say, "A firm handshake is a valuable real-world skill. When you interview for college or a job, the first impression you give can make a huge difference, and one of those first impressions will come from your greeting." When you introduce an activity, you might say, "I'm going to teach you a game. Later on today, we're going to use this game to practice some challenging math content."

Morning Meeting Ideas

Build on the first day's Morning Meeting with straightforward, low-risk meetings this week that will help create a sense of predictability and a tone of belonging, significance, and fun. And even though it's tempting to assume that older students will know how to do a certain skill or routine, continue to take some time for modeling to help ensure students' success going forward.

■ *Greeting*—Because upper elementary grade students may be self-conscious this first week, keep greetings simple and low-risk: around-the-circle verbal greetings or partner handshakes. These basic greetings help students develop key social skills such as greeting others by name, using a friendly tone, and listening to others.

■ *Sharing*—Partner chats in which you name the topic are a safe initial sharing structure for fifth and sixth graders, enabling them to talk with one other person without worrying that all eyes are on them or feeling pressured to think up a "cool" topic on their own.

To ensure that students make connections with different classmates, consider giving all students cards and having them find their match. For example, cards could be aligned with some early math content, so the person with the 5 x 7 equation card pairs up with the person with the 5 x 7 array card.

Safe and Inviting Sharing Topics for Week One

➤ Favorite book, movie, or song

➤ A place you want to visit someday

➤ Favorite afterschool activity

➤ Pets or animals

➤ Family members

➤ Least favorites

■ *Group activity*—Fifth and sixth graders enjoy games as much as (or maybe even more than!) first graders, but they can also be leery about games that could result in making mistakes in front of each other. Activities and songs such as Human Protractor, A Warm Wind Blows, and "Peanut Butter, Grape Jelly" get everyone moving, connect to academic skills, and involve little risk. Later in the year, acting games like charades and What Are You Doing? become possible as students build trust and competence working together. (See Appendix B for song lyrics and directions to activities and learning structures mentioned in this chapter.)

■ *Morning message*—Explain that all students are expected to read the message to themselves before the meeting begins. To help them engage with the message this week, include an intriguing question or a preview of the day. By the end of the week, consider including a more interactive part of the message to which students add ideas directly. Be sure to explain how this works and note that all students are expected to add at least one idea. See a sample message on the next page.

Happy Friday, Sixth Graders!

9/5/——

Can you believe the first week is almost over? It's been fun, and I think we're all ready for a relaxing weekend!

We've been exploring multiplication this week. Today we're going to embark on The Great Factor Challenge. In the space below, write a number between 1 and 100 that we could break down into factors.

HAGF! (Have a Great Friday!)
Mr. Hilliard

Middle of the Day

Recess

With their day one experience behind them, many students will welcome an option for free play at recess. Some may want to play soccer, while others prefer to walk and chat with friends. However, for other students, especially those without favorite games or strong social connections, recess can be a time when they feel especially alone or bored, or worse, shunned or teased.

Offering some options this week that welcome everyone's participation (and are facilitated by an adult) ensures that recess is safe and inclusive for everyone. Captain's Coming, Elves, Wizards, and Giants, and similar activities are low-risk options for upper elementary students—offering them a chance to get some exercise and have fun with their peers while learning how to engage positively with others.

Lunch

Because of the importance of peers for this age group, we want to structure lunch as well as recess to foster prosocial interactions. As on the first day, set up lunch this week so that everyone has a group to join and something positive to discuss. Continue to provide a few conversation starters or help facilitate a round of Uncommon Commonalities, an activity where a group of students tries to see how many things they can find that they have in common but that aren't readily obvious. Throughout this week, help students successfully navigate this potentially challenging time by reinforcing positive behaviors frequently and reminding and redirecting as needed.

Quiet Time

It's best to keep choices relatively limited for the rest of this week, although we can start adding options as soon as the class seems ready. What's most important this week is continuing to be clear and consistent about expectations. Students should quickly choose what to do, settle into a spot, and work quietly and independently for the duration of quiet time.

Quiet Time Tip

I've found that if I use quiet time to work silently myself, serving as a model for students, they're more likely to make the most of this time.

Ending the Day

Dismissal Logistics

As with the first day of school, students will need a little more time for end-of-day routines this week than they will later in the year. Think through exactly how you want these routines to be carried out and then model, re-model, and practice with students this week. How will the room get cleaned? Where should chairs be placed? How will students know where to head after school? When do they pack up their backpacks? These logistics require some time to set up even with older students, but if we invest the time during this week, dismissal will run much more smoothly throughout the year.

Closing Circle

To reinforce the importance of this time, again emphasize how looking back over the day and celebrating accomplishments builds class community and helps students reflect on their learning. Keep closing circle activities simple the rest of this week so that students feel comfortable and successful. For example, you might play a round of Just Like Me or A Warm Wind Blows, or repeat the Morning Meeting sharing structure you used to pair students up and then prompt them to reflect on what they enjoyed doing today or what they're looking forward to tomorrow.

Teaching Academics

It can be tempting, especially in the upper elementary grades, to start right in on complex schoolwork and projects during week one. Yet when we take the time this week to teach the necessary skills and routines that rigorous academic work requires, students will go much further with their learning in the end. For efficiency's sake, we can incorporate a lot of this teaching within our academic lessons. So for the rest of this first week, continue to build the learning community as you teach students skills for collaboration and communication—and get them excited and energized about their academics.

Materials

To decide which materials to introduce this week, think about the work students will actually be doing for the next few days. For example, if students will be using calculators, introduce them using a Guided Discovery or Interactive Modeling, depending on the learning purpose. (See Appendix A for more on these teaching techniques.)

Useful Materials to Introduce in Week One	
Interactive Modeling Ideas:	**Guided Discovery:**
• Computer/tablet (logging on and off, storing) • Printer (loading paper) • Assignment book	• Color tiles (or other math manipulatives) • Dry-erase boards, markers, erasers • Atlases, maps, globes

Academic Routines

On day one, we established a few essential academic procedures. For the rest of this week, we focus on other key procedures to help students start moving toward greater independence with their academic work. This independence will help them grow as students and also enable us to differentiate our instruction. After all, it's students' ability to function independently that enables us to provide individual coaching and meet with small groups.

This means that we need to teach students academic routines for working with autonomy and independence. In addition to the routines you introduced yesterday, here are a few others to introduce this week:

- What to do when you finish a task
- Handling materials (taking out and putting away)
- How to get help if you're stuck
- Keeping track of assignments

We can teach these routines using Interactive Modeling and then re-model, remind, and reinforce as students work toward mastering them.

Academic Choice

Upper elementary students are capable of amazing projects as the year progresses. I've seen students give 45-minute presentations that incorporate active and interactive components such as games, puzzles, and quizzes. Other students have written a short book of poetry, created complex models, or performed elaborate skits to demonstrate what they've learned in a unit of study. The foundation for such sophisticated projects is established in these first few weeks of school through Academic Choice (see Appendix A).

On day one, we gave students some basic, but meaningful, academic choices that they could manage successfully. Now they're ready to learn more about making smart choices for their learning. By scaffolding choice—that is, giving limited options for relatively short tasks and teaching students how to decide among these—we set students up for success with more complex academic choices later in the year.

For example, this week students can make simple choices about what art supplies to use to illustrate their learning goals (or "hopes and dreams"). Perhaps they can choose a place to work during certain academic times. Or we might give three short tasks during math and let students choose the order for completing them. With any of these choices, we can help students learn how to make smart choices by giving them just two to three options and by asking open-ended questions and offering suggestions.

Academic Choices for Week One

➤ Where to work

➤ Which supplies to use

➤ In what order to do simple tasks

➤ What work to do

➤ Which topics to write about

- "As you decide where to read today, think about what you need as a reader. Do you need a space away from others? Do you need a chair, or are you more comfortable on the floor?"

- "You can use colored pencils or markers to illustrate your hopes and dreams paper. If you want strong, bold lines, you might want to use markers. If you'd prefer to be precise with your drawing, the pencils might be a better option."

We can also deepen students' thinking about how to make smart choices in the future by asking them to reflect on how well their choices worked out.

- "Tomorrow, you'll again choose the order in which you complete your math tasks. Think about the order you chose today. How well did that work? Do you think you should try a different order tomorrow?"

- "Reflect on your writing spot choice. Were you able to focus on writing? Tomorrow you'll choose a spot again, so think about which spot will help you do your best writing."

Teaching Collaboration

Great cognitive growth occurs through social interaction; our students will learn more together than they can ever hope to learn separately. High-quality, productive interactions are also essential if students are to meet the demands of a rich and rigorous curriculum. It's our job to teach students how to work together effectively, and we can begin this week by teaching students how to work with partners.

In general, students will be more successful working in pairs this week than in larger groups, which require a more complex set of social-emotional skills and, if attempted too early, can result in some students taking over and others withdrawing. Yesterday, we introduced some essential skills for partner chats. Here are a few ideas for expanding on this teaching for the rest of the week.

- *Use Interactive Modeling*—We can model specific attributes of productive partner work, just as we model how to carry a chair safely. Any time students work with a partner, whether it's during Morning Meeting, math, language arts, or another con-

Communication Skills to Teach This Week	
Listening Skills:	**Speaking Skills:**
• Face your partner.	• Wait until it's your turn to speak.
• Use supportive body language and facial expressions.	• Use confident body posture.
• Listen for (and remember) key details.	• Look at your partner.
• Summarize your partner's sharing in your own words.	• Stay on topic as you share.
	• Speak in complete sentences.

tent area, we can model (or re-model) and have students practice essential communication skills, such as those listed in the chart above.

■ *Use Morning Meetings*—When students share at Morning Meeting, we can give them practice with the same skills they'll use during any content period. We could also have partnerships carry over—pairs who share with each other at Morning Meeting can work together during math, language arts, science, or social studies.

■ *Assign partners and vary them*—This first week of school, we know we can't just say, "Okay, everyone, find a partner!" Later in the year, once we've taught students how to find a partner efficiently and with consideration for others, they may be ready for this. Early in the year, though, we want to deliberately assign partners (trying to match personalities and interests) or simply draw names from a hat. Whatever method you choose, mix partnerships during the first six weeks so that students learn to collaborate with diverse partners, and be sure to observe how well students work with each other.

Rigorous and Relaxed Learning

One of our primary goals at the beginning of the year is to foster a sense of steady engagement while tackling challenging academics. For example, writing an autobiographical sketch can help students share about themselves and learn about their classmates. A playful round of Human Protractor can get everyone laughing while they practice mathematical thinking. Making a map of the classroom in social studies can give students a chance to explore with a partner while learning key mapping skills.

Positive Teacher Language

As I talked with a colleague about building self-motivation and grit in students, she said something quite profound: that how students see themselves is important, but most important is how they think *we* see them. When students know that teachers have high expectations and believe that they're capable of meeting those expectations, this perception has a profound impact on how they learn and develop.

Envisioning Language

On the first day of school, we gave students academic tasks that helped them feel competent. We also used envisioning language to inspire them about this year's learning. For the rest of this week, we continue to use envisioning language to convey our belief that students will be successful this year. For example:

Envisioning Language	
To convey belief in students as learners:	"Think of something you love to learn. It might be basketball, video games, or the flute. Did you realize that you already have an incredible skill set when it comes to learning and challenging yourselves?"
To convey belief that students will engage positively in their work:	"Okay, readers, let's join together in our circle. Be ready to share something you enjoyed about your book today."

Reinforcing Language

Although older students may be looking for more approval from their peers than from us now, they still count on us to guide and coach them. Just as we did on day one, we want to make use of the power of teacher language all this week by reinforcing students' progress and efforts. For example:

Reinforcing Language	
To the class:	"Everyone worked with a new partner today. I saw lots of examples of people cooperating with each other and helping each other stay on task."
To a pair of students (privately):	"Your thoughtful questions about that chapter helped you both think more deeply about the main character's motivation."
To an individual student (privately):	"Hashaam, I saw that you offered to help Anika when she was getting frustrated with the math problems. That was kind and supportive."

Homework

To set students up for success with homework, introduce it slowly this week. We don't want to assume that students know how to do homework productively. Instead, they need to be taught our homework expectations, see us model key homework routines, and get practice with these routines in school. For example, model and practice:

- Writing down assignments

- Checking that each assignment is completed

- Passing in completed homework

- Getting help when needed (for example, by emailing or calling you or a classmate)

Use short, in-class homework assignments that students complete at school all this week. This allows students to ease into the homework routine. Then, next week, we'll help students (and families) get set up for the "real" homework routines that they'll manage on their own.

Teaching Discipline

We took the initial steps of teaching discipline on the first day with our class. For the rest of this week, we carry on this work by helping students build positive relationships and by setting a collaborative tone. Also this week, we begin to involve students in creating the rules.

Building Positive Relationships

We know that a profound shift often happens as elementary students move into fifth and sixth grades. Like their younger-grade counterparts, they still want to have positive connections with their teachers, but now they also crave deeper connections with peers. It's not surprising that they struggle with cliques, teasing, and anxiety about popularity. Recognizing this, we can help students develop positive relationships by:

- *Emphasizing that we all work together*—For the classroom to be productive, collaborative, and inclusive, every student needs to know and be able to work with every other student. Morning Meeting, energizers, and interactive learning structures (even simple partner chats) help students become more comfortable and trusting of one another rather than relying on just one or two friends. Getting-to-know-you activities, such as Just Like Me and other personal surveys (like the one we did on the first day of school), allow students to share about their lives and learning in safe ways.

- *Strengthening peer connections*—When students have positive relationships with their peers, they'll display more prosocial behaviors and focus more on their learning. If we see students who seem reserved, we can mix up recess activities and the seating at lunch to make sure they're always included.

- *Connecting with students*—We can gain insights into students' lives and also connect with them when they share during Morning Meeting and throughout the day. When students know us and feel we have their best interests in mind, they're more likely to trust us when it comes to solving a problem or taking on an academic challenge.

Routines for Positive Discipline

Later in the year, we'll expect upper grade students to be quite independent. For this week, though, we continue the teaching and practicing of routines that we started on the first day of school. Brief review sessions may be all that are needed for these students to strengthen previously taught routines. However, we still use Interactive Modeling to introduce new routines, especially ones that are multifaceted, such as the care of technology resources.

Using positive teacher language to point out students' progress and efforts will also help solidify routines into habits and build community. For example: "You all put the tablets away carefully and efficiently on the cart yesterday. That helped the other class get to use them for their entire time slot."

Learning Goals

In the first half of the week, we can help students begin to articulate learning goals, or what many teachers call "hopes and dreams," for the school year, both social and academic ones. These should be individual goals that students can actually work on in school. To introduce this process, you might state your own hopes and dreams for them this year or share previous student examples, and then have students brainstorm ideas together before settling on their own. I also review students' hopes and dreams to ensure that the goals are realistic and specific. If not, I'll have a brief coaching conference with the student.

Once students have decided on a learning goal, have them write it down and illustrate it. Because these goals will guide the creation of class rules, you'll want to set a deadline for this process, a goal that will move things along while also giving students time to make sure they're finding a goal that is truly important to them. The end of this first week or early next week is a realistic timeframe for upper grade students. When everyone's ready, display their goals and give the class time to read what their classmates have shared.

Even if you're planning to use existing rules—perhaps ones shared by your team, grade level, or whole school—rather than creating new ones with students, you'll still want to connect those rules to students' hopes and dreams for learning. Doing so will help them see the rules as positive guidelines that create a safe, supportive classroom in which they can achieve their goals.

Sample Learning Goals

Academic Goals:

- I'd like to read a book that's at least 300 pages long.

- My hope is to research a famous person who's made a difference in the world.

- I'd really like to try some new science experiments this year.

- My goal is to learn to multiply and divide fractions.

Social Goals:

- I want to get better at working on group projects.

- My goal is to make some new friends this year.

- I hope to get better at taking risks in front of a group.

- My goal is to join or start an after-school program.

Establishing Rules Together

To begin a discussion about creating rules as a class, you might say, "You've had a chance to read everyone's learning goals. Let's start thinking of some rules that can help us work together really well and allow everyone to reach their goals."

First, have students brainstorm rules with partners and then as a whole group while you record ideas. Coach students in framing rules so they're stated positively. For example, if a student says, "We shouldn't swear and be mean to each other," you might suggest, "How can you restate that rule so it lets everyone know what to do?" The rule might then become "Use kind and supportive words with each other."

Allowing the brainstorming session to unfold over several days gives students more time to come up with new ideas. By devoting time to the rules creation process this week, you'll help students better understand the value of having rules in place. Most likely, by week's end you'll have a long list of possible rules that range from "Show respect" to "Pick up trash" and everything in between. Next week, you'll work with students to consolidate all those ideas into three to five essential rules.

Responding to Misbehavior

Just as we did on the first day of school, we want to address any misbehavior this week right away, while maintaining a calm, respectful tone so students continue to feel safe and valued. One way to do this is to give a clear, respectful, matter-of-fact redirection as soon as we notice them going off track with their behavior. For example:

Off-Track Behavior	Redirecting Language
After a classmate shares about playing the trumpet, Stefan mutters, "The trumpet sucks."	"Stefan, we make only respectful comments in this classroom."
After Minori enters the classroom, she lets her coat drop to the floor and leaves it there.	"Minori, hang up your coat before you read the morning message."
Tablets have just been introduced. Joey starts opening various apps when he's supposed to be listening to instructions.	Have Joey give you the tablet. Return it a few minutes later with a reminder: "We're just using this one app for now."

LAST THOUGHT

5–6

We're laying important groundwork throughout this first week of school. We're setting a tone of safety and collaboration, building initial skills of independence, and getting students excited about their learning. In the coming weeks, we'll build on this foundational work and continue to pave the way for students' success.

Week Two

Goals for Week Two

Last week, we taught and practiced initial routines, worked at learning names and making positive connections, and began the year's first academic work. It's often during the second week that the school day starts to take on a more comfortable feel as procedures and routines develop into habits. Our goals for this week are for every student to:

- *Continue to build connections with all classmates* and feel part of a positive learning community.

- *Have opportunities to practice and polish routines* introduced in week one and learn additional key routines.

- *Experience more academic choices* and work on multi-day assignments or projects.

- *Gain more confidence in speaking and strengthen listening skills,* working with partners and as part of the whole group.

- *Work together to finalize the classroom rules* in Grades 3–4, or finish learning goals (or "hopes and dreams") for the year in grades K–2.

Overview for All Grades

During the second week of school, we see the classroom start to blossom. The first student work is posted on the walls. Books, science journals, sight word cards, writing notebooks, math journals, and other learning tools are accumulating in desks and cubbies. And it's not just the room that seems to be bursting with energy. First graders approach the beginning of the day with purpose—hanging up backpacks and attending to morning jobs with industry. Third graders hurry down the hall, eager to reconnect with teachers. Fourth graders excitedly focus on the daily schedule: "Yes! We've got science this afternoon!" and "Look what we're doing in math today!" Meanwhile, the sixth graders try to enter the classroom coolly, but we know their hidden vitality is ready to be uncapped.

As with the first week of school, the work of building community—and developing children's social-emotional skills—is integrated with the teaching of academic content and skills. Students practice listening to each other and talking clearly at Morning Meeting and when they share their writing or their math thinking. Taking time in these early

107

weeks to connect students' learning goals to classroom rules and expectations sets students up for success with the rigorous and collaborative academic work to come.

This week is also a time to continue boosting academic momentum. We start digging into work that takes more than one or two class periods to accomplish. We might work toward the first published piece of writing or a science project that takes several days to complete. This deliberate stretching out of work lends a greater sense of significance and purpose to the learning.

At the same time, pushing students too hard too soon can have a negative impact on our newly formed learning communities. Kindergartners who have to read for too long at a stretch will soon be rolling on the floor. Second graders may chatter away if we ask them to be silent for extended periods. Fifth graders told to complete tough homework on their own may break down in tears.

Because it's only week two, we need to remember that kindergartners are still much like last spring's preschoolers; second graders are like "older" first graders; and so on for each grade. Of course, this is not true of every child, but it's a general caution we should be aware of throughout the first six weeks of school.

So for this week, we take a few deep breaths and remind ourselves that it's still early in the school year. Slow, steady progress is what's needed.

Kindergarten, First & Second Grades

Although you still have plenty of routines, materials, and interactive learning structures to introduce, the second week of school has two overriding themes for primary grade students:

- *Automaticity*—Routines become habits: After snack is finished, all trash goes in the trash can. When quiet time begins, everyone works independently. Before the closing circle, backpacks are packed. Building automaticity leads to greater class cohesion and a smooth flow to each day that allows more time for learning.

- *Stamina*—To truly gain mastery of academic content and skills, students need to build up their muscles for doing reading, writing, math, and other learning on their own. Also, for us to work with students in small groups or individually, the rest of the class has to be able to function independently for a solid chunk of time. We can help every child build the stamina for independent work, taking care to be patient as we do.

MONDAY

8:15 Arrival routines Introduce morning task

8:35 Morning Meeting
- Greeting: Around-the-circle "Good morning"
- Sharing: Around-the-circle (weekend event)
- Group activity: Sing "Peanut Butter, Grape Jelly"
- Morning message: What do you remember about the hundreds chart?

9:00 Math Review hundreds chart • Class math challenge • Explore numbers (one more, one less; ten more, ten less; etc.) • Model: Asking a peer for help

9:50 Snack; outside time or energizer Continue to practice/reinforce routines and expectations; build repertoire of energizers

10:10 Special

11:00 Reading Introduce and model retelling stories (key details) • Build reading stamina (start with a few minutes and gradually increase) • Practice retelling (conferences; partners)

11:30 Establishing rules Add to students' list of learning goals (or "hopes and dreams")

11:45 Recess Introduce some new games this week (see Appendix B)

12:05 Lunch Assign table groups

12:30 Quiet time Limited choices (reading, drawing, math)

12:45 Read-aloud Open-ended questions (partner chats)

1:00 Energizer (see Appendix B)

1:10 Writing Build writing stamina • Introduce short personal stories (a time I was sick/hurt) • Practice writing process (think, write, share)

1:40 Vocabulary Introduce word wall • Add to word wall

2:00 Science Guided Discovery: Building materials (e.g., blocks) • Partners plan/build together

2:45 End-of-day logistics and closing circle (What I'd like to do this week)

3:00 Dismissal

TUESDAY

8:15 Arrival routines

8:35 Morning Meeting
- Greeting: Around-the-circle "Good morning"
- Sharing: Around-the-circle (writing topic)
- Group activity: Skip Counting (sitting and standing)
- Morning message: Keep thinking about writing topic

9:00 Math Introduce counting with tallies • Practice counting with tallies • Count by fives, tens, etc.

9:50 Snack; outside time or energizer

10:10 Special

11:00 Reading Continue focus on retelling • Continue to build reading stamina • Practice retelling (conferences; partners)

11:30 Establishing rules Add to students' list of learning goals

11:45 Recess

12:05 Lunch

12:30 Quiet time

12:45 Read-aloud Continue with open-ended questions (partner chats)

1:00 Energizer

1:10 Writing Continue to build writing stamina • Practice writing process • Explore writing topics (favorite place; animal or pet; family story)

1:40 Vocabulary Add to a word wall • Energizer: Alphabet Aerobics

2:00 Science Guided Discovery: Building materials (e.g., cardboard tubes) • Partners build together

2:45 End-of-day logistics and closing circle (favorite school supply)

3:00 Dismissal

WEDNESDAY

8:15 Arrival routines

8:35 Morning Meeting
- Greeting: Partner greeting
- Sharing: Around-the-circle (favorite recess activity)
- Group activity: Alphabet Aerobics
- Morning message: Learning goals

9:00 Math Counting with tallies; money

9:50 Snack; outside time or energizer

10:10 Special

11:00 Reading Introduce informational text; retelling; reading stamina

11:30 Establishing rules Work on learning goals; storing in-process work

11:45 Recess

12:05 Lunch

12:30 Quiet time

12:45 Read-aloud

1:00 Energizer

1:10 Writing Continue to build writing stamina; practice writing process

1:40 Vocabulary Using word wall

2:00 Science Challenge: What can you build?

2:45 End-of-day logistics and closing circle (song; see Appendix B)

3:00 Dismissal

THURSDAY

8:15 Arrival routines

8:35 Morning Meeting
- Greeting: Partner greeting
- Sharing: Partner chat (ideas for science work today)
- Group activity: Pop Up Number
- Morning message: Tallying

9:00 Math Counting with tallies; money

9:50 Snack; outside time or energizer

10:10 Special

11:00 Reading Continue focus on informational text; retelling; reading stamina

11:30 Establishing rules Complete learning goals

11:45 Recess

12:05 Lunch

12:30 Quiet time

12:45 Read-aloud

1:00 Energizer

1:10 Writing Strengthening writing by adding details

1:40 Vocabulary Using word wall

2:00 Science Challenge: What can you build?

2:45 End-of-day logistics and closing circle (favorite read-aloud part)

3:00 Dismissal

FRIDAY

8:15 Arrival routines

8:35 Morning Meeting
- Greeting: Partner greeting
- Sharing: Partner chat (What I'm looking forward to in school today)
- Group activity: Favorite from week
- Morning message: Tallying

9:00 Math Solving "Which is more?" money problems

9:50 Snack; outside time or energizer

10:10 Special

11:00 Reading Continue focus on informational text; retelling; reading stamina

11:30 Establishing rules Present and display learning goals

11:45 Recess

12:05 Lunch

12:30 Quiet time

12:45 Read-aloud

1:00 Energizer

1:10 Writing Strengthening writing by adding details

1:40 Vocabulary High-frequency words

2:00 Science Share and display work

2:45 End-of-day logistics and closing circle (What I liked about school this week)

3:00 Dismissal

Flow of the Day

Beginning the Day

Arrival Routines

After modeling and practicing (many times!) the arrival routines last week, students now have a pretty clear idea of what to do when they enter the room. Still, continuing to greet students at the door can help you reinforce what they should do to prepare for each day's learning.

"Good morning, Maya! I see you remembered to hang up your sweatshirt."

"Hello, Giovanni. It's great to see you! Remember to get your name tag."

"Good morning, Manny! I see you have your name tag on. Do you remember what comes next in our morning routine?"

Giving the whole class feedback can help further reinforce morning routines. For example, just before calling children to the circle for Morning Meeting, you might say, "I saw students remembering to hang up coats, get their name tags on, and do quiet reading at their seats." If part of the morning routine is still shaky, you might take a few minutes to quickly model and practice it again.

Arrival Tasks

Young students benefit from having concrete tasks to accomplish first thing every morning, especially if the class trickles into the room throughout arrival time. Students could do many kinds of fun tasks as they enter the room (see examples at right). Setting up and teaching the routines for these tasks is part of the work of this week.

No matter which choices you offer, each should have a learning purpose and allow for some quiet social interaction if students wish. Choosing tasks that children can complete and feel successful about will help set a positive, can-do tone for the day.

Arrival Task Ideas

Class Hundreds Chart

Create a 10 x 10 array. Challenge students to place cards numbered from 1 through 100 in the correct boxes to create a hundreds chart.

Sign-In Chart

Children can practice writing their names (with proper capitalization) on a dry-erase board.

Independent Work

Give students limited choices of activities to do at tables or desks (for example, read, write/draw, do a math problem). Use materials that are easy to access and clean up so the transition to Morning Meeting is smooth.

Morning Meeting

Morning Meetings this week build on the first week's solid start. For Monday's meeting, help ease students into the school routine by using greeting, sharing, and group activity structures that you introduced last week. As the week progresses, continue to blend consistency and familiarity with novelty. On a day when the sharing structure is new, for example, the greeting and activity could stay the same.

■ *Greeting*—Have students practice passing a simple handshake around the circle while saying, "Good morning, [classmate's name]." If most students are using clear voices, greeting each other by name, and shaking with their right hand, the class may be ready to try simultaneous partner greetings later in the week. This adds complexity, because everyone is talking and greeting at once. Throughout the week, continue reinforcing the key speaking and listening skills (looking at the person, using a friendly voice, greeting others by name, waiting to speak) that students need to be successful.

■ *Sharing*—Continue practicing the foundational skills of sharing in week two, especially keeping to the assigned topic, taking turns, and listening to others. If students are ready, introduce partner sharing:

• Pair students up, give them a topic, and assign one person in each group to go first.

• The first sharer talks briefly about the topic (15–30 seconds).

• Ring the chime. The first sharer stops and you direct the second sharer to start.

• After 15–30 seconds, ring the chime again, signaling the second student to finish.

After a few days, you might start challenging students to remember what their partner said. "We're getting really skilled at sharing stories with a partner! Who can remember one thing your partner said?" In the coming weeks, students will be ready to learn how to ask relevant questions and make respectful comments after listening to someone's sharing.

■ *Group activity*—On the first day back after the weekend, singing a song learned the week before can be reassuring. The class might sing "Peanut Butter, Grape Jelly" again and add new foods after singing "peanut butter" ("peanut butter, raisins," "peanut butter, crickets!"). Listing these new foods on the anchor chart for the song is a fun way to record students' ideas for singing at another time.

A simple movement activity to use this week is Skip Counting by multiples: "Two!" (everybody stands), "Four!" (everybody sits), and so on. (See Appendix B for directions to activities and learning structures and for song lyrics mentioned in this chapter.)

■ *Morning message*—A consistent structure for the morning message helps students of all reading abilities engage more effectively with the text. Early in the year, consider keeping a few lines of the message nearly identical each day. For example:

September 9, 20––

Good Morning!

We will practice counting today.

Have a great day!

Ms. Devino

September 12, 20––

Good Morning!

What hope and dream will you choose?

Have a great day!

Ms. Devino

Morning Snack

Make sure to reinforce what went well for students last week. For example, "Last week we got really good at getting our snacks and moving right to our seats!" For things that need some extra coaching and practice, you might say, "This week, we're going to focus on cleaning up our areas. We'll take a little extra time today to make sure we do that well." You might also realize that part of the structure needs to change. Perhaps the trash can was too far away, making it hard for students to clean up efficiently, so you move it to a more central location.

Middle of the Day

Recess

Having adults actively facilitate games remains an important support for young children, helping them learn the expected norms of recess and ensuring a safe, fun time for every child. You might want to introduce a version of Freeze Tag called Category Tag, in which a category is named ("colors" or "animals") and students avoid being "frozen" by calling out an item in the category before the tagger can tag them. If the class is ready for greater complexity, they might enjoy Blob Tag or Captain's Coming. However, a class still struggling with cooperation and safe outdoor play might do better with simple games such as Red Light, Green Light.

Lunch

Assigned seats continue to help set a safe tone this week. Depending on your reading of the class, you might opt to keep table groups the same all week so that children get a chance to know a small group of other students really well, or you might decide to keep mixing groups up, helping students get to know more of their classmates. From time to time, you can use your continued presence in the lunchroom to help teach and reinforce lunchtime routines so they become automatic. Once that happens, lunch is more likely to be a calm time for all students to socialize and actually eat their lunches—something that can be surprisingly difficult to do for some young students.

Quiet Time

This week, the main goal of quiet time is to continue building stamina and establishing routines. Some students will still find it hard to stay in one spot and work quietly. Challenge students to see how long they can make it ("We made it for three minutes yesterday. Let's try for four today!") and brainstorm ideas for how to stay focused. You could add these ideas to an anchor chart and review them at the beginning of each quiet time.

The more we help students get into the quiet time routine by reinforcing their efforts when they meet expectations, and reminding and redirecting when needed, the more helpful this time will be for them. Their success in building stamina now will allow for greater choices and flexibility later in the year.

> **Quiet Time Tip**
>
> As in week one, it's best to keep quiet time choices simple and limited in number this week. You might offer three choices: reading, drawing, or working with math manipulatives.

Ending the Day

Dismissal Logistics

Often, we try to cram in just a few more academic minutes at the end of the day, but a hurried or disorganized dismissal can leave children and adults feeling rattled, even after a great day of school together. Now and through the rest of the year, we want to give students the time and structure they need to bring the day to a peaceful close.

As students continue building independence with dismissal tasks, a class chart of who goes where after school can be a big help, both for students and teachers. Consider a series of simple bus pictures, each with the bus number and the names of children who take that bus. If students go to different places depending on the day of the week, a weekly calendar with students' names and destinations is another option. Having a class afterschool chart is also useful when a substitute teacher is facilitating dismissal.

Afternoon Jobs

In some classrooms, students have designated jobs at the end of the day. Two children might help stack chairs, two others might tidy up the area around the sink, and so on. Each week, jobs rotate so that all students have a turn doing each job. In other classrooms, all students pitch in and help neaten up the room as needed. Whatever system you adopt, make sure students have enough time to successfully complete their jobs and get packed up in time for a closing circle.

Closing Circle

During this second week, continue using closing circles to build students' sense of safety and community. You may also want to add a little complexity while still keeping things brief. For example, if the first week's closing circles primarily consisted of a sharing about something from the day or singing a song learned earlier, you might do both of these things this week. Or you might begin looking ahead to the next day's learning by introducing a new activity—one that students will do during Morning Meeting or a content time. However you decide to wrap up your learning together, a closing circle brings calmness to a time of day that can often feel rushed.

Teaching Academics

This week, we continue to build on what we began in the first week of school. Teaching students how to use materials and how academic routines should work remain priorities. We also want to continue teaching students skills needed to work productively and positively with others. A new emphasis this week is on building stamina—helping students extend the amount of time they can spend on academic tasks. Of course, throughout everything we do, we keep building a positive and exciting tone for learning.

Academic Materials and Routines

Last week, we introduced some key materials and routines to begin helping students work and learn in all content areas. This week, we can focus on helping children establish habits that will lead to greater confidence and independence. To do this effectively, we want to use plenty of reinforcing language when children are on the right track (speaking privately to individual students) and reminding language when they're about to begin anything that requires them to use a material or routine we've already taught.

Building Confidence and Independence	
Reinforcing Language	• "I was watching as you put the math counters back in the storage bin. You did that really carefully so that all of the counters got into the right place." • "Jamilla, you were looking right at Robert as he shared. That showed him that you were listening!" • "Second graders—you just read quietly for ten straight minutes! We're really building stamina as readers."
Reminding Language	• "You're about to use tape in science to put cardboard tubes together. What do you remember from last week about using tape?" • "As you head to your writing spots, remember what we've been practicing. Make sure you have a pen or pencil, find a spot where you can work well, and get right to work."

Also this week, we want to teach some new materials and routines, using Interactive Modeling and Guided Discovery just as we did in week one (see Appendix A to learn more about these techniques). For example, perhaps you're starting a science unit on engineering where students will explore the strengths of different materials. You could use Interactive Modeling to teach how to take out, use, and store the materials. You might use a Guided Discovery to explore the many ways that cardboard can be folded and shaped.

Keep in mind that it's unrealistic to expect that you can model and practice every new routine and explore every new material in advance. Instead, model or explore only the ones that are essential for the current learning tasks, more complex than usual, or going to be used most frequently going forward. You can always go back and re-model a routine if children struggle with it or lead a new exploration to stretch their capacity to use a material more creatively.

Academic Choice

Following last week's introduction of Academic Choice (page 63), we continue to offer students simple choices this week to help them further develop their decision-making skills. Also this week, we can begin teaching the specific skills students will need in each of the three phases—planning, working, reflecting—for Academic Choice to go smoothly and for children to reap its full benefits. The following chart shows some of these skills.

Skills to Teach for Academic Choice	
Planning	• Making a thoughtful choice • Signing up on a chart to show choice • Making a simple plan for doing their work
Working	• Finding a good work spot • Checking their plan as they work • Sticking with their choice
Reflecting	• Answering reflective questions such as "How did I do at sticking to my plan?" and "How focused did I stay on doing my work?" • Giving encouraging feedback to classmates • Rejoining the circle as a whole group to reflect on what they learned

To teach these skills, model them for students using Interactive Modeling and "think-alouds." For example, you might model how to share an idea with a partner using Interactive Modeling. To show how to find a good working spot, you might hold up a "think-aloud" sign to indicate your thought process as you demonstrate: "I need to find a place that's quiet and comfortable. Let's see . . . that chair by the window looks like a nice spot, but it's crowded over there, so that might not be so comfortable for me. I think I'll try the beanbag chair and see how that works today."

Teaching Collaboration

Learning the skills needed for working well together is critical to children's academic progress. In week one, students began learning how to take turns and exchange ideas with a partner. This week, we continue to teach collaboration skills that are essential to a caring, cooperative learning community.

Speaking and Listening Skills

Now is the time to focus more intensively on modeling and practicing speaking and listening skills that are essential to collaborative work, such as listening respectfully to others, showing interest as others share, and speaking with confidence. Just about every time of the day offers chances to teach and practice these key academic conversation skills. For example:

- *Morning Meeting*—Students practice how to take turns speaking as we share ideas around the circle.

- *Read-aloud*—Students share ideas with a partner about the reading and practice listening closely.

- *Writing*—As students share their stories about pets, family events, and trips, they practice the skill of staying on topic.

Short and focused Interactive Modeling sessions embedded in academic lessons help students see exactly how to put these speaking and listening skills to use and give them a chance to practice them while doing core academic work.

Productive Pairings

As we pair students up for collaborative work, we always want to carefully consider how and why we're putting them together. Our pairings will reflect what we've learned through careful observation during the first few days of school. We might decide to pair some students to foster connections and friendships based on what they want to learn; we might form other pairs to encourage students of differing strengths to help each other as they work.

Names on Word Wall

The class word wall, a display that will help everyone recognize, spell, and know the meaning of key words, can be an especially helpful learning tool this week. Children can add their names to the wall, which signifies that everyone is an important member of this learning community.

Throughout the week, we'll solidify children's learning of names by playing Alphabet Aerobics and using a few people's names each round. This activity also makes a great energizer that can be used anytime during the day when students need to move a bit. Doing this activity with students' names posted on the word wall also helps students get in the habit of checking this display when unsure about spelling a word.

Building Stamina

To help her first graders read independently early in the year, a colleague of mine challenged them to see how long they could focus on books. As soon as she saw students start to wiggle and look distracted—after just two minutes—she called everyone to the circle, so the time felt positive and successful. "We made it for two minutes!" she exclaimed while the students beamed. Then she added a challenge, "Let's see if we can do it again!" Two more minutes passed and they again celebrated in the circle. By the end of the week, they were up to five straight minutes of reading.

You can use this same basic approach to help students build stamina in each content area. As the working periods increase, consider offering short stretch breaks or doing a quick energizer to let children recharge and refocus. Though this periodic moving, transitioning, and energizing might seem distracting from our adult perspective, it's exactly what young children need early in the year. By January, these same students will likely be able to focus and work on their own for twenty straight minutes. This increasing stamina makes them more powerful learners, and it also enables you to have more productive teaching times with small groups and individual children.

As you help students build stamina, keep in mind that they'll do their best when they find the work enjoyable. Besides having some choice and opportunities for movement, children need to be engaged with the book they're reading, the math problem they're solving, or the science content they're learning. For example, a reluctant reader might be excited about outer space, so you could provide some appropriately leveled books about that topic. Or if your class loves to play games, you could make sure to weave some activities with dice and cards into math practice.

Remember to keep your expectations in line with what children are developmentally ready to handle—squirming is a clear sign that they've reached their limit! And, above all, be patient. Developing stamina takes time. The more steadily and calmly we support students, the more they'll view building stamina as a positive challenge.

Teaching Discipline

As students continue settling into school, we keep up last week's work of forming a respectful and joyful classroom culture and teaching expectations and routines. We also extend our work on the naming of learning goals and introduce interim rules—ones we'll use until we create our own as a class.

Building Community

When students feel that they're part of a community—when they're comfortable with their peers and feel a sense of belonging and significance—they're better able to regulate themselves for the common good. That is, they can behave in ways that meet expectations and support their own learning and that of their classmates.

Here are some ways to build a positive classroom community while helping children grow academically and socially this week:

- *Hold daily Morning Meetings*—When students greet and welcome each other, share, and do an activity together first thing in the morning, they're making connections, building an identity as a group, and practicing academic skills.

- *Use energizers and songs*—Sprinkling these throughout the day gives students another way to have fun together, practice self-control, and recharge the energy they need for learning.

- *Make class graphs*—Birthday charts, tooth charts, and "How many letters are in your name?" graphs reinforce the message that everyone is valued in this class.

- *Sing birthday songs*—Teaching a variety of songs lets students choose how the class recognizes their birthday and reinforces the importance of their presence in the classroom.

- *Plan joyful and interactive learning*—Activities that are enjoyable and collaborative help students learn to work together while having fun.

Learning Goals

In week one, we began listing things students hope to learn at school this year. For the first two or three days of this week, continue to add to the list with short brainstorming sessions. Stretching this process out over a few days gives ideas a chance to percolate and sends the message that sorting out our learning goals (or hopes and dreams) is important work, not something to rush.

By midweek, everyone should be ready to choose one learning goal that they feel is most important to them. Children can write and illustrate their goal on a half-sheet of paper (with help from adults as needed). For example, Luis writes, "I hope to learn about history" while Danae writes, "I want to learn to spell hard words."

On Friday, students will get to share their goals with the whole class. This can serve as their first official work sharing, so model how to hold the paper up and speak in a clear voice. After everyone has shared, students can proudly post these papers on the "Hopes and Dreams" bulletin board. Next week, these will help lead students into a discussion about their classroom rules.

Early Rules

If we're going to create classroom rules together during the third week of school, what rules do we use in the meantime? There are many options. For example, you can use:

- *Last year's rules*—Using the rules the previous class created for the first few weeks of school provides a set of rules to refer to as needed and helps set a positive tone. Letting students know that these rules are temporary and that they'll soon create their own helps build anticipation.

- *School rules*—Schoolwide rules can work as class rules until students have created their own. In fact, after the classroom rules have been created, it's helpful to make connections for students between those rules and the schoolwide rules that guided your first few weeks together.

- *Common expectations*—Some teachers opt not to have class rules posted in the first few weeks of school. Instead, they refer to a set of common expectations: "This year, we're going to take care of each other. What's a way we can do that as we move our bodies in this next activity?" "In this classroom, we'll use kind words. What are some kind words we could use after someone shares their work?"

Any of these options can work as long as expectations are clear and the room is physically and emotionally safe.

Responding to Misbehavior

This week, as always, a quick and respectful response to small misbehaviors will help teach positive behaviors and reinforce that the classroom is a safe place. Specific redirecting language, spoken in a direct, nonnegotiable tone, communicates what positive action the child needs to do now. We want to convey that it's the action that needs correcting, not the child. The message sent: This room is a safe place. See the chart below for some examples of clear, direct responses to misbehavior.

Off-Track Behavior	Redirecting Language
Mariah starts to poke Takeba.	"Mariah, hands to yourself."
Chris grabs a book from Julio during quiet time.	"Chris, give the book back to Julio. At the end of quiet time, you may ask him if you can borrow it."
A table is left messy after snack time.	"Table three, head back to your table and clean up the way we've practiced."

In the next chapter, you'll learn more about effective responses to misbehavior.

By the end of the second week of school, things are starting to come together. Students and teachers alike are feeling more comfortable and confident. Students are beginning to show more independence and more skills in working with one another. Next week, this work carries on as we help students enhance their capacity to learn independently and collaboratively— and build a classroom community that will soar throughout the year.

Third & Fourth Grades

This week, we notice that students start to feel at ease with us and their classmates, sharing more and more with us and each other. We also see signs that they're building automaticity as they settle into the daily routines. And we see them increasing their stamina as they work on their own for longer periods of time.

We want to ride this wave of momentum, but we want to do so deliberately and not go too fast. So this week, we keep building connections and strengthening our learning community. We introduce new routines while continuing to reinforce those previously taught. And we continue to pace the academic work to match students' needs and abilities, building on each success and moving forward thoughtfully, step by step.

MONDAY

8:15 Arrival routines   Establish morning tasks

8:30 Morning Meeting
- Greeting: "Good morning" and handshake around circle
- Sharing: Partner chat (one event from weekend)
- Group activity: A Warm Wind Blows
- Morning message: Preview of this week's learning

9:00 Math   Introduce Human Protractor and angles • Guided Discovery: Protractors • Teaching math homework routines

9:50 Snack; outside time or energizer   Introduce team challenges and working snack time

10:10 Reading   Teach: Preparing for conferences • Building reading stamina (start with a few minutes and gradually increase over the week) • Working with partners

11:00 Establishing rules   Reflect on and add to rules list

11:20 Writing   Add to writing topics • Writing choice (new topic or continue piece from last week) • Build writing stamina • Share writing

11:45 Recess   Introduce some new games this week (see Appendix B)

12:05 Lunch   Assign table groups this week

12:30 Quiet time   Continue with limited choices (reading, drawing, math/protractors)

12:45 Read-aloud   Understanding character; open-ended questions (partner chats)

1:00 Energizer   (see Appendix B)

1:10 Special

1:55 Science   Introduce environmental studies unit with focus on local animals • Teach and practice: Observation skills • Introduce project: Class terrarium

2:30 Homework   Review assignment • Practice routines

2:45 End-of-day logistics and closing circle   (What I'm looking forward to this week)

3:00 Dismissal

TUESDAY

8:15 Arrival routines   Introduce homework in-bin

8:30 Morning Meeting
- Greeting: "Good morning" and handshake around circle
- Sharing: Partner chat (math topic)
- Group activity: A Warm Wind Blows
- Morning message: Homework reminders

9:00 Math   Scavenger Hunt: Finding angles • Guided Discovery: Measuring angles • Homework: Angles

9:50 Snack; outside time or energizer

10:10 Reading   Teach: "Thinking while reading" by using sticky notes • Continue building reading stamina and working with partners

11:00 Establishing rules   Categorize rules as a class

11:20 Writing   Introduce timeline for writing (revise, edit, etc.) • Writing time and building stamina • Sharing writing

11:45 Recess

12:05 Lunch

12:30 Quiet time

12:45 Read-aloud   Continue with understanding character; open-ended questions (partner chats)

1:00 Energizer

1:10 Special

1:55 Science   Continue with unit using informational text • Teach: Informational text analysis • Explore informational texts related to unit study

2:30 Homework   Review assignments and routines

2:45 End-of-day logistics and closing circle   (Local animal I might want to research)

3:00 Dismissal

Week Two Sample Schedule ■ Grades 3–4

WEDNESDAY

8:15 Arrival routines

8:30 Morning Meeting
- Greeting: Partner greeting
- Sharing: Partner chat (animal to research)
- Group activity: Human Protractor
- Morning message: Angles

9:00 Math Measuring angles

9:50 Snack; outside time or energizer

10:10 Reading Conferences; taking notes; building stamina

11:00 Establishing rules Finish categorizing rules

11:20 Writing Writing and revising; building stamina; sharing

11:45 Recess

12:05 Lunch

12:30 Quiet time

12:45 Read-aloud

1:00 Energizer

1:10 Special

1:55 Science Continue with unit (local animals) and observation skills

2:30 Homework Review assignments and routines

2:45 End-of-day logistics and closing circle (song; see Appendix B)

3:00 Dismissal

THURSDAY

8:15 Arrival routines

8:30 Morning Meeting
- Greeting: Partner greeting
- Sharing: Partner chat (non-fiction topics you want to explore in reading)
- Group activity: Human Protractor
- Morning message: Angles

9:00 Math Guided Discovery: Drawing angles

9:50 Snack; outside time or energizer

10:10 Reading Review informational texts; conferences; stamina

11:00 Establishing rules Complete rules poster

11:20 Writing Editing and completing final draft; building stamina

11:45 Recess

12:05 Lunch

12:30 Quiet time

12:45 Read-aloud

1:00 Energizer

1:10 Special

1:55 Science Continue with informational texts

2:30 Homework Review assignments; begin one if time

2:45 End-of-day logistics and closing circle (thoughts on read-aloud book)

3:00 Dismissal

FRIDAY

8:15 Arrival routines

8:30 Morning Meeting
- Greeting: Mix-and-mingle greeting
- Sharing: Partner chat (upcoming weekend)
- Group activity: Song or poem
- Morning message: Reflect on week

9:00 Math Drawing angles

9:50 Snack; outside time or energizer

10:10 Reading Informational texts; conferences; stamina

11:00 Establishing rules Sign and display rules poster

11:20 Writing Writing reflection and sharing

11:45 Recess

12:05 Lunch

12:30 Quiet time

12:45 Read-aloud

1:00 Energizer

1:10 Special

1:55 Science Start research on local animals

2:30 End-of-day logistics and extended closing circle (reflect on week/preview next week)

3:00 Dismissal

Flow of the Day

Beginning the Day

Arrival Routines

Third and fourth graders generally welcome the comfort and stability of a consistent morning routine. An anchor chart like the one shown below, displayed in a prime viewing location, can help students remember the multiple tasks they need to complete in preparation for Morning Meeting and the day ahead.

We keep students on course by paying attention to them during this time and using reinforcing, reminding, and redirecting language as needed. As Maria comes to the circle area we might say to her privately, "You remembered the entire routine today." To Charles, who just dropped his backpack on the floor, we might say, "Do you remember where your backpack goes?" And to Kenya, who's tapping her finger on the fish tank, we might say, "Kenya, it's time to read the message."

Of course, throughout the year we'll need to adjust the morning routine. We may add "Turn in homework" to our anchor chart once homework routines are established or allow a few more minutes for stowing outdoor clothing when cold weather arrives.

> **Classroom 204's Morning Routine**
>
> ➤ Hang up coats and backpacks.
> ➤ Sign up for lunch.
> ➤ Read the morning message.
> ➤ Meet in the circle.
> ➤ Turn in homework.

The personality of the class may also prompt a change. A class that gets overly silly during arrival time may need a concrete academic task to do while they wait for Morning Meeting, such as completing a math puzzle or practicing spelling high-frequency words. By observing students at the beginning of each day, we learn what's working and what needs adjusting.

Morning Meeting

This week, students continue to practice key social-emotional and academic skills in Morning Meeting, boosting their feelings of belonging and significance. Meetings that are lively, friendly, and purposeful prime students for a great day of learning. Here are some ideas to try in week two:

- *Greeting*—Start this week with the familiar "Good morning, _____," and a handshake sent around the circle. We might say, "What are some things we should do when we greet someone?" to help students remember to use the friendly voices and just-right handshakes they practiced last week.

  By midweek, students will likely be ready for a bit of variation. Perhaps on Wednesday, you might invite them to greet the person on either side of them. On Friday, they might mix and mingle for a minute, shaking hands and greeting a number of classmates.

- *Sharing*—In week one, we used the around-the-circle sharing format. This week, most third and fourth graders are ready to try simple partner chats. Here's how to set students up for success:

  - *Model and practice one or two skills at a time.* A great skill to start with is sharing a main idea and one or two supporting details, which connects to literacy objectives. Use Interactive Modeling (see Appendix A) to teach this skill. Later in the week, if students are ready, you might model how to ask and answer questions after someone shares.

  - *Choose familiar topics.* Pick ones everyone can connect with ("What's one fun thing you did this weekend?") or that connect to the day's academic content ("What's an animal you might like to study in science?").

  - *Use a timer.* Give each partner about thirty seconds to share.

- *Group activity*—This week, try to choose activities that can be adjusted throughout the year, not just for variety's sake but also to support academics. For example, the Human Protractor can connect to math units in geometry, fractions, place value, and number sense. Reading a silly poem or tongue twister can help students practice word recognition, reading fluency, and choral reading. (See Appendix B for directions to the activities, learning structures, and songs mentioned in this chapter.)

- *Morning message*—This is a good week to invite students to write responses on the messages, as shown in the examples on the next page. When messages are brief and engaging, students are eager to read and interact with them.

Be sure to reinforce Morning Meeting expectations this week, with a friendly tone of voice that conveys faith in children's best intentions. For example: "I noticed that we all used a kind voice today as we greeted each other." "You all looked at your partners and listened when they were sharing."

Greetings, Learners!   9/8/——

This week, we'll be learning some cool stuff! We're going to work with angles in math and study local animals in science. We'll also start our reading conferences. What's something you're looking forward to? Write it below:

Have a great week!
Mr. Banitis

Dear Geometry Whizzes,   9/12/——

You've learned a lot about different angles this week. Draw an angle in one of the boxes below.

Have a great day!
Ms. Hooper

Acute	Right	Obtuse

Morning Break

During this second week, use snack time to discuss the transition to a "working snack," which most third and fourth graders will be ready for in the third week of school. Students can eat while they brainstorm ideas and set expectations together. Here are a few questions and suggested guidelines to consider as you set up the expectations for a working snack routine in your classroom.

Suggestions for a Working Snack Routine	
When can students eat?	Students could eat during independent or small group work times, as long as the snack doesn't get in the way of the work, but not during class lessons or when they're being active audience members or listeners (such as during Morning Meeting or a writing conference).
Where can students eat?	Dry and neat snacks (granola bars, carrot sticks, etc.) are okay at tables or on the floor. Any potentially messy snacks (yogurt, drinks, etc.) are best restricted to tables.
What can students eat?	As long as no one has a nut allergy, one option is to allow students to eat pretty much whatever they bring from home (while sticking to any school rules about candy or soft drinks). In addition, you could keep some healthy class snacks handy, and let parents know that they can drop off snacks for the whole class if they're willing and able to do so.

Including a brief outdoor break or energizer helps students refocus for the rest of the morning's learning.

Middle of the Day

Recess

This week, we can work on helping students become more independent with recess. However, students will still benefit from having an adult facilitate a game of tag or another group activity. I remember once facilitating a game of Blob Tag at recess with eighty third graders. When five students hadn't yet been captured, the others all joined together in one long chain, sweeping the field for the remaining runners and laughing the whole way.

By facilitating recess activities, we not only help students have fun in the moment, we also establish a safe and inclusive tone so that they can engage positively and learn how to play together.

Lunch

Students are still getting to know their classmates and solidifying lunchroom routines, so we support them this week by continuing to assign table groups. To help students make connections with as many classmates as possible, consider mixing up the table groups each day.

If we join students for lunch this week, we can help them stay positively engaged with each other and on the right track with lunchtime routines. Eating with students is also a great way to keep strengthening our relationships with them. Whether you're able to eat with students or not, providing conversation starters and reminders of how to include everyone at the table helps keep lunch safe and enjoyable for all students.

From time to time, take a few minutes to debrief with students about how recess and lunch went. You might say, "On a scale of one to five, where one is 'stinky-bad' and five is 'perfect-fantastic,' how do you think recess and lunch are going so far?" In addition to starting a conversation that can help improve the middle of the day, we're helping students practice self-reflection, an important skill that translates to many different social and academic settings.

Quiet Time

Especially on the first day of this week, students may need some reminders about moving efficiently to their quiet time spot and working there independently. This provides us with a prime opportunity to reinforce the notion that "we say what we mean and mean what we say." For example, I remind students that they're expected to stay in their spot for all of quiet time. If a student raises her hand and asks to get up to find a new book, I might say, "Not now. Everyone needs to stay in their spots. Reread a chapter or write a summary of what you just read." Allowing students to ignore expectations sends a mixed message and leads some students to test limits with more intensity and frequency.

Continue to keep quiet time choices relatively few in number and easy for students to manage this week. Reading and writing are always sound options, as is drawing. You may also want to consider allowing students a choice of exploring a new supply or tool introduced during science, social studies, or math.

Ending the Day

Dismissal Logistics

Although it's tempting this week to reduce the time allowed for dismissal logistics, students are still just getting used to school. They'll do better if we keep giving them a few extra minutes so they can complete their afternoon tasks without feeling rushed or stressed.

As at the beginning of the day, an anchor chart like the one shown here for end-of-day routines can help students keep track of things as they transition from school to home. It can also help students be more independent, especially as logistics begin to include various after-school programs and events.

Before Closing Circle

➤ Pick up at least three things in room.

➤ Pack backpack.

➤ Check bus number.

➤ Meet in the circle.

Closing Circle

Picture this end-of-day meeting: "I can't wait to start studying my animal," says Georgia. "I'm looking forward to the read-aloud," states Juan. Steven leans in to Mrs. Walker, a paraprofessional who works with the class, and whispers in her ear. Mrs. Walker then says, "Steven is looking forward to measuring more angles."

Students continue to share a brief sentence around the circle in response to the prompt, "What are you looking forward to about tomorrow?" This calm and thoughtful moment before the hubbub of dismissal helps students end the day on a reflective note and with positive anticipation for tomorrow's learning.

Throughout this week, we'll keep practicing essential closing circle routines and skills: getting to the circle on time, thinking of ideas to share, listening to each other, and speaking clearly and concisely. A lively song or activity—one previously taught at Morning Meeting—can add a spark of energy and send everyone out the door with a smile.

Teaching Academics

Several goals for academic work remain constant from week one to week two. During week two, we continue to open the classroom, introducing new areas, supplies, and routines as we teach academic content. We also keep the focus on teaching collaboration skills as students work primarily with partners this week.

A new academic goal for this week is to begin building academic stamina so that students can maintain focus and energy for longer periods of time. And, of course, the goal of creating a supportive, exciting tone around academics continues this week and throughout the year.

Materials

Students will need some direct teaching about each new material introduced this week. A new bin of informational textbooks to accompany the environmental unit in science will get more use if it's introduced and explained. A Guided Discovery (see Appendix A) can help students explore protractors with purpose and interest so they're ready to measure angles. Interactive Modeling might help introduce a new electric pencil sharpener or show students how to use the whiteboard markers when interacting with the morning message.

Academic Routines

Students are learning so much so quickly in these first few weeks of school that it's easy for them to get overwhelmed or confused, or just not be able to hang on to that much information at once. As with materials, they'll need some direct instruction and plenty of support with each new routine introduced.

We can build much of that instruction right into our academic lessons. For example, as part of the day's reading lesson, we might model what a teacher-student conference will look like, so that all students will know what to expect and how to prepare for their own conference. Or we might model how to use question words when talking with a partner about an informational text, or how to post a problem and solution on a math bulletin board.

For routines to become routine, they need to be practiced correctly. We can reinforce students' efforts when things are going well, remind students when they seem to be forgetting, and redirect them when things get off track, always using a tone that says we're all learning and practicing together.

Solidifying Academic Routines	
Reinforcing Language	"Fourth graders—I noticed that during math period, people were remembering how to use the rulers carefully, placing them on a table when they were writing down measurements. It also looks like all the rulers got put back in the ruler bin."
Reminding Language	"All right, everyone, we're about to join in the circle for our reading lesson. Who can remind us what we need to bring so we're all ready to go?"
Redirecting Language	"Freeze, everyone! Several people were moving too fast and the volume was getting too loud. Remember, when we settle in for read-aloud time, we move at a walking pace and talk quietly."

Academic Choice

One of the most important routines for students to practice in week two is how to make choices and follow through with them. Just as you did in week one, offer simple academic choices throughout this week so students continue to practice having some control over their learning. For example, students might choose between two different kinds of angles to practice drawing. They might choose one part of their story to revise in writing as they work toward their first final draft.

This week, we introduce students to the three phases of Academic Choice (see Appendix A): planning, working, and reflecting. Helping students get used to these phases—making thoughtful choices and plans, working productively on their plan, and reflecting on their plan and work—prepares them for more complex choices and learning later on. The chart on the next page gives a few suggestions for how to use Academic Choice effectively this week.

Suggestions for Using Academic Choice	
Planning	• Give students a few minutes to think about what choice might be best for their own learning. Guide students in doing this through partner chats, quiet reflection, or writing. • Invite students to show their choices, using a sign-up board or sticky notes.
Working	• If the learning task allows it, let students choose where they'll work. For example, if the task involves painting, you'll want everyone at their tables. If they'll be reading or writing, let them choose a spot where they feel comfortable and can focus. • Let students know how much time they'll have for working, and give five- and one-minute warnings.
Reflecting	• Pose a few questions to prompt students to reflect on how their choices worked out, something they learned, something that was challenging, and something they enjoyed. • Vary how students share their reflections (writing, partner chat, whole-class sharing).

Teaching Collaboration

As we continue getting to know our students this week, we can better tailor our teaching of collaboration skills to address their particular needs. Continue to stick with partner work, allowing students to practice and master the key speaking and listening skills they learned during the first week. Next week, they'll likely be ready to work in small groups.

Deepening Skills of Partner Work

Think about what went well during partner work in the first week, and what was challenging. Were students generally respectful, looking at their partners as they listened? Did they remember what their partners said? Depending on what you observed, you might model a specific skill again, such as showing respectful body language or paraphrasing. This reteaching doesn't need to be time-consuming and can be woven into the introduction of academic lessons. For example, before students partner chat about the read-aloud chapter they just listened to, do a quick reteaching on respectful body posture and looking at the speaker.

Productive Pairings

Although it's still early in the school year, you're already seeing which students might work well together and which ones might struggle. Or you might notice that two students share a strong interest in a book series or science topic. By thoughtfully pairing students whose strengths, abilities, or interests are complementary, you can set them up for success in developing essential skills for working cooperatively all year long.

Interactive Learning Structures

This week, help students master partner chat skills by introducing simple learning structures, such as Inside-Outside Circles and Swap Meet. These structures help mix students randomly, allowing everyone to work with diverse partners, and they can be reliably used all year to foster active and interactive learning. The following examples highlight some ways you can use these structures in week two.

- *During math,* students can use Inside-Outside Circles to share about the Academic Choice activity they just completed: "With your next partner, share about a problem you tried that was challenging. Remember to look at the other person as you share."

- *During writing,* students can use a Swap Meet to brainstorm ideas for topics they might write about: "You're going to have three minutes to swap ideas with different classmates about places you would like to visit. See how many different people you can connect with as you share ideas."

Building Stamina

By mid-year, we can expect third and fourth graders to sustain independent reading for thirty minutes or more and writing for twenty minutes or more. Regardless of content area, if the activity is engaging and appropriately challenging and offers some autonomy, students can astonish us with how long they can work productively.

This kind of stamina is critical if students are to successfully tackle challenging work and be prepared to overcome whatever obstacles they may meet in their later lives. It's with those mid-year and lifelong goals in mind that we continue to work on building stamina in the third week of school.

Build Stamina Gradually

At the beginning of the year, students are still adjusting from a summer schedule, which for many might have been quite unstructured. We must therefore bring their stamina along slowly, helping them build on successes. During writing workshop, we might increase the amount of sustained writing time a little bit each day, adding energizers to break up the writing period. Students are much more likely to gain confidence and pride in their ability to sustain writing when they meet with incremental successes along the way.

Emphasize Stick-to-itiveness

One way to help build stamina is to give assignments that require students to work continuously for a set period of time, rather than completing a specific number of pages, problems, or tasks. For example, you might ask students to read a science article for ten minutes and then to highlight some main ideas, summarize the article, or write questions they have about it.

Homework

The work of scaffolding homework continues this week as we shift more of the responsibility onto students. Giving reminders and using plenty of reinforcing language will help students be successful with reading and following directions, packing homework neatly in backpacks, and turning work in when they arrive in the morning. We also want to keep observing students as they practice homework in school so that we get a sense of how long assignments really take to complete.

Homework Practice Tips

Throughout this week, set aside time at the end of the day for in-school homework practice. Then, by the end of the week, students may be ready to start homework in school and finish it at home.

Teaching Discipline

Teaching discipline is an ongoing, year-long process. We continue to teach classroom behavior expectations and respond to misbehavior with brief, firm, and respectful redirections. We also continue to nurture the supportive community so crucial to discipline by building positive relationships with students and helping them do the same with each other.

This week, our main focus is the creation of classroom rules. This shared articulation of how we want our class to be lends power and purpose to discipline in the classroom. (For an overview of the rules creation process, see Appendix A.) Here's how this process might look.

Brainstorming Rules

Last week, students began brainstorming possible rules that would help everyone work toward their learning goals. Spending a few more days on this brainstorming gives students the chance to stretch their thinking and deepen their understanding of the importance of rules. Keep in mind the following as students generate rules.

- *Frame ideas positively*—Students will likely have lots of ideas of what not to do: "Don't swear." "Don't be mean." "Don't leave trash all over the place." As you chart students' ideas, coach them to reframe negative ideas as positive ones: "If we're not going to be mean to people, how should we treat each other?" The student might restate the rule as: "We should be nice."

- *Generate a wide variety of ideas*—You may find students getting stuck in one arena as they brainstorm possible rules, usually about how to treat others. "Be nice to people," says one student. Another adds, "Yeah, we should treat others nicely." A third chimes in, "You should only say nice things to people." At this point, help them shift their thinking: "We have a lot of good ideas for rules about how to treat other people. What are some other rules that could help us create a class community that learns well together?" If needed, prompt students for rules that relate to how they do their own work, how they can work and learn with others, and how they can take care of the classroom.

As students brainstorm, list their ideas on a chart. If they miss anything you think is important, add it to the chart.

Categorizing the Rules

After generating a list of possible rules, it's time to group the rules into categories. Depending on whether the class seems able to keep its focus, I do the brainstorming and categorizing on the same day or on two separate days. Either way, I begin the discussion by saying, "We have quite a list of possible rules here. I don't know about you, but I'll have a hard time remembering twenty-two different rules!" I continue, "Now, we're going to combine these ideas so our class rules are easier to remember. Everyone find your sharing partner from this morning's meeting and talk about which rules seem to go together."

After a few minutes of partner chatting, we come back together and pairs share their ideas. As a class, we then work at combining and condensing the brainstormed list into three to five categories. One way to do this is to color-code students' ideas on a chart with different-colored markers. Or you might use different symbols to denote possible categories.

This process may take a little time, and I've found that students have better focus and energy if we do this work in a few short sessions (ten to fifteen minutes each) rather than all in one sitting.

Stating the Rules

Once all rules have been categorized, each category is then stated as a rule. For example, the category "our own learning" might become "Focus on our own work." Each year the categories may differ, but if the final rules have something to do with respecting and caring for 1) ourselves, 2) others, and 3) the learning environment, they'll apply to just about any situation at school.

As much as possible, I try to use students' actual words in stating the rules. Below are examples of final sets of rules:

Classroom 204's Rules	Team Hawk's Rules	Our Rules to Learn By
Be nice to others.	Be respectful of people and things.	Respect yourself and others.
Take care of our classroom.	Do your best.	Keep the school safe and clean.
Get help when you need it.	Be safe.	Be honest.

Publishing the Rules

By the end of the week, we're ready to make our class rules official. I might say, "We've done a lot of work to get to these three rules. It's important that we all agree on them. Show a thumbs-up if you agree that these rules will help us work together this year." If anyone doesn't give a thumbs-up, I ask him or her to explain and then tweak the rules until everyone is ready to agree. A few student volunteers then create a poster of the rules to display. They leave a space for everyone to sign them, thus showing our agreement that these rules will serve as our guide for how to work together as a class.

Responding to Misbehavior

One key to effective management in third and fourth grades is to respond to small misbehaviors quickly and respectfully, before they mushroom into larger issues. Doing so consistently in these early weeks of school goes a long way toward creating a safe and supportive tone in the classroom. For example:

Off-Track Behavior	Redirecting Language
Two students are jostling each other in line.	"Liam and Garrett, stop. Our rule is 'Be safe and calm.'"
A student leaves her reading materials on the floor.	"Chrissy, put your reading bag away."
A student whispers loudly enough for those around her to hear, "Jimmy doesn't know five times five? He's stupid."	"Cara, respectful comments only."

In the next chapter, you'll learn more about effective responses to misbehavior.

The second week of school is a busy one! Keep coming back to the ideas presented in this chapter so that the week is more manageable and enjoyable for both you and your students. Then, as students leave the classroom Friday afternoon, think back on all that you've accomplished—students are learning and feeling good about school. In the next chapter, we'll look at more ways to continue having a positive impact on every student in your classroom.

Fifth & Sixth Grades

Fifth and sixth graders yearn for independence. They want to have choices about what they learn, who they sit with, and what they do at recess. A key part of our job is supporting them in their growth toward greater autonomy—and this effort begins in earnest during the second week of school. As we go about this work, we want to keep in mind the idea of balance.

We can set students up for success by gradually giving them more responsibilities, although we'll still need to model appropriate behaviors and ensure that everyone is included throughout the day. In so doing, we'll pave the way for a community of students who can work both independently and collaboratively, treat each other with empathy, and reach challenging goals.

143

Week Two Sample Schedule ▪ Grades 5–6

MONDAY

8:15 Arrival routines Establish morning tasks

8:30 Morning Meeting
- Greeting: Neighbors greet
- Sharing: Partner chat (one event from weekend)
- Group activity: Hands Up
- Morning message: Reminder of working snack

8:50 Math Finish factor challenge • Identifying prime and composite numbers • Writing down math assignments

9:50 Outside time or energizer

10:05 Reading Review routines • Introduce conferences and share schedule • Working with partners

11:00 Establishing rules Add to rules list and begin categorizing

11:20 Writing Brainstorm topics for autobiographies • Explore characteristics of autobiographies

11:45 Recess Introduce some new games this week

12:05 Lunch Vary table groups throughout this week

12:30 Quiet time Expand choices this week

12:45 Read-aloud Introduce story graphs

1:00 Energizer

1:10 Special

1:55 Social studies Introduce geography unit with focus on land features • Teach mapping skills

2:30 Homework Review assignments • Practice completing assignments in school

2:45 End-of-day logistics and closing circle (one positive from today)

3:00 Dismissal

TUESDAY

8:15 Arrival routines Practice homework drop-off

8:30 Morning Meeting
- Greeting: Mix-and-Mingle
- Sharing: Inside-Outside Circles (autobiographical categories)
- Group activity: Hands Up
- Morning message: Prime numbers

8:50 Math Introduce calculators • Largest prime number challenge • Sharing/publishing prime number challenge solution

9:50 Outside time or energizer

10:05 Reading Introduce reading fiction • Teach character interactions (grade 5); how plot unfolds (grade 6)

11:00 Establishing rules Finish categorizing

11:20 Writing Explore creating autobiographies (sketch mapping) • Writing time

11:45 Recess

12:05 Lunch

12:30 Quiet time

12:45 Read-aloud Creating story graphs

1:00 Energizer

1:10 Special

1:55 Social studies Teach more about land features • Practicing mapping skills • Teach how to create a map

2:30 Homework Starting assignment in school; finishing at home

2:45 End-of-day logistics and closing circle (partner chat on autobiographies)

3:00 Dismissal

WEDNESDAY

8:15 Arrival routines

8:30 Morning Meeting
- Greeting: Inside-Outside Circles
- Sharing: Partner chat (how you unwind after school)
- Group activity: Find Your Match (factor strings)
- Morning message: Prime factorization example

8:50 Math Factor strings; prime factorization

9:50 Outside time or energizer

10:05 Reading Reading fiction (text analysis)

11:00 Establishing rules Name rules and reach agreement

11:20 Writing Writing auto-biographies; conferences

11:45 Recess

12:05 Lunch

12:30 Quiet time

12:45 Read-aloud Adding to story graphs

1:00 Energizer

1:10 Special

1:55 Social studies Continue with geography unit; creating a map

2:30 Homework Starting assignment in school; finishing at home

2:45 End-of-day logistics and closing circle (A Warm Wind Blows)

3:00 Dismissal

THURSDAY

8:15 Arrival routines

8:30 Morning Meeting
- Greeting: Neighbors greet
- Sharing: Inside-Outside Circles (three places you want to visit)
- Group activity: Find Your Match (prime factorization)
- Morning message: Check in on autobiography

8:50 Math Factor strings; prime factorization; challenge activity

9:50 Outside time or energizer

10:05 Reading Reading fiction (text analysis); conferences

11:00 Establishing rules Complete and display rules poster

11:20 Writing Writing auto-biographies; conferences

11:45 Recess

12:05 Lunch

12:30 Quiet time

12:45 Read-aloud Adding to story graphs

1:00 Energizer

1:10 Special

1:55 Social studies Continue with geography unit; creating a map

2:40 Homework First at-home assignment

2:45 End-of-day logistics and closing circle (students' choice)

3:00 Dismissal

FRIDAY

8:15 Arrival routines

8:30 Morning Meeting
- Greeting: Mix-and-mingle
- Sharing: Partner chat (reflection on learning this week)
- Group activity: Students' choice
- Morning message: Rules and lunch

8:50 Math Sharing/publishing one problem solved this week

9:50 Outside time or energizer

10:05 Reading Reading fiction (text analysis); book shopping

11:00 Establishing rules Discuss ways to follow rules

11:20 Writing Planning process for completing autobiographies

11:45 Recess

12:05 Lunch

12:30 Quiet time

12:45 Read-aloud Adding to story graphs

1:00 Energizer

1:10 Special

1:55 Social studies Finishing and presenting maps

2:40 End-of-day logistics and extended closing circle (reflect on week/preview next week)

3:00 Dismissal

Flow of the Day

Beginning the Day

Arrival Routines

By the second week of school, daily school logistics compete for our attention in the morning. Emails are waiting for replies, paperwork needs to be filled out, and piles are stacking up on shelves. It's tempting to tackle some of these first thing, but we're better off putting them aside and being truly present for students as they enter the room.

Continue to greet students as they arrive, using their names, making eye contact, and trying to quickly assess how they're doing. Welcoming students each morning helps them feel significant and sets a positive tone for the entire day.

Morning Meeting

Just as adults like to socialize before starting work, upper-grade students benefit from some relaxed social time as they begin their day. You can help meet this need by having them read and respond to the morning message and then chat quietly until Morning Meeting begins.

If the class has a hard time handling unstructured social time, you may want to give them a concrete task such as solving math or word puzzles while they wait for Morning Meeting to start. However, avoid starting the day with difficult or mandatory assignments before Morning Meeting because that can introduce a negative tone.

This week, we repeat some activities to give students a sense of competence and confidence and introduce new ones to add variety and keep interest high.

- *Greeting*—Fifth and sixth graders may take a while to feel comfortable greeting their classmates. Each day this week, use a straightforward greeting—perhaps a simple variation of "Good morning" and a handshake. One day, students might greet a few neighbors; on another day they might do a mix-and-mingle greeting, where everyone says hello to as many people as they can in one minute.

  This week, it's also best to avoid greetings that put students on the spot, such as coming to the center of the circle to greet someone. Later in the year, once students know and trust each other more, this will be more appropriate.

Useful Sharing Topics for Week Two	
Social Topics	**Academic Topics**
• What's one positive thing that happened over the weekend?	• What are three places that you're including in your mapping project?
• What's one thing you're looking forward to about the coming weekend?	• What are three topics you plan to include in your autobiographical sketch?
• What's one way you like to unwind after school?	• What do you think the main character will do next in our read-aloud book?

■ *Sharing*—As in week one, sharing this week is quite structured. Each day we'll engage in some form of partner chat—the same kind of sharing structure students will use during the week's academic work. Continue to choose topics that everyone can feel comfortable sharing about, such as those shown in the chart above.

■ *Group activity*—For the second week of school, keep activities fun yet low-risk. In addition to those introduced last week, consider the following ideas:

• Try Hands Up, a lively chant that has students name an idea that fits a category, such as "seven" for prime numbers or "tundra" for geographic features.

• Introduce Find Your Match, which gets students moving and can easily connect with a language arts strand. Or, to support math skills, give some students cards with a number (56) and others cards with a prime factorization (2 x 2 x 2 x 7) and have them find the classmate with the matching card.

(See Appendix B for directions to the activities, learning structures, and songs mentioned in this chapter.)

■ *Morning message*—This week, the expectation is that students read the morning message and interact with it—answering a question, adding an idea, or tallying something—before the meeting begins. Messages with an inviting tone and a quick task related to their learning will help students look forward to the day ahead (see example at right).

Good Morning, 6th Graders!

I hope you all had a relaxing weekend. We've got a lot of fun work ahead of us this week!

Cheers!
Mr. Xu

Thinking Challenge:
We started our "working snack" last week. How do you think it went? Show your thoughts by putting a tally mark in a column below.

Not well   So-so   Great!

Middle of the Day

Recess

Continue to offer some structured and adult-supervised activities at recess so all students have a safe landing place during this time. For example, you could facilitate a tag game; modeling appropriate tagging again as needed will help students meet with success. You might also introduce other games that encourage lots of movement and aren't overly competitive, such as Continuous Kickball.

During this week, remind students of the playground rules and routines, such as staying within playground boundaries and lining up. A simple reminding question before students head out for recess—"Who can remind us what the playground expectations are?"—can help ensure that everyone has fun.

Lunch

Once classroom rules are established (see page 155), students can brainstorm specific ways to follow the rules during lunch. Doing so will help guide their behavior and enable them to move toward greater autonomy in the cafeteria. You may still want students to sit in assigned lunch groups all this week. If so, try mixing students randomly as well as pairing them with someone who shares a common interest, hobby, or afterschool activity. Try to briefly visit lunch a few times this week to see how everyone is doing, especially in meeting the expectations for including others.

Quiet Time

Fifth and sixth graders can begin to handle a wider variety of choices this week. Consider creating a list of options and expanding it as the year progresses. This week, for example, students could decide to read, write, draw, use learning tools that you've already introduced, or work on an ongoing assignment. Also remind students that they should choose something that they can comfortably do in the amount of time available. Next week, you might add another option or two. Continue to reinforce that this time is for a silent, independent activity—a time to refocus and rejuvenate for the afternoon's learning.

Ending the Day

Dismissal Logistics

As the second week unfolds, we'll have a better sense of how much time is needed for students to complete tasks prior to dismissal and make a smooth transition to the closing circle. Later in the year, students may be able to pack up backpacks, stack chairs, straighten out the room, and join in the circle in just five minutes. However, they may need a bit more time now, at least for this week. And you may need to make other adjustments, such as doing the closing circle before these logistics, if some students have to leave before the final bell.

Whatever end-of-day routines are needed, we'll want to hone them this week to ensure that the class can function successfully and more autonomously all year long. This means that as students get ready at the end of the day, we're circulating among them to reinforce, remind, and redirect as needed.

Closing Circle

"Let's take a moment and review our day. What's one thing you really enjoyed today? What are you looking forward to tomorrow?"

A few moments of reflection can help students consolidate today's learning and anticipate tomorrow's, perhaps with the same sharing structure used in Morning Meeting. Ending the day with a closing circle helps our time together feel more cohesive and complete, which is especially important for pre- and young adolescents.

Teaching Academics

During the second week, we continue the foundational work we began in week one: helping students master academic routines, introducing needed materials, teaching essential collaboration and communication skills, and creating a joyful and supportive environment for learning. This week, we also begin to stretch work times out and build up students' academic stamina so that they can work longer and more independently.

Materials

This week, continue to purposefully introduce materials that students will be using for the first time or in a different way than they have previously. Again, this teaching works best when integrated into academic lessons. For example, if students will be using dice or calculators for the first time in math this year, introduce them during the first part of the lesson by using Interactive Modeling or Guided Discovery (see Appendix A). You may also want to teach students how to use math tools, such as rulers, protractors, and compasses, when beginning a math lesson or settling into quiet time.

Academic Routines

Fifth and sixth graders find comfort in predictable rhythms at school. Clear and consistent routines are a big part of this—and a key to their academic success. Although students may be familiar with certain routines from the previous year, everyone will benefit from learning this year's expectations, especially new students.

Reinforce Existing Routines

This week, we want to make sure we're being consistent with the expectations we taught last week. For example:

- If students are supposed to bring their book, pen, sticky notes, and reading journal to readers' workshop, a brief reminder can help them stay on track: "We're about to start our reading lesson. Who can remind us what we need to bring?"

- If a student forgets, a quick reminder lets him know that he's still responsible for meeting the expectations: "Jamie, go get all your reading materials so you're ready for our lesson."

Students will be less likely to forget or push limits if they know "we mean what we say and say what we mean" when it comes to the expectations of being prepared for every lesson.

Teach New Routines

Just as we did last week, model and practice each new routine and skill introduced this week. For example:

- If laptops or tablets are going to be used for the first time this year, students need to know how to sign them out, log in to the school's system, create and save files, and use software or apps.

- In collaboration with the school librarian, we might set up a system for students to use the library on their own, being sure to teach how to sign out, work efficiently in the library, and reenter the classroom appropriately.

- As students take on work that lasts for more than one day, we can set up a routine for where to store in-process work, such as a designated shelf or bin.

Academic Choice

During week two, students continue to practice making meaningful choices about their work when they decide, for example, what elements to include in their maps for social studies, topics to flesh out in their autobiographical sketches, and books to read during independent reading.

All of these choices are straightforward, few in number, and easy to manage, both for students and for teachers. Students are increasing their abilities to make responsible decisions about their learning and reflecting more deeply on their work (what went well, what they could improve, and so on). Throughout this week, they gain a greater sense of autonomy as we reinforce the message that this work is their work.

The three phases of Academic Choice (see Appendix A) give structure to how we offer choices to students and help ensure that they're learning to make thoughtful decisions and reflect on their work. The chart below gives an example of an Academic Choice lesson on creating a factor string.

Suggestions for Using Academic Choice	
Planning	Students are offered ten different numbers to break down into factor strings. They need to choose five that they would like to solve, thinking about which ones might offer them an appropriate level of challenge.
Working	Students have ten minutes to create factor strings for the numbers they chose.
Reflecting	Students choose one factor string they created to share with a partner. They explain how they came up with it and whether they found their work hard, easy, or in-between.

Teaching Collaboration

All the work we've done in week one to help students build relationships, make connections, and learn how to work effectively together provides the backbone for their successful academic learning. Here are a few ways we can continue this work in week two.

Working With Partners

This week, students will still likely be more successful working in pairs than in small groups. Partner work will help them solidify the essential skills needed for productive group work later on—sharing responsibility, taking turns listening and speaking, and compromising.

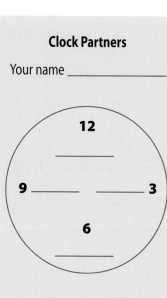

One way to assign partners efficiently is to use Clock Partners. The first time you use this structure, assign all partners yourself, either basing them on your observations of students in the first week or assigning them randomly. When it's time for a partner activity, call out, for example, "Everyone find your six o'clock partner!" During the next day or two, have students work with the same partner for each activity. Then, over the next few weeks, rotate through until students have had a chance to work with all four of their clock partners.

Another useful structure to try is Inside-Outside Circles. Here are two ways you might incorporate this structure into your lessons this week:

- *For writing workshop,* use Inside-Outside Circles to have partners briefly share about an assigned topic for writing, and then shift the inside circle a step to the right or left so that each student has a new partner to share with.

- *During a Morning Meeting,* use Inside-Outside Circles for sharing and then use it again during social studies as a way for students to discuss their mapping project.

Teaching Communication Skills

As students engage in a variety of partner chats this week, we can continue to build their speaking and listening skill sets. Just imagine how rich classroom discussions in all academic areas will be later in the year when we take time in the first six weeks to give students a strong base of skills to work from!

For this week, refer back to the skills listed on page 97 to decide which ones students still need more work on and which new ones they're ready for. Consider teaching and practicing these skills during sharing at Morning Meeting. Later, during an academic lesson, you might say, "Remember at Morning Meeting how we practiced staying on topic and using complete sentences? When you talk with your partner about your book, make sure to practice those same skills."

Building Stamina

Later in the year, we can reasonably expect fifth and sixth graders to sustain attention for long periods of time. They'll likely be able to read for forty minutes or more, write for thirty minutes or more, and focus on content-area projects for over an hour at a time. The second week of school is when we start coaching students to develop their muscles for this type of persistence, gradually increasing the challenge so students learn to stretch their attention and focus. You might say, "Yesterday, we read independently for seventeen minutes. Today, let's go for twenty!"

However, we can only expect students to sustain longer and longer work periods if they're truly invested in the content and tasks. To make learning more lively—more active and interactive—while also building stamina:

- *Give students opportunities to express themselves* through their work. For example, in writing workshop, students could write autobiographical sketches and then in peer conferences learn about each other through this writing; in social studies, students could create a map of a fictitious land while applying what they've learned about land-forms and mapping skills.

- *Sprinkle in energizers* that give students practice with academic skills during a content period. You can also use an interactive learning structure such as Inside-Outside Circles to incorporate movement while partners share about their learning.

Positive Teacher Language

Throughout this week, just as we did last week and as we'll keep doing for the rest of the year, we use positive teacher language to establish a positive climate for learning. Reinforcing, reminding, and redirecting language, spoken with warmth and respect, helps set a safe and supportive tone. Open-ended questions show students that their ideas and opinions are valued. Consider how each of the examples of teacher language on the next page helps foster a classroom where students are more apt to take the risks needed for learning.

Creating a Climate for Learning	
Reinforcing Language	"Jaqui, you really took your time on your math work. You double-checked each problem and focused on your work."
Reminding Language	"We're about to come back to the circle to share writing. Remember to have a sticky note on the paragraph you want to share with a partner."
Redirecting Language	"Timothy, we're reading silently right now, so this isn't a time to ask me a question. You can do that when silent reading time is over."
Open-ended Questions	"Think about the main character in our read-aloud. She has a tough choice to make. If you were in her position, what's something you might do next, and why?"

Homework

Our goal this week is to successfully transition students to doing homework on their own at home. Releasing this responsibility in stages sets students up for success with this independent work. For example:

- *Monday*—Students complete a short "homework" assignment in class, pack it in their backpacks (as if they've just finished it at home), and bring it in the next day, placing it in the homework bin as part of their morning routine.

- *Tuesday and Wednesday*—Students start an assignment at school, pack it up, finish it at home, and bring it in the next day.

- *Thursday*—They'll most likely be ready for their first true at-home assignment.

Homework Practice Tip

You may also want to guide students in writing down assignments throughout the day. This can help them record assignments more accurately, prepare them for when they change classes in middle school or high school, and avoid a frantic finish to the day.

Teaching Discipline

This week, we focus on finalizing class rules and guiding students in seeing how the rules can be applied throughout their day together. We also carry on with the work we started last week in helping students get to know each other and build positive relationships.

Consolidating the Rules

In week one, students reflected on their learning goals for the year and shared them with the class. They also brainstormed a list of possible rules that would help create a classroom environment where everyone would feel invested in the rules and supported in reaching for their hopes and dreams. This week, students will complete the brainstorming session and whittle the list down to a manageable number of rules—three to five works well.

There's no perfect process for combining the many brainstormed rules into a few final ones. In fact, it can be challenging to do so because students may have varying opinions about which rules connect. That's okay. The messiness is part of the process. We're getting students to think more deeply about the rules as we lead them to question, debate, and struggle together. Here's one idea for doing this consolidation that works well with fifth and sixth graders:

- *Have students share ideas* together as a whole class. Consider mixing in some partner chats to make sure everyone has a chance to talk.

- *Guide students in offering ideas* of which rules seem to fit together, and work to incorporate all the brainstormed rules into a few broad categories. For example, "I think 'being respectful to everyone' and 'saying please and thank you' can go together in the 'respect' category."

- *Once the categories are finished,* name each one. These names then become the final rules (see example at right).

Sample Class Rules

- ➤ Respect yourself and others.
- ➤ Treat everyone with kindness.
- ➤ Give your best effort.
- ➤ Take care of our classroom and school.

Publishing the Rules

Reaching consensus as a class and acknowledging that the rule-making process is finished helps students get emotionally invested in the rules. A simple "thumbs up, thumbs down, thumbs to the side" can be one way to see if everyone is satisfied with the rules. If some students have their thumbs down or to the side, invite them to explain why and then guide the class in revising the rules (usually reworking the wording is all that's needed) until everyone is satisfied.

Once consensus is reached, you might want to ask a few student volunteers to make a poster of the rules to display in the classroom. Have everyone sign the poster to show mutual agreement that the rules will help guide their work together (but not as a promise to never break them, which would be unrealistic). You might even do a fun activity, such as singing a song or doing a favorite energizer, to celebrate finalizing the rules.

Connecting the Rules to Learning

When fifth and sixth graders view teachers as the focal point for rules, following the rules becomes more about "obeying" them and pleasing the teacher than learning self-discipline. If teachers reinforce this view, even unintentionally, some students may turn into "teacher pleasers"—doing the right thing just to keep their teacher happy—while others may break rules to challenge the teacher's authority.

Instead, when we're giving reinforcements, reminders, and redirections, we want to specifically and objectively refer to the applicable rule. The following chart offers ideas for using teacher language to focus students on the rules, instead of on the teacher, as a guide to developing self-discipline and learning ethical, responsible behavior.

Translating Rules Into Action	
Instead of a teacher-centered approach	**Use a rules-centered approach**
"I'm going to be watching for students to walk respectfully in the halls to art class."	"One of our rules is 'Be respectful of others.' How might that look and sound as we walk past other classrooms to art?"
"I want to see everyone listening carefully to each other during your writing conferences."	"How can our rules help us have productive conferences today?"
"I expect you all to be kind and respectful to Mr. Rodriguez when I'm in my meeting today."	"What are some specific ways you can follow our class rules when Mr. Rodriguez is here?"

By asking students to connect global rules ("Be respectful") to concrete behaviors ("Walking quietly in the hallways avoids disturbing other students' learning"), we guide them in applying the rules they've worked so hard to create together. The intentional use of the plural possessive pronoun "our" also reinforces where the rules came from and who owns them: Teachers may be the ones in charge of helping everyone follow the rules, but we created the rules together and they belong to us all.

Responding to Misbehavior

Once rules are in place, we can shift how we respond to misbehavior. When we remind and redirect students, we can now connect to the class rules. For example:

Connecting Behavior to Class Rules	
Reminding Language	"Everyone's about to work with partners. How can we follow our rule 'Take care of each other' so that everyone can hear?"
Reminding Language	"One of our rules is 'Be respectful to yourself and others.' As you listen to your partner today, how will you do that respectfully?"
Redirecting Language	"Alexis, a class rule is 'Be safe' and that includes in the halls. Head back to the door and walk this time."
Redirecting Language	"Whoops! Looks like people are struggling with our rule 'Keep the classroom clean.' Everyone return to your tables and help clean up before we transition to math."

We continue to address any misbehavior in a calm, respectful tone, and we're crystal-clear about how our room will look, sound, and feel in support of our rules. Next week, we'll teach students how logical consequences can help support our learning community and promote positive behavior.

Increasing Independence

Once the rules are established, the class has a framework for a discussion about being more independent. For example, students may be eager to have more flexible seating at lunch, so this week you might connect independence during lunch to the rules: "I've been assigning table groups so that everyone is included at lunch. Now that our rules are set, let's talk about how to apply our rules 'Be respectful' and 'Take care of each other' when you decide which classmates you'll sit with at lunch. What are some ideas you have for that?"

Students might agree to invite anyone who is eating alone to join them at their table and to include everyone at their table in the conversation. Then, after lunch, take a few minutes to reflect as a whole group on how well these ideas worked and what adjustments, if any, are needed. Use this same process to generate ideas for following the rules at other times of the day.

As you work on granting students more independence, observe carefully to see how they're doing. I've made the mistake of giving students too much autonomy before they were ready. Each time, I had to rein things back in, taking away privileges I had granted too soon. Paradoxically, for students to have more autonomy in April and May, they usually need to have less in August and September.

LAST THOUGHT

5–6

The second week of school is both exhilarating and exhausting. Students are eager to dive into great work, but they still need plenty of support and guidance. In the coming weeks, they'll continue to grow in confidence and independence, readying themselves for the challenging schoolwork ahead.

Week Three

Goals for Week Three

The third week of school is a transition week, when our goals start to shift. Whereas during the first two weeks we were focused on introducing and setting up routines, now we're thinking more about consolidating learning and gaining momentum—increasing the complexity and risk-taking of students' learning while constantly monitoring and adjusting as needed. So our goals for this week are for every student to:

- *Continue to build stamina in all content areas* and take steps toward greater independence during academic lessons as well as recess and lunch.

- *Continue to practice routines* so that they become automatic and enable engaging learning to happen all day, every day.

- *Experience the rules coming to life in the classroom*—students in grades K–2 create their classroom rules and start to see how they come into play throughout the day; students in Grades 3–4, who created their rules last week, deepen their sense of how the rules positively influence their daily life at school.

- *Learn about logical consequences* and start to take responsibility for their mistakes as they strengthen positive behavior skills.

Overview for All Grades

When we teach children how to ride a bike, we start off cautiously and stay right behind them, even if they have training wheels and are never really in danger of falling. Then comes the day when we take the training wheels off. We give a little push and off they go. We may still run behind their bikes, grabbing and then letting go of the seat for a few seconds at a time, but soon we only hold on to the seat to get them started. And then, at last, we back off. Or almost. We still keep them in sight so if they fall, we can help them get right back up.

This transition to independence for new bike riders is much the same for students and their teachers in week three. Now, it's time for us to start letting go—bit by bit—all the while encouraging and reinforcing, and still staying nearby in case they take a spill and need our help to get going again.

This week is a time to help students gradually move to greater independence. It's also a time to guide them in taking more academic risks. Learning is inherently risky. It can be hard to ask a question, stumble over a word when reading aloud, or participate in a group conversation about a new topic. This means that the classroom must be a safe place—one where taking risks is always okay.

During the first two weeks, we worked hard to build a sense of safety in the classroom. Now that it's been established, we can start gently pushing children to try some positive risk-taking. At Morning Meeting, we might do an activity in which students take turns at the center of the meeting circle—and have to think quickly in front of the class. Or we might invite a student to read the morning message aloud to the class. We should keep the risks small, though, and let students volunteer to be "in the middle" or to share with everyone. And we want to give all students opportunities to take some risks and feel supported in doing so.

This week, just as when teaching a child to ride a bike, we want to closely observe our students, anticipating the right level of support to give them and then readjusting in the moment. We might take our hand off the seat, but we must still be at the ready to help steady them whenever we're needed.

With time and patience, students will be riding on their own more and more—gaining confidence in taking on exciting new challenges with their learning—while we coach and cheer them on!

Kindergarten, First & Second Grades

I recently visited a first grade classroom mid-year, and everywhere I looked, I saw children functioning independently and successfully in 20-minute reading and writing blocks. Later, I asked the teacher, "How did you get here?" She responded, "Very slowly."

The third week of school is often when we start to feel that we're making progress toward this kind of classroom. Yet, like my first grade colleague, we must move step-by-step, matching the pace of students' learning with their readiness. Introducing one or two new routines in reading is enough for this week. Next week we can add another, and one more the week after, gradually adding complexity and challenge as students are ready. As we go forward this week, we acknowledge and build on students' small successes.

MONDAY

8:15 Arrival routines

8:30 Morning Meeting
- Greeting: Use one that went well last week
- Sharing: Model dialogue sharing
- Group activity: Sing "Black Socks"
- Morning message: What do you know about dice?

9:00 Math Introduce and model number stories (simple word problems) • Introduce and model dice as a math tool

9:55 Snack; outside time or energizer Continue to reinforce/review routines and expectations; build repertoire of options (see Appendix B)

10:10 Special

11:00 Reading Introduce and model working in small groups • Class brainstorm: Ideas for staying focused and working independently

11:30 Establishing rules Reflect on list of learning goals (or "hopes and dreams") • Brainstorm rules

11:45 Recess Introduce free play options this week

12:05 Lunch Continue to assign and mix up table groups

12:30 Quiet time Expand choices this week (if children are ready)

12:45 Read-aloud Practice retelling and related skills this week

1:00 Energizer

1:10 Building vocabulary Continue adding to word wall • Alphabet Aerobics

1:30 Writing Continue building writing stamina (expand writing time) • Write personal stories (choose one from last week to keep working on)

2:00 Social studies Introduce and explore concept of community

2:45 End-of-day logistics and closing circle

3:00 Dismissal

TUESDAY

8:15 Arrival routines

8:30 Morning Meeting
- Greeting: "Good morning" in Chinese
- Sharing: Model dialogue sharing with questions
- Group activity: Act out math equations or number stories
- Morning message: Using "at" words (bat, cat, and so on)

9:00 Math Creating number stories • Academic Choice (addition with counters, dice, coins)

9:55 Snack; outside time or energizer

10:10 Special

11:00 Reading Practice working in small groups (focus on retelling and related skills this week) • Individual and small-group conferences

11:30 Establishing rules Finish brainstorming • Start to categorize

11:45 Recess

12:05 Lunch

12:30 Quiet time

12:45 Read-aloud

1:00 Energizer

1:10 Building vocabulary Using "at" words • Word Family Caterpillar

1:30 Writing Continue to build writing stamina • Write personal stories (focus on adding details)

2:00 Social studies Explore places in local community

2:45 End-of-day logistics and closing circle

3:00 Dismissal

WEDNESDAY

8:15 Arrival routines

8:30 Morning Meeting
- Greeting: Gentle fist bump
- Sharing: Model dialogue sharing with questions
- Group activity: Act out math equations or number stories
- Morning message: Addition stories

9:00 Math Continue with number stories; introduce and model dominoes

9:55 Snack; outside time or energizer

10:10 Special

11:00 Reading Practice working in small groups • Individual and small-group conferences

11:30 Establishing rules Finish categorizing; name the rules

11:45 Recess

12:05 Lunch

12:30 Quiet time

12:45 Read-aloud

1:00 Energizer

1:10 Building vocabulary Using word wall and "at" words

1:30 Writing Continue to build writing stamina; write personal stories; add details

2:00 Social studies Explore jobs and transportation in local community

2:45 End-of-day logistics and closing circle

3:00 Dismissal

THURSDAY

8:15 Arrival routines

8:30 Morning Meeting
- Greeting: "Good morning" in French
- Sharing: Dialogue sharing with questions
- Group activity: Number stories
- Morning message: More "at" words

9:00 Math Continue with number stories; Academic Choice (subtraction with counters, dice, coins)

9:55 Snack; outside time or energizer

10:10 Special

11:00 Reading Practice working in small groups; individual and small-group conferences

11:30 Establishing rules Signing and posting the rules

11:45 Recess

12:05 Lunch

12:30 Quiet time

12:45 Read-aloud

1:00 Energizer

1:10 Building vocabulary Using word wall and "at" words

1:30 Writing Continue to build writing stamina; write personal stories; add details

2:00 Social studies Create a class map

2:45 End-of-day logistics and closing circle

3:00 Dismissal

FRIDAY

8:15 Arrival routines

8:30 Morning Meeting
- Greeting: Gentle high five
- Sharing: Dialogue sharing with questions
- Group activity: Just Like Me
- Morning message: More "at" words

9:00 Math Creating problems for others to solve

9:55 Snack; outside time or energizer

10:10 Special

11:00 Reading Practice working in small groups; individual and small-group conferences

11:30 Establishing rules Introduce logical consequences

11:45 Recess

12:05 Lunch

12:30 Quiet time

12:45 Read-aloud

1:00 Energizer

1:10 Building vocabulary Using word wall and "at" words

1:30 Writing Continue to build writing stamina; write personal stories; add details

2:00 Social studies Gather artifacts and prepare for first field trip

2:45 End-of-day logistics and closing circle

3:00 Dismissal

Flow of the Day

Beginning the Day

Arrival Routines

By the third week of school, students have likely settled into the morning routine. Everyone knows what to do, for the most part, and is doing it with a good measure of independence. We still want to greet students as they enter the classroom, and we may still need to help a few stay on track with their morning tasks. But now we can shift to spending more time connecting with individual students and the class as a whole.

As we observe students unpacking backpacks, signing up for lunch, chatting as they work on morning tasks, and reading the morning message, we can take the pulse of the entire class. Perhaps they seem particularly wound up, so we decide to change the lively greeting we'd planned to a calmer one. And if we know, for example, that a student is having a tough time at home, we can make a point of checking in with him or her privately. A few moments of quiet conversation lets us offer support and gauge the student's readiness for learning today.

Morning Meeting

Morning Meeting primes the pump for the social, emotional, and academic learning of the day. This week we can prepare children for that learning, and slightly bump up the complexity of the meeting, by introducing some low-level risks. Doing so can help children feel safe enough to take a risk later in the day when, for example, it's time to read a piece of writing aloud to a peer. Here are some low-level risks you might include in this week's Morning Meeting components:

- *Greeting*—Varying greetings a bit this week can add subtle layers of complexity while still helping children practice the most essential elements of greeting (giving a friendly smile, using names, and looking at the person). For example, students can:
  - *Shake hands and say, "Good morning" in a language other than English ("Bonjour," "Ni hao," "Hola").* You might create a chart of greetings in various languages; each time you introduce a new language, add it to the list.

- *Use handshake variations.* A gentle fist bump or high five might be a good place to start.

Each of these simple greeting variations will add a little excitement and support students' risk-taking in safe and manageable ways.

- **Sharing**—You may feel students are ready for dialogue sharing, where one student shares a piece of news and other students respond with questions. Be sure to model this sharing yourself a few times, keeping it brief (just a few sentences) and giving students practice asking thoughtful questions with prompting as needed. Displaying a list of question starters (Who _____? Where _____? and so on) can help young students develop their questioning skills. To keep this sharing manageable, limit the number of sharers to two or three each day and have them take no more than three questions each.

- **Group activity**—Students are probably ready this week to try activities that require them to be "on the spot." Ask for volunteers so that students who are more anxious can ease in slowly. For example, here's how you could have students act out math equations as a fun way to get ready for math later in the day:

  - *Introduce it:* "We need six volunteers for this next problem. Who's ready to try it?" Place two of the volunteers to one side of the circle and the other four opposite them.

  - *State the problem:* "Two bugs are sunning themselves on logs, when along come four friends to join them. How many bugs are on the logs now?" The six children move together and the class counts together to answer the problem.

Later in the week, you might try a slightly more daring activity if your class is ready—one with a little more movement or that involves acting something out in front of the group. Use your growing knowledge of your students to judge when they're ready for a bit more challenge.

- **Morning message**—Continue to maintain some consistent patterns to your message each day so that all students can "read" most parts, especially kindergartners and first graders. Second graders this week are likely ready for more variety. For all grades, vocabulary building is a helpful new element to include in messages this week. For example, if the class is studying a set of domain-specific words, use some of these words in the message. Then have students find and underline those words. Repeating the same words in other messages this week will help all students master them.

Morning Snack

Once students are generally doing well with basic snack routines, and depending on your sense of the class as a whole, you may decide to add a new element to morning snack time. For example, you might give table groups a discussion topic to chat about as they eat, such as "What's something you're looking forward to about science later today?" Or you might offer the choice of a fun activity, such as Just Like Me. (See Appendix B for directions to the activities, learning structures, and songs mentioned in this chapter.) Whatever you decide, make sure that it's simple enough so that students get a true morning break.

Middle of the Day

Recess

This week we can help students move toward greater independence at recess, although we still want to observe them and gauge their readiness. If a class is playing well together, before they go to recess you might agree on two or three games that they can play on their own, emphasizing the importance of safety, fairness, and inclusion. Adults should still check in on these new games and coach as needed.

This shift to a slightly less structured recess is another example of letting go of the bike but still running alongside. For a class that isn't quite ready for this level of independence, you might introduce some new games, such as Elbow Tag and Excuse Me, Please and join in so children get more practice with cooperation, inclusion, and kindness.

Lunch

If a group has been relaxed and friendly at lunch, they may be ready to try flexible seating. Perhaps they might sit at any of four tables as a class, or they might join other classes. Set children up for success by modeling and practicing lunchtime etiquette such as how to ask to join a table and how to invite someone to sit with you. Once class rules are established, you might also brainstorm ways to follow those rules during lunch. As with recess, it's still important for adults to actively supervise and coach students as they transition to more independence.

Quiet Time

Are students coming in from lunch and settling right into quiet time? Do they stay focused and on task? If so, they're likely ready for more choices. Perhaps they could use any of the math tools you've introduced. Or they might like to use the sort cards the class has been exploring during vocabulary or reading time.

As you increase quiet time choices, consider what supports students might need to be successful. You might add just one or two choices to start, or students could make their choice and get materials ready before leaving for recess. You may also want to use a sign-up board to help students make a choice efficiently while allowing you to more easily keep track of what everyone is doing.

Ending the Day

Dismissal Logistics

Like arrival time, this time of the day may start to feel more automatic during week three. You'll still need to coach students, but you might not have to be so specific. For example, in the second week of school, you might have said, "Okay everyone, remember to check our afternoon job chart. You need to pack your bag, clean your area, get your coat, and meet in the circle." Now your reminder might be: "Time for afternoon jobs. Check the chart if you need a reminder."

Closing Circle

Like a bookend to Morning Meeting, a closing circle continues to lend stability to the end of the day. Even a five-minute meeting can benefit children by providing the security of a simple structure that's repeated while offering some flexibility and novelty. By week three, you'll have a solid sense of the overall class personality and needs, and you may be ready to settle on a closing circle routine. For example:

1. Sing a song or do a brief activity (two to three minutes).

2. Share with a partner or around the circle, either reflecting on the day or previewing tomorrow (two to three minutes).

Teaching Academics

By the third week of school, academic routines are getting firmed up as students gain a stronger sense of how academic times work. The room starts to take on a more settled feeling and, as a result, an important shift begins to take place: We can gradually increase the complexity of lessons and activities as students are ready to take on a bit more autonomy and responsibility.

For example, as students sustain independent reading for longer periods, we can start to establish more formal literacy groups and think about doing a readers' theater or class play. Now that students have access to more materials, bigger projects are possible. An entire wall might be devoted to social studies work on communities, with drawings, diagrams, and models. Or you might set up a class store project to help students practice working with money as they learn new math concepts.

Continuing to Set a Positive Tone

As we begin to build complexity and students become more independent, we keep offering whatever supports they need. In week three, we continue teaching new routines, carefully introducing new materials, and reinforcing what we have previously taught. We also nurture a supportive learning environment, using positive teacher language and integrating opportunities for movement and fun energizers.

Consider How You Address the Class

Now is a good time to remind ourselves that the way we refer to our students as a class helps shape how they view themselves as learners (see examples on facing page). Consider how many times during the day we have to get students' attention and do so by using a class name. We want to consistently use names that will help students develop a positive identity; that identity will in turn have a positive impact on their learning.

Addressing the Class	
Avoid	**Rationale**
"Boys and girls"	Is gender our students' most important characteristic? Is this what we want them paying attention to?
"Ms. Petersen's Class"	This emphasizes the teacher as the defining feature of the class. It also sounds as though the students belong to the teacher.
"Little Duckies," "Kiddies," "Peanuts"	Any name that makes students sound cutesy or like pets may be off-putting and feel disrespectful to some.
Instead, try	**Rationale**
"First graders"	Straightforward and descriptive, this is an easy substitute for "boys and girls."
"Scientists," "Readers," "Mathematicians"	Used when teaching a particular content area, these all show students that they're engaged in meaningful work.
"Mountain Lions," "Magicians," "Team Thinkers"	Consider having your class brainstorm and choose a class name that can be used throughout the year.

Display Photos of Students at Work

Another way to build a positive classroom tone is by helping students see themselves as capable learners. Throughout the day, snap photos of students engaged in their work, perhaps as they're making a map of their city or town as part of their first social studies unit, or using dice or dominoes to create math problems. Then post these around the room.

Make sure that all students are represented in photos and other displays. Students' visions of themselves as workers—as mathematicians, readers, writers, and so on—will be strengthened when they see themselves actually doing important work.

Academic Choice

We can focus on one of this week's goals, that of increasing complexity, by adding to the choices we give students when they're doing academic work. In weeks one and two, they might have had just two choices when they practiced counting and tallying—for example, working with buttons or plastic discs. This week, we might add dominoes, dice, cards, and other materials, using Guided Discovery and Interactive Modeling (see Appendix A) to help children explore and learn how to use these tools.

If students are ready, we could also offer multi-choice activities. For example, students might get to choose not only which material to use as they practice addition but also how to show their work, either through numbers or pictures.

Stamina and Small-Group Work

Last week, we worked with students on increasing the number of minutes they could read or work on a math problem independently. This week, we continue that effort, helping children work more autonomously and for longer periods of time—and we also shift our teaching a bit: Whereas in the first two weeks we closely monitored the classroom, this week we can back off a little, observing from more of a distance.

Classroom Organization Tip

Better organization on our part can help students be more successful academically. Carefully labeled storage bins can help students find the materials they need to produce richer work. A sign-up sheet lets us keep track of students' academic choices and guides us in coaching them. These are just two examples of how a calm, orderly environment supports students in taking on more complex learning.

This shift means we can begin our first group work this week. As we work with a small group, however, our attention is as much on the rest of the class as it is on the group. For example, if we introduced retelling stories to partners last week, we might have students practice that same skill in small groups. As we sit with one group at a time, we can face out toward the rest of the room so we're still observing the class as a whole.

As students become more capable of working in groups with less direct support, we can use group work more frequently, varying the group members and differentiating instruction as needed throughout the year.

Teaching Collaboration

For small groups of students to be successful, we must teach them the skills they need to work together cooperatively.

Speaking and Listening Skills

As we move into week three, we help children hone their speaking and listening skills. Notice which skills your students need more practice with and which ones they seem to be mastering. For example, suppose children are listening well but still struggling a bit with speaking. While continuing to help them solidify their listening skills, focus more on essential speaking skills (using a clear, confident voice, looking at the audience, and staying on topic). Also think about new skills they may be ready to try, such as how to refocus if their attention wanders.

Another way we can continue to build students' collaborative skills is by using interactive learning structures. For example, Fishbowl is especially useful for helping young children learn how to work well together.

Fishbowl Directions and Tips

1. With a few students who will be the demonstrators, practice a specific skill in advance, such as how a book club group can take turns sharing.

2. The demonstrators sit or stand together, with the rest of the class surrounding them as if looking into a fishbowl.

3. The demonstrators show how to use the skill while the other students notice what they are doing well.

- Choose students for the small group carefully and inclusively, or consider enlisting older students (perhaps from the previous year's class) as "outside experts" for the demonstration.

- Make sure the small group has practiced and can demonstrate the desired behavior well.

- Give the audience a clear viewing task ("Watch how the group takes turns").

- Keep the demonstration short (less than five minutes).

Teaching Discipline

Last week, we worked with students over several days to help them elaborate their learning goals and choose one thing they'd like to accomplish this school year. By moving through this process together, these young students have not only clarified their individual goals but also started to come together and build trust, in one another and in us. The time is ripe for creating classroom rules!

Creating Classroom Rules Together

Here's a simple process you can follow:

- *Generating ideas*—Gather as a class by the bulletin board where you've posted students' learning goals, or "hopes and dreams." Introduce the process: "Look at all these goals for this year! We're going to have to really work together as a class to make these things happen. Let's think about some rules that will help us work together."

After some initial ideas have been charted—"Don't be mean!" "Raise your hand!"—pause the group. "We're off to a great start with these ideas. Since our rules will tell us what *to* do instead of what *not* to do, let's see if we should change the wording of any of these ideas a bit. If we're not going to be mean, how will we treat each other?" Students are likely to suggest wording such as "Be nice." Go through the list and reword a few more ideas before wrapping up the session for the day.

The next day, pick up where you left off, adding some more ideas and changing wording as needed so they're stated positively. You might also suggest some ideas here and there to help fill in some gaps. For example, if you notice there aren't many ideas about caring for the room, you might add "Pick up snack trash."

- *Categorizing ideas*—Once there's a sizeable list of ideas, perhaps twenty or more, it's time to group them into categories to make the list manageable. Over a couple of days, work as a class to combine ideas and trim the list. This takes some time and can be a little messy. That's okay, because as the class wrestles with this task, they're thinking more deeply about the ideas. As a result, the rules they ultimately settle on with you will hold greater value for them. Here's one way to bring the large list of brainstormed ideas down to just a few.

  1. Begin with the long list of brainstormed rules: "Wow! We have a lot of ideas for rules! Let's combine some so we have a smaller number that will be easier to remember."

  2. Notice pairs in the same category: "I think that 'Be nice to each other' and 'Say nice things to each other' go together." Color-code these two ideas to show that they go together.

  3. Ask students for items to put in that category: "What are some other rules that say something about being nice to others?"

  4. Once all ideas in that category are exhausted, move on to another category and repeat until all ideas are included in three or four broad categories.

- *Naming the rules*—Now it's time to name the categories. These names will become the final list of classroom rules, so they should be short, easy to remember, and stated positively. For example, the category about being nice might become the rule, "Use kind words." Every year these rules will be different, reflecting the distinct personalities and characteristics of each class. Following are examples of rules from three different classrooms:

Class Rules	Room 102's Rules	Eagle Nest Rules
Be safe.	Use materials with care.	Take care of our classroom and school.
Use kind words.	Be helpful to others.	Treat everyone nicely.
Work hard.	Get help when you need it.	Keep everyone safe.
Work as a team.		

Students then sign the rules to show their agreement that these rules are fair and will help guide their work together as a class. It's important to keep clear in your own mind that signing the rules doesn't mean that students will never break them! Mistakes with behavior happen. But the rules will serve as a touchstone to remind students of their commitment and help them get back on track. Once everyone has signed the rules, post them in a prominent place at student eye level so students can easily see them and adults can conveniently refer to them.

Putting the Rules Into Action

With the rules now in place, it's time to start making them concrete for students—helping them see how to apply the rules to different situations. Referring to the rules throughout the flow of the day illustrates how they guide our actions and help us create a supportive, safe, and caring learning community. For example:

Referring to the Rules Throughout the Day	
Reinforcing Language	"Did you notice how calm and focused we were during quiet time? You were following our rule about working hard."
Reminding Language	"As we start using dice in our classroom, how can we follow our class rule about respecting materials?"
Redirecting Language	"Brian, remember our rule about being safe. We walk when lining up. Try that again."

Introducing Logical Consequences

Students feel more secure knowing that their teacher will make sure that the rules are followed and everyone is safe, and logical consequences help us do that. We can use three types of logical consequences to stop misbehavior and help students see the connection between their behavior and its effect on themselves and others. These three types of logical consequences are:

- *Time-out*—This technique helps children take a break and regroup mentally and emotionally, before they are completely out of control, and enables the rest of the class to keep learning.

- *Loss of privilege*—If children aren't following the rules during an activity, a logical consequence would be that they lose the privilege of doing that activity for a while or are directed to do it in a different way. For example, if two partners are goofing around during science, they might lose the privilege of being partners for the rest of science time.

- *Break it, fix it*—Whether on purpose or not, if children damage something, make a mess, or hurt someone's feelings, they take responsibility for the results of their behavior. For example, if a child spills some milk during snack, the consequence might be that he or she cleans up the spill. (Note that it would not be a logical consequence for the child to have to clean up the entire room.)

To open a discussion about logical consequences, you might begin with a read-aloud, such as *Alexander and the Terrible, Horrible, No Good, Very Bad Day*; *Andrew's Angry Words*; or *Lily's Purple Plastic Purse*. All three books open the way for a talk about having a bad day, being in a bad mood, or other scenarios where following rules is hard. We could ask, "When is it hard for you to follow rules?" Or we might say, "We're all going to have times when following rules is hard. We might be upset about something. We might just forget our rules. This year, logical consequences will help us get back on track."

Then, give a few everyday examples to help students understand how logical consequences will help them fix a problem or correct a mistake. (In giving examples, it's not necessary to use the terms "loss of privilege" or "break it, fix it"). For example:

- *Time-out*—"If someone calls out and interrupts the speaker, a time-out can help them regain self-control."

- *Loss of privilege*—"If someone is making a mess with the paints, they might have to work with crayons instead."

- *Break it, fix it*—"If someone gets marker on a table, they'll need to clean it off."

The intention here is to set the appropriate tone and convey two key points to students: first, that when rules are broken teachers will help everyone get back on the right track; and second, that mistakes are part of learning and we all make them, including teachers.

Another important idea to convey is that experiencing a consequence doesn't mean someone is "in trouble" or that the teacher is upset. It's simply a way for students to learn how to better follow the rules—rules that guide them in creating a classroom community where everyone can reach for their hopes and dreams. In the next chapter, you'll learn more about logical consequences and their use in the classroom.

Students' increased confidence now shows as they move through the room with purpose and work and play with new friends. By Friday, the class feels like it's been together for more than just three short weeks. Much of the heavy lifting of the first six weeks of school is behind us and, in the coming weeks, our attention and energy continue to shift. We still have new routines to teach and new supplies to introduce, but we can spend more time actually using class routines and materials to do amazing school work. We're seeing all of our hard work pay off!

Third & Fourth Grades

By the third week of school, third and fourth graders are pretty well settled into the school routine. It's important to recognize, however, that we're still at the very beginning of the school year. Throughout this week, we're reinforcing students' progress and helping them see their successes and growth.

Our steady leadership and guidance helps the class make an important shift this week—toward starting to ride by themselves a bit more, gaining confidence and competence as they balance on their own and begin to pick up speed.

MONDAY

8:15 Arrival routines

8:30 Morning Meeting
- Greeting: Use one that went well last week
- Sharing: Dialogue sharing (two students) and asking questions
- Group activity: A class favorite from the first two weeks
- Morning message: Working snacks

9:00 Math Introduce math project (polygon display) • Define/explain terms (triangles, quadrangles, etc.) • Academic Choice: Work independently and continue to build stamina

10:00 Outside time or energizer Continue to reinforce/review routines and expectations; build repertoire of options (see Appendix B)

10:15 Reading Review/re-model working in small groups • Work independently in small groups while individual conferences take place

11:00 Establishing rules Small group discussions • How we can follow rules during assemblies, with guest teacher, etc.

11:15 Writing Teach revision process • Revising work on own

11:45 Recess Introduce more options this week

12:05 Lunch Work toward open seating by end of week

12:30 Quiet time Expand choices this week (if children are ready)

12:45 Read-aloud Choose a new genre for this week

1:05 Special

1:50 Science Choose local animal to research and help with class terrarium project • Use of KWL charts

2:30 Homework Start homework in school; finish at home

2:45 End-of-day logistics and closing circle

3:00 Dismissal

TUESDAY

8:15 Arrival routines

8:30 Morning Meeting
- Greeting: High five
- Sharing: Dialogue sharing (three students) and asking questions
- Group activity: Find Your Match (geometry)
- Morning message: When can it be hard to follow rules?

9:00 Math Explore triangles • Continue to work independently and build stamina

10:00 Outside time or energizer

10:15 Reading Continue working independently in small groups while individual conferences take place

11:00 Establishing rules Introduce logical consequences

11:15 Writing Introduce peer conferences • Revising work on own

11:45 Recess

12:05 Lunch

12:30 Quiet time

12:45 Read-aloud

1:05 Special

1:50 Science Continue with local animal research and class terrarium • Update KWL charts

2:30 Homework Start homework in school; finish at home

2:45 End-of-day logistics and closing circle

3:00 Dismissal

Week Three Sample Schedule ▪ Grades 3–4

WEDNESDAY

8:15 Arrival routines

8:30 Morning Meeting
- Greeting: "Bonjour" or "Buenos días"
- Sharing: Partner sharing with questions
- Group activity: What's the Change? (science)
- Morning message: Triangles, quadrangles

9:00 Math Explore quadrangles; continue to work independently and build stamina

10:00 Outside time or energizer

10:15 Reading Independent small groups; individual conferences; open new book section(s)

11:00 Establishing rules Introduce, model, and practice time-out procedures

11:15 Writing Revising work on own; observe and coach peer conferences

11:45 Recess

12:05 Lunch

12:30 Quiet time

12:45 Read-aloud

1:05 Special

1:50 Science Plan how to present animal research; help with class terrarium; update KWL charts

2:30 Homework Tips for homework success; first homework at home

2:45 End-of-day logistics and closing circle

3:00 Dismissal

THURSDAY

8:15 Arrival routines

8:30 Morning Meeting
- Greeting: Pinky shake
- Sharing: Partner sharing with questions
- Group activity: Coseeki (science)
- Morning message: Research project check-in

9:00 Math Explore parallelograms; continue to work independently and build stamina

10:00 Outside time or energizer

10:15 Reading Independent small groups; individual conferences; open new book section(s)

11:00 Establishing rules Practice time-out; discuss rules and lunch

11:15 Writing Revising work on own; observe and coach peer conferences

11:45 Recess

12:05 Lunch

12:30 Quiet time

12:45 Read-aloud

1:05 Special

1:50 Science Work on animal research and class terrarium

2:30 Homework Discuss homework successes and challenges; homework at home

2:45 End-of-day logistics and closing circle

3:00 Dismissal

FRIDAY

8:15 Arrival routines

8:30 Morning Meeting
- Greeting: High five and "Bonjour" or "Buenos días"
- Sharing: Partner sharing with questions
- Group activity: Category Challenge (math, science)
- Morning message: Check-in about time-out

9:00 Math Create display of learning about polygons

10:00 Outside time or energizer

10:15 Reading Independent small groups; individual conferences; open new book section(s)

11:00 Establishing rules Check-in on time-out; discuss rules and lunch

11:15 Writing Introduce and practice editing and proofreading

11:45 Recess

12:05 Lunch

12:30 Quiet time

12:45 Read-aloud

1:05 Special

1:50 Science Present work on animal and reflect on it using KWL charts

2:30 Homework Discuss homework successes and challenges

2:45 End-of-day logistics and closing circle

3:00 Dismissal

Flow of the Day

Beginning the Day

Arrival Routines

After two weeks of school, third and fourth graders will most likely have mastered the morning routines. This week, we work at helping them stay on the right track. As students enter the room and get settled in for the day, we notice what they're doing well: "I see everyone is remembering to read the morning message and check the schedule before you join the circle for Morning Meeting." We also offer reminders as needed: "Jawad and Christopher, remember to check off your lunch choices before you join the circle." This calm, direct attention helps solidify routines so they continue to run smoothly.

Morning Meeting

This week, encourage students to take some small risks during Morning Meeting to help prepare them to take academic risks later in the day. For example, a student who can get up in front of classmates during an activity in the morning will feel more confident in sharing a piece of writing with them during writing time.

Still, risk should be added slowly and cautiously. One way to do this throughout week three is to introduce the idea of "challenge by choice"—students volunteer when they're ready to take a risk, such as by offering to be the first to try a variation of a game or to sign up to share in front of others. Here's a plan for gradually increasing risk that you can adapt for your own Morning Meetings this week:

- *Greeting*—Introduce variations on the basic handshake greeting, such as high fives, pinky shakes, or greetings in different languages. Give students the option of using the basic handshake greeting or trying a variation when it's their turn. Whichever variations you choose, model how to do them and continue to emphasize the essential elements of all greetings—looking at the person, smiling, and using names.

- *Sharing*—Introduce dialogue sharing, in which one student shares a bit of personal news or offers brief thoughts about a teacher-assigned topic and then other students respond. This week, help ensure students' success in responding appropriately by teaching them how to ask questions. Later in the year, teach how to respond with comments, which are trickier.

This kind of sharing and responding needs to be carefully taught to be most effective. Consider modeling dialogue sharing a few times before inviting students to try it, and use a sign-up sheet to limit sharers to two or three each meeting. The following chart offers a few ideas to emphasize as you teach dialogue sharing:

During Sharing	
Sharer's Jobs	**Audience's Jobs**
• Keep sharing brief and on topic.	• Look at the speaker.
• Share only school-appropriate content.	• Listen with interest.
• Face the audience.	• Ask respectful questions.
• Finish with, "I'm ready for questions."	

- *Group activity*—Consider teaching an activity that lets students take a risk in front of everyone when they're ready. For example, in Category Challenge, one volunteer stands in the middle of the circle and is given a category. While the class passes a pen around the circle, the volunteer names as many items in the category as she can. Start with simpler categories ("colors" or "foods") and then move to more challenging ones ("states" or "words that start with 'th'"). (See Appendix B for directions to the activities, learning structures, and songs mentioned in this chapter.)

- *Morning message*—Continue to check that all students are reading the message first thing in the morning. When going over the message together, you can give students an opportunity to take a risk in front of the class by inviting volunteers to read the message aloud. Or ask for a volunteer to read some of the challenging words first. Asking students for ideas on what to do if a reader is stuck can also help this feel like a safe risk to take.

Morning Break

Last week, we set up the guidelines for a working snack, in which students can have a quick snack at almost any time during the day. This week, we make sure that students are meeting expectations, especially with cleaning up and ensuring that snacking doesn't interfere with their work. If students are struggling a bit with this, we can scale back and limit the snack to set times. As during week two, we continue to provide a brief outdoor break or energizer to help students reenergize and refocus for the rest of the morning.

Middle of the Day

Recess

During recess this week, our role can transition to one that's less directly facilitative while still being supportive. For example, on one or two days, we could still suggest or even initiate some group games. On other days, we might only stroll through the playground, checking in on different areas, supervising and coaching as needed. If we see a student having difficulty connecting with others, we could help him engage with a group and remind other students of how they can be inclusive and take care of classmates during recess.

Lunch

We also transition to a less directly facilitative role in the cafeteria this week, as we continue to help students transfer classroom rules to other areas of the school. Before the class heads off to lunch, for example, help them generate ideas for how rules can guide lunchtime behavior: "What's one way to 'Be kind' in the lunchroom?" or "What might 'Respect school property' look like in the cafeteria?" We might then pop into lunch for a few minutes at a time to see how they're doing and offer support as needed.

Quiet Time

If we find that students are doing well with the simple choices offered so far, we can add in a few more this week. Consider offering the option of working on an ongoing project, such as revising a piece of writing, researching animals for science, or exploring shapes for math. And keep reminding students of the expectations for this time, reinforcing their successes to keep them headed in the right direction, and redirecting when needed. For example:

- *Reinforce:* "I noticed that as you entered the room for quiet time, you settled in quickly and efficiently. You were following our rule about taking care of each other."

- *Remind:* "Okay, everyone, as we head back to the room, remember the quiet time behavior we've been practicing this year."

- *Redirect:* "Sophia, head right to your spot for quiet time. You can check in with friends later in the afternoon."

Ending the Day

Dismissal Logistics

By the third week of school, dismissal logistics are flowing pretty smoothly. Overall, students know what their jobs are and are well practiced in doing them. We continue to guide and support, fine-tuning as needed. If we started to use an anchor chart in week two, we keep referring to it and can even enlist students to help refine it.

Closing Circle

This week is a great time to start having students practice self-reflection as part of the closing circle. "Think about how lunch and recess have been going. On a scale of one to five, how do you think our class is doing at following our rules?" Then invite the class to briefly share successes and ideas for possible improvements. Doing so reinforces that, instead of merely complying with teacher demands, they're working together toward the ideals they helped define during the rules creation process.

We want to make sure that closing circles this week—and throughout the year—remain upbeat. Even when students are discussing improvements, the tone can be positive, looking toward the future rather than dwelling on the past.

Teaching Academics

By the third week of school, academic momentum is really beginning to build. While we continue to teach students what to do and how to do it when introducing a new material or routine, we can now start to structure activities that last more than one class period and try some small group work.

Academic Choice

One way we can increase academic complexity this week is by offering a wider array of choices about how students learn or what they learn. For example, perhaps last week students had two choices about how to practice geometry concepts: pattern blocks and drawing with rulers. This week we add to that repertoire through Guided Discovery explorations (see Appendix A) of geoboards and tangrams. As we open new shelves of books in the class library, students can have richer and more varied choices about what kinds of books to read: historical fiction, biographies, and informational texts about science topics.

Because choosing from a wider variety of options can be harder for students, we need to teach them strategies for effective decision-making. We might model how to narrow down choices through the process of elimination. Or we might discuss how to reflect on choices made one day so that tomorrow's choices will be more informed.

Multi-Day Projects

As academic assignments become more layered, students begin to feel that what they're learning is more significant, and schoolwork takes on a more serious and purposeful tone. Here are some ideas for this kind of extended academic work:

- *Writing*—After several days of working on building writing stamina and starting a few different pieces of writing, students can choose one piece to start reworking into a final draft. Throughout this week, we can get students thinking ahead: "On Friday, you'll choose one of your first pieces of writing to bring to a final draft. Start thinking about which one you might choose."

- *Science*—A class studying local animals might take on a project that extends over several days. Students might choose one animal to learn about—their first foray into independent research. Each student could set a goal for the number of facts they want to gather and then create a simple display to share what they learned.

- *Math*—A week-long investigation of polygons lends itself to a sense of accomplishment as each day students build on previous learning. A culminating activity at the end of the week—a polygon display on a hallway bulletin board, for example—highlights the study.

Building Independence

"Can I go to the bathroom?" "My pencil broke!" "Ms. D., I'm finished! Now what do I do?" For learning to really soar during the year, we need to deliberately teach students to take care of small needs like these independently. Here are a couple of strategies we might use to do that this week:

- *Class discussion*—Hold a brief class discussion in which you let students know that it's their job to be more independent. This can strengthen the tone of trust you are building in the room as you essentially say, "I trust you to be responsible." Have students brainstorm ways they could take care of minor problems (can't find supplies, not sure about directions, etc.) when you are busy. Post this list in a place where students can easily refer to it.

- ■ *Notice and address class challenges*—Do students keep asking for help with a particular minor problem? See if there might be a simple fix. For example, I know one teacher who made a box of bandages available so her students could get them independently for small nicks, without having to ask her or make a trip to the nurse's office.

- ■ *Teacher language*—Even the way we address our class can help build a sense of independence. For example, instead of calling the class "Mrs. Jacobson's class," which may reinforce a sense of dependency on us, consider referring to the class as "learners," "scientists," or other terms that convey a sense of competence.

By building on students' successes and increasing challenges gradually, we can help them become more self-reliant and responsible.

Teaching Collaboration

This week we build on the collaborative skills students have been working on, helping them continue to practice key speaking and listening skills. In addition to working with partners, this week students learn how to work in small groups.

Working in Small Groups With the Teacher

Throughout the year, we'll need to work with small groups of students, one group at a time. This week we set up this routine by inviting a few students at a time to meet with us for five minutes or so about some academic content or to check in with them about an assignment. This is an opportunity for us to coach students on taking turns talking, staying on topic, and other essential skills for small-group discussions.

However, for these small groups to run smoothly and for students to develop independent work skills, the rest of the class needs to be able to work without our direct help or constant vigilance. After all, if several students are off task or a line of students keeps appearing at our elbow, the small-group work won't get very far. So while we're working with the small group, we're also observing the other students as they work on their own, reinforcing their efforts to stay focused and giving reminders and redirections as needed. Our focus is on setting clear expectations, boosting students' stamina for staying focused, developing a repertoire of strategies for them to use to solve minor problems on their own and following through with students who are off task.

Before meeting with the first small group, I often gather the whole class into the circle area. We brainstorm ways to solve problems independently if I'm busy with a group, and explore how remembering our rules can help everyone do their best learning. Then, at the end of the small-group work time, we reflect as a whole class: "The goal today was to stay focused on your own work while I met with small groups. How did we do with that? How did our class rules help us?"

By reflecting and making connections to the rules, we're building the class's capacity to work on their own while also building their capacity to engage in rich and productive small-group work throughout the year.

Next Steps With Small Groups

Later in the year, students will need to work in small groups with less direct supervision. They'll use many of the skills they've already been practicing with partners, including looking at the speaker and staying on topic. However, to ensure that they're ready for the challenges to come, some new skills need to be introduced now. For example, we might model and have students practice in small groups:

- Sharing "air time" equally

- Speaking one at a time

- Linking comments to others' ideas

Many interactive learning structures can serve as vehicles for practicing these more advanced, more independent small-group interactions. Maître d' (see opposite page) is one that works especially well with third and fourth graders. You might consider teaching it during Morning Meeting as a sharing structure or activity and then using it later in the day during an academic period.

Maître d' Directions and Tips

1. Direct students to get into groups of different sizes, depending on the "table grouping" you call out (for example, "Tables for three," "Tables for four").

2. Give a topic for discussion: "Discuss one new fact you learned from the article we just read."

3. After two minutes, announce a new table grouping and topic.

- Share ideas for how class rules apply (for example, "Focusing on the topic supports our rule, 'Take care of your own learning'").

- Model as needed (how to move efficiently into new table groupings, how to take turns sharing ideas).

- Use an auditory signal to get students' attention when it's time to move to a new grouping.

- You may want to encourage table groups to stand as they talk so they can move a little more.

Homework

In general, the third week of school is ideal for transitioning third and fourth graders to at-home homework. At the beginning of the week, students can start homework at school and then finish it at home—getting into the habit of thinking about their homework at the end of the day, neatly packing it away, and bringing it back the next day. By the end of the week, students should be ready to try doing homework completely at home. Each day, spend a little time debriefing with students about how homework is going, inviting them to share helpful strategies and any challenges they're having.

Keeping Homework Manageable

One of the best ways we can support students in developing positive homework habits is to keep homework light and manageable. For third and fourth graders, homework is ideally about simple practice to reinforce skills, not multi-day projects, challenging extensions of work, or unfinished in-school work. A few math problems, a few sentences to write, or a short scavenger hunt at home (to find a few examples of concepts learned in school) is plenty.

In addition to five to fifteen minutes of this kind of homework, encourage students to read for enjoyment. This approach to homework sets students up for success—helping them have a more positive homework experience and building their confidence and sense of responsibility.

Teaching Discipline

Third and fourth graders generally know what's expected of them in terms of behavior by the third week of school. Still, we want to be sure to teach and practice routines and expectations, especially new ones, and continue to build a positive community.

This week, we also start to shift our approach so that students experience living the rules that we agreed to last week and taking more ownership of them. In addition, we introduce logical consequences as our tool for helping students stay on track with their behavior and learning when they go off course.

Making the Rules Come Alive

I remember the first time I created rules with a class of fourth graders. After brainstorming ideas, categorizing them, and reaching consensus on the few rules we'd adopt for the year, I metaphorically dusted off my hands and thought, "Phew, that's done."

Now I know better! Once the classroom rules have been created, the teaching of discipline has truly only just begun. This process—bringing the rules to life—will last all year long.

Referring to the Rules

After posting the rules, refer to them frequently and in a positive way. After all, the rules have been framed as goals that guide us toward positive behavior and enable us to function well as a learning community. The teacher's role is to help students connect the rules to how they speak, act, and treat others.

An effective way to do this is by phrasing reminders as prompting questions, which will help students think proactively about how the rules can help shape their behavior and work. For example:

- "We're about to head to the art room. What are some ways we can follow our rules as we walk in the halls?"

- "In just a moment, you're going to clean up your math supplies and meet in the circle to share your work. How can we follow our rule 'Be safe and kind' as we do this?"

- "During writing today, some people may be having peer conferences. It might be hard to stay focused on writing if two other writers are chatting nearby. How might you 'Take care of yourself' if you are struggling to stay focused?"

In addition to helping students think proactively about their behavior, we're also highlighting for them that our rules poster is a living document that helps guide us throughout the day.

Relying on the Rules in Challenging Times

By recognizing that certain times of day or situations may be more difficult for students than others, we can coach them in how to meet these challenges by using the class rules. Challenging times might occur every day (recess, lunch) or only occasionally (assemblies, days with guest teachers, field trips).

To help students proactively use class rules to navigate these trickier times, try holding small-group discussions. The goal for each group could be to brainstorm responses to two questions:

1. Why is this time so challenging?

2. What are some specific ways we could follow our rules during this time?

By thinking about challenging times in advance, students are more likely to behave appropriately, stay on track with their learning, and assume more ownership of the rules. Ultimately, students should follow the rules not to please us, but because that's how we take care of each other in a supportive learning environment.

Logical Consequences

Now that our rules are formally posted, and with a firmer foundation of classroom community and trust, we can talk explicitly about the following logical consequences and how they will help support the rules:

- *Time-out*—This technique helps students regroup mentally and emotionally just as they are starting to lose self-control, while enabling the rest of the class to continue with their learning.

- *Loss of privilege*—If students are struggling to meet expectations during a certain activity, a logical consequence might be that they lose a privilege connected to that activity. For example, if a student is being careless with a tablet or other device, he might lose the privilege of using the tablet or device for the rest of that period.

- *Break it, fix it*—When students break something, make a mess, or hurt someone's feelings, whether on purpose or not, they can learn to take responsibility for their mistake. For example, if a student accidentally knocks over a bin of math manipulatives, the consequence is that she stops and picks them up.

A good starting point for teaching logical consequences to third and fourth graders is to hold a class discussion about times when rules are hard to follow. To get the conversation going, I like to share one of my own struggles following rules. "I'm usually pretty good at being kind to others," I might say, "but a rule that's often hard for me is 'Take care of our classroom.' I'm so busy during the day that sometimes I leave piles of stuff around instead of putting them away where they belong. Which rules do you think will be easier for you to follow? Which ones might be harder, and why?"

Because we all struggle with rules from time to time, logical consequences are best explained as ways to help in those situations: "Even though we all try to follow our rules, sometimes we make mistakes or forget what we should do. It happens. This year, when I see that you're struggling with our rules, I might give you a logical consequence to help you get back on track."

Then, because third and fourth graders are largely concrete thinkers, give them a few simple examples—ones that could happen to anyone and that they won't associate with "getting in trouble"—to help them see the connections between rules and logical consequences. (I don't use the terms "loss of privilege" or "break it, fix it" in my teaching this week.) For example, "Suppose we're lining up for recess and a student leaves their trash on a table. What should that student do?"

Before I open up the floor for their ideas, I stress that logical consequences are for fixing a problem, not for punishing a student. We then share ideas and discuss examples, such as:

- *Time-out*—A student calls out answers without raising her hand. *She takes a time-out to settle down.*

- *Loss of privilege*—A student is distracting tablemates instead of working. *The student who's being distracting moves to a separate work spot.*

- *Break it, fix it*—A student knocks a classmate's pen off the table as he walks by. *The student who knocked the pen off picks it up.*

Depending on your class, you might hold this discussion in one session or extend it over several short ones. Either way, the goal remains the same: to help students think about consequences and their usefulness in helping everyone take responsibility for following rules. The bottom line is that when rules are broken, something happens, but it's about getting back on track for learning, not about being embarrassed or punished.

Positive Time-Out

Time-out is a logical consequence that needs some extra explanation and teaching if it is to serve as a positive—not punitive—strategy. The following ideas can help guide you in setting up time-out for use with third and fourth graders:

- *Set a positive tone*—A short explanation of how time-out will work helps student understand its benefits: "There will be times when we lose focus or self-control and do something that breaks the flow of our own learning or other people's learning. For example, someone might start feeling antsy and talk to a neighbor in the middle of someone else's sharing at Morning Meeting. Time-out will help us get back on track quickly and easily."

- *Model*—You can use Interactive Modeling (see Appendix A) to teach students the protocols for using time-out efficiently without disrupting others. When planning this modeling, consider how you expect students to go to time-out, what you expect them to do there, and when and how they should return. Also, teach the rest of the class to stay focused on their work when someone is going to time-out. This will also help that student regain control.

- *Practice*—After the initial modeling, give students practice in using time-out. Let students know that over the course of the next few days, time-out will be used only for rehearsal—when they're in control and following the rules. I actually use a running log to make sure that everyone has had a chance to practice. This explicit trial run helps reinforce the idea that time-out is a learning tool and that it's for everyone.

LAST THOUGHT

3-4

This week, while students are working more collaboratively and independently, we continue to observe, assess, and coach. We reinforce successes, redirect small misbehaviors before they escalate, and frequently take the class's pulse: What's working well? What's still bumpy? What are students ready for—and when should we slow down a bit? We start to feel that we're really getting to know individual students and the personality of the class. And with that knowledge, we can start to make more-informed decisions about what and how we'll teach in the coming weeks.

Fifth & Sixth Grades

Although fifth and sixth graders will verbalize that they're ready for teachers to back off—"We can play at recess on our own, you know!"—we need to be observant and at the ready behind the bicycle this week. Students can take on more challenging work, activities, and learning structures, but they're still learning how to work well together. They can verbalize how rules apply in various settings, but they're not yet able to consistently apply those rules on their own.

Older children continue to need our coaching and reinforcing of their step-by-step successes just as younger ones do. This week, we jog behind the bike and lend a steadying hand as needed.

Week Three Sample Schedule ▪ Grades 5–6

MONDAY

8:15 Arrival routines

8:30 Morning Meeting
- Greeting: Use one that went well last week
- Sharing: Dialogue sharing (teacher as only sharer; listeners' role this week is to ask questions)
- Group activity: Category Challenge (multiplication facts)
- Morning message: What was a highlight from your weekend? What's something you're looking forward to in school this week?

8:50 Math   Introduce/review traditional multiplication • Academic Choice all week: Students choose between two algorithms to practice

9:50 Outside time or energizer   Continue to reinforce/review routines and expectations; build repertoire of options (see Appendix B)

10:05 Reading   Review/re-model working in small groups with focus on academic conversation skills • Work independently in small groups while individual conferences take place

11:00 Establishing rules   Introduce logical consequences

11:15 Writing   Introduce/review using laptops and word processing program • Begin drafting autobiographical sketches

11:45 Recess   Introduce more options this week

12:05 Lunch   Continue with open seating this week

12:30 Quiet time   Expand choices this week

12:45 Read-aloud   Practice academic conversation skills; choose a new book or genre for this week

1:05 Special

1:50 Social studies   Introduce country studies • Guided Discovery of materials as needed

2:45 End-of-day logistics and closing circle

3:00 Dismissal

TUESDAY

8:15 Arrival routines

8:30 Morning Meeting
- Greeting: Around-the-circle
- Sharing: Dialogue sharing (teacher only; listeners ask questions)
- Group activity: Category Challenge (multiples)
- Morning message: List a multiple of 6, 7, 8, or 9.

8:50 Math   Multiplication (partial products) • Students make up own problems; practice for 20 minutes to build stamina

9:50 Outside time or energizer

10:05 Reading   Reflect on yesterday's reading • Continue working independently in small groups while individual conferences take place

11:00 Establishing rules   Introduce and practice time-out

11:15 Writing   Introduce peer conferences • Continue work on autobiographical sketches

11:45 Recess

12:05 Lunch

12:30 Quiet time

12:45 Read-aloud

1:05 Special

1:50 Social studies   Continue with country studies • Brainstorm reasons for choosing a country; list countries as options for study

2:45 End-of-day logistics and closing circle

3:00 Dismissal

Week Three Sample Schedule ■ Grades 5–6

WEDNESDAY

8:15 Arrival routines

8:30 Morning Meeting
- Greeting: Ball Toss
- Sharing: Dialogue sharing (three students share; listeners ask questions)
- Group activity: Acting out division problems
- Morning message: Language arts connection

8:50 Math Introduce/review traditional division; students choose among algorithms to practice

9:50 Outside time or energizer

10:05 Reading Reflect on yesterday's reading; independent small groups; individual conferences

11:00 Establishing rules Reflect on rules and logical consequences

11:15 Writing Writing/revising on own; observe and coach peer conferences

11:45 Recess

12:05 Lunch

12:30 Quiet time

12:45 Read-aloud

1:05 Special

1:50 Social studies Continue with list of countries; start list of research topics and questions

2:45 End-of-day logistics and closing circle

3:00 Dismissal

THURSDAY

8:15 Arrival routines

8:30 Morning Meeting
- Greeting: Ball Toss (and in reverse)
- Sharing: Dialogue sharing (three students share; listeners ask questions)
- Group activity: Hands Up chant
- Morning message: Math connection

8:50 Math Division (partial quotients); students make up own problems; practice for 20 minutes

9:50 Outside time or energizer

10:05 Reading Reflect on yesterday's reading; independent small groups; individual conferences

11:00 Establishing rules Reflect on rules and logical consequences, including time-out

11:15 Writing Writing/revising on own; observe and coach peer conferences

11:45 Recess

12:05 Lunch

12:30 Quiet time

12:45 Read-aloud

1:05 Special

1:50 Social studies Students write proposals for countries they want to study

2:45 End-of-day logistics and closing circle

3:00 Dismissal

FRIDAY

8:15 Arrival routines

8:30 Morning Meeting
- Greeting: Spider Web
- Sharing: Dialogue sharing (three students share; listeners ask questions)
- Group activity: What Are You Doing?
- Morning message: Research project connection

8:50 Math Multiplication and division practice; choice of what needs most practice; create and solve own problems

9:50 Outside time or energizer

10:05 Reading Independent small groups; individual conferences; assign first book group for next week

11:00 Establishing rules Reflect on rules and focus on time-out

11:15 Writing Revising/editing/proofreading; preview next week's work

11:45 Recess

12:05 Lunch

12:30 Quiet time

12:45 Read-aloud

1:05 Special

1:50 Social studies Research country chosen; explore websites; introduction to note-taking sheet

2:45 End-of-day logistics and closing circle

3:00 Dismissal

Flow of the Day

Beginning the Day

Arrival Routines

How are morning routines going? Do students know what to do when they enter the room? Does the beginning of the day feel calm and orderly?

This week, we can make sure students' transition to school continues to go smoothly by tapping into their need to socialize. Think about how you could slightly adjust the morning routine so students have a few minutes with their peers. For example, you might invite them to chat quietly with classmates or work on the morning message task with a partner. A smooth morning transition will help students feel relaxed and ready for Morning Meeting—and pay dividends all day long.

Morning Meeting

If students seem to be feeling safe and your class is developing into a caring community, Morning Meetings can start to build in risk and complexity. It's important, though, to do that building thoughtfully, giving students choices about how much risk they take on.

- *Greeting*—Begin the week with a greeting that's worked well and that students enjoy. Later in the week, introduce ones that are a little more involved, such as the Ball Toss or Spider Web greeting. When trying a new greeting, support students by reviewing how the class rules can help everyone have fun and feel welcomed. Ultimately, what's most important about any greeting is that everyone feels a sense of belonging and significance, so continue to emphasize using each other's names, looking at the person, listening, and speaking with friendly voices. (See Appendix B for directions to the greetings, activities, learning structures, and songs mentioned in this chapter.)

- *Sharing*—By the third week, fifth and sixth graders will likely be ready for dialogue sharing, in which one person shares a piece of news and the class responds with questions and comments. Students may share about a wide variety of topics, from the sport they play to the death of a grandparent. This form of sharing enables students to learn more about each other and practice a more complex set of speaking and listening skills.

Through modeling and practice, dialogue sharing can deepen a class's sense of community. Here are some tips:

- *Use Interactive Modeling* (see Appendix A) to teach sharers how to be brief and use complete sentences, and listeners how to respectfully ask purposeful questions and make relevant comments.

- *Introduce dialogue sharing in stages.* Be the only sharer for a couple of days before inviting students to try. Introduce asking questions this week and the skill of making comments next week.

- *Keep content safe.* Talk with students about appropriate sharing topics for school and help them brainstorm ideas. At first, preview their sharing topics to make sure they're school-appropriate.

- **Group activity**—This week, mix in new activities with ones you've already introduced. As activities begin to involve more risk, we can introduce the idea of "challenge by choice," where students can vary their level of participation according to the amount of risk they'd like to take—to be at the center of the game or to take a more supportive role. Activities well suited for this kind of choice include naming items in a category (Category Challenge) and improvisational acting (What Are You Doing?).

Dear Creative Writers,

Today in Writers' Workshop, we'll talk more about how to change "tired" words into "wow" words to help our stories come to life for readers. In the box below, take a look at some of the "tired" words we found in our read-aloud book yesterday. Turn one into a "wow" word.

TIRED WORDS	WOW WORDS
look	
good	
bad	
little	
big	grand
went	

Let's have a great day of learning!

Mrs. Martinez

- **Morning message**—Fifth and sixth graders will likely need frequent reminders to develop the daily habit of reading and responding to the morning message. Time spent solidifying this habit early in the year is well spent: Reading the message is essential, and trying to reestablish this routine later in the year is more difficult.

The more engaging your messages, of course, the more likely that students will read and interact with them. Try to tie each message directly to the students' day and include something for students to do (add ideas about math content, predict tomorrow's weather, and so on). The previous page shows a message that can help engage students in their upcoming reading and writing lessons.

Middle of the Day

Recess

If things are generally going well on the playground, this is a good time to start moving away from directly facilitating recess activities. You might offer a group option two days this week and spend the other days circulating, observing, and coaching.

As you do this, keep an eye out for students who are sitting by themselves or just wandering around. These may be signs that students are being bullied or excluded or are having a hard time joining others. Be sure to check in with these students. "How's it going, Koji?" you might ask. "Are you just taking a walk or are you looking for someone to play with?"

Tight friendship groups, especially among girls, are a hallmark of this age. It's up to us to make sure they stay positive and kind. As we walk toward a group sitting together and giggling, we want to notice their body language and tone and whether they change topics as we approach. "Hey, everyone," we might say to engage openly with them. "How's it going? Mind if I join you for a bit?" As we observe, interact, and intervene (when needed), we're letting students know that we're still a presence on the playground—there to make sure everyone is safe and included.

Lunch

We can start to diminish our presence in the cafeteria this week. Before we do, however, we'll want to assess what's going well and what still needs work. Are routines solid? Are students disposing of trash properly, following bathroom procedures, and using appropriate voice volume? Are students showing respect to one another and to the adults present? These questions can help guide the level of support we offer students going forward. Depending on what you observe, you might:

- Pop in and out during lunchtime.
- Begin lunchtime with students and then leave halfway through.
- Continue to eat lunch with students.

When in doubt, it's better to err on the side of caution by giving more support for a longer time, rather than decreasing it too quickly.

Quiet Time

If quiet time routines are going smoothly, consider adding more options for students this week. They could work on something they've already started, such as revising drafts, doing research, or working on a class project. You might want to introduce a sign-up chart for students who want to practice math or language arts skills using a computer program or app. You could also have students focus on areas that most interest them, such as reading books in a favorite genre, or on any content areas they want more practice with, such as math facts or vocabulary building. Again, add choices only as students are ready.

Ending the Day

Dismissal Logistics

I find that as schoolwork increases, students often need more time to organize backpacks and clean up in the afternoon, so this week is a good time to assess how the end-of-day routines are going. Do students have enough time to get packed up before the closing circle? Do any students need extra support, such as a personal checklist, to stay on track? Try to preserve the time needed for final routines to ensure that transitions go smoothly and the day ends pleasantly.

Closing Circle

As with Morning Meeting this week, we can continue using closing circles for quick activities that reinforce math facts or other skills students are learning. We can also increase our repertoire of closing circle activities by recycling activities, energizers, and sharing structures used during the day. Remember, though, to keep the focus of closing circles on having an upbeat ending to the day—a chance for the class to come together to celebrate or reflect on the day and look forward to tomorrow.

Teaching Academics

By the third week of school, fifth and sixth graders will have many basic academic routines down pat. However, any time we want to change a routine, either to adjust for the particular needs of the class or to add a little complexity as students are ready, we need to set students up for success by teaching, modeling, and letting them practice. We also need to reinforce what students are doing well to solidify behaviors they already know. For the most part, though, the intense early-year work of establishing routines and teaching about materials is greatly reduced. We can now turn our attention to other things.

Academic Choice

Academic Choice (see Appendix A) can take on more depth this week, now that students have had a couple of weeks' practice choosing among limited options. For example, during the first week of school we might have opened up only a few bookshelves; by the third week, we can open up the entire classroom library so that students can choose any book from any genre.

As students enter adolescence, they're quicker to dismiss work that seems irrelevant or uninteresting. "Why do we have to do this?" or "This is stupid," they may grump. For these students, academic engagement is especially important at this point in the school year. So throughout this week, we can emphasize student responsibility and give them some real control over their work through more—and more complex—choices. For example:

- *In math,* teach two different algorithms for solving multiplication and division problems and use Academic Choice to help students decide which one makes the most sense for them to practice. Then, for homework, students can make up their own problems and practice using the method they've chosen.

- *For more effective peer writing conferences,* ask students to set conference goals and prepare specific questions.

- *In social studies,* have students choose three countries they'd like to study and write a brief explanation of their interest in each one. Then, with your guidance, they can select the one that best fits their learning goals.

Although we're offering students more control this week over what and how they learn, we never hand over *all* of that responsibility. Students don't get to decide whether or not they learn how to multiply and divide, but they can choose a method that works best for them (with our guidance and coaching, of course). All students will engage in writing conferences and book groups, but they can choose some goals for writing and some of the books they read. Fifth and sixth graders will appreciate that extra measure of choice.

Teaching Collaboration

For the first two weeks of school, students primarily worked on the skills involved in effective partner work. This week, if you think your class is ready, begin the year's first small-group work. Thoughtfully pace your introduction of the skills needed for this collaborative work. Having plenty of time to practice will help students feel more confident in taking on academic challenges throughout the year.

Small-Group Work

To set students up for success working in small groups:

- *Build on previously learned skills.* Students have already learned a lot about working with others. We can help them transfer these skills to new situations and boost their sense of competence and confidence. "Today we're going to share about our reading in trios. Think about what you've practiced when sharing with one partner. What are some things you can do to be a good listener in a small group?"

- *Teach new skills.* Although some skills from partner work directly transfer, students need to develop additional skills for working in a small group. Group members will need a system for taking turns. Students will need to shift their bodies and eyes from speaker to speaker instead of focusing on just one person. Brainstorm ideas as a class about what groups will need to do to be successful, and then model and practice key skills together.

- *Continue to facilitate groupings.* Whether groups are formed randomly by drawing names or are put together specifically to match (or separate) certain students, teachers should still be the ones creating groups. This will keep the classroom climate supportive as students develop the more complex skills needed for group work.

Interactive Learning Structures

You can also introduce some new learning structures this week to help students further develop their skills for productive small-group collaboration. For example, you might teach a new sharing structure or group activity during Morning Meeting and then use it later in the day during an academic period. Here's one structure that helps fifth and sixth graders form groups quickly and work well with a wider variety of classmates:

Commonalities Directions and Tips	
1. Name a category, such as "number of buttons on your clothes."	• Choose neutral categories, avoiding ones that might highlight sensitive areas such as height or weight.
2. Students group themselves with others who have the same number of buttons (including none).	• Set a group size (say, five or less). A group of eight with something in common could split into two smaller discussion groups.
3. Students then discuss an assigned topic or work on an assigned short task.	• Make sure students find a group. If someone can't find others who have the named attribute in common, help them find a group to join.
4. Begin another round with a new category.	

Building Stamina

By now, most students will have developed more school stamina and can handle longer work periods, so this week we can adjust our schedules to reflect this shift. If students no longer need us to set aside time in the afternoon to help get them started on their homework, we can use that time for additional content instruction or practice.

At the same time, we want to keep an eye on the energy level of the room and make adjustments in the moment. If we increase writing time from twenty to thirty minutes, we should also keep assessing students' ability to handle this increase. If we see their attention fading and restlessness increasing, we can give them a quick movement break or have them engage in an interactive learning structure that gets them moving and collaborating.

Increasing Student Independence

In week three, most students will likely have a solid grasp of the essential academic routines, so we can help them move toward taking on more responsibility for working independently. We need to do more than just say, "You're in fifth grade now—it's time to take more responsibility!" Instead, we want to create the conditions and teach students the skills they need so this can happen, building on the work we've done since the first week of school.

Of course, our goal is not to have students be completely independent of us. It will always be our job to teach key concepts and skills, coach students who need extra help, manage class energy levels, and tend to classroom issues such as hurt feelings or conflicts over materials. But we do want students to access materials on their own, check their own work, know what to do once they finish a task, respectfully ask a peer for clarity about an assignment, and so on. Learning how to manage these tasks on their own prepares them to take on more challenging academic work throughout—and beyond—this school year.

Helping students hone their self-management skills also enables us to work intensively with small groups. This week, before we pull a small group together for direct instruction or coaching, we might briefly discuss as a class how students can work successfully on their own, with partners, or in their own small groups. Together, we might also brainstorm strategies for solving minor problems so as not to disrupt others. This week, as we work with a group or an individual student, we'll still want to position ourselves so that we can watch the rest of the class and offer support as needed. At the end of the work period, we can reflect together on how things went.

Even the way we address the class can support their developing sense of independence. For example, instead of referring to the class as "Mr. Harland's class," which suggests dependence on us, we can refer to students as "mathematicians" or "researchers." Terms such as these convey confidence and competence.

Building Complexity

Along with more independence, students are also ready for more complex work in the third week of school. Work that feels more substantial is exciting and challenging, with the potential to boost students' interest and sense of accomplishment. This week we want to:

- **Start longer-range projects.** It's not too early in the year to begin a project that will take a couple of weeks to complete. In fact, this kind of work tends to feel more significant to upper elementary students. Here's how you might set up such a project on writing autobiographical sketches.

  - In the first two weeks of school, students start this work by writing several short pieces about things they like to do, family members, and other personal topics.

  - In week three, students keep adding pieces to their autobiographical work and start thinking about additional topics or details they want to include. They practice adding details to their writing through "tell me more about" conferences: they read their writing to a partner, who suggests where they could expand their writing by saying, "At this point in your writing, tell me more about…."

  - In the following week, students continue this work and complete final drafts.

> ### Assessing Students' Ability to Work Independently
>
> As this week ends, take some time to assess how student independence is coming along. What's going especially well? What still needs some work? This second question can help guide your planning for the coming weeks.

- *Integrate content.* The connecting of content throughout the day lends a sense of cohesion and continuity to students' learning and sets a purposeful tone for their work. For example:

  - If students are learning about maps in social studies, they could draw maps of places connected with their autobiographical writing.

  - Students could create a class graph of key events from their read-aloud book, a skill they're also practicing during reading workshop.

  - As a warm-up for the math lesson later that day, students could explore prime numbers and prime factorization during Morning Meeting.

Homework

As students take full responsibility for doing homework at home, continue to set them up for success by keeping assignments manageable and flexible. A few tips:

- *Keep it short and sweet*—Practicing five math problems for homework is likely to be as effective as practicing twenty, and if students have only five to complete, they'll probably do so with a more upbeat attitude and greater sense of competence.

- *Offer some choice*—If a homework assignment has ten questions, students could choose five to answer. Or invite students to write their own questions, letting them self-differentiate by making the work as difficult as they can handle.

- *Provide support*—What should students do if they get stuck? Some teachers give students their phone number so they can call for help. Another idea is to have a buddy system, where every student has a classmate to call. Or have them simply write a question mark on their paper and ask for help the next day. Avoid counting on parents to help, since they may be unable to do so because of work or other factors.

- *Limit time going over homework*—Although we need to check that homework was done, we don't need to spend class time correcting work unless an assignment directly ties in with the day's lesson. In addition, for students who couldn't do the work for whatever reason, correcting homework in class can lead to feelings of anxiety or disengagement.

Teaching Discipline

This week, we focus on finalizing class rules and guiding students in seeing how the rules can be applied throughout their day together. We also carry on with the work we started during the first two weeks of school in helping students get to know each other and build positive relationships.

Referring to the Rules

Last week, with the rules in place, we fostered positive conversations about discipline and how the rules can help guide our behavior in various situations, such as at recess and lunch. This week, keep finding ways to bring the rules front and center. For example:

- "How can we follow our rule about taking care of ourselves as we work on this next math challenge?"
- "How will our rule 'Respect yourself and others' help us during writing conferences?"

When teachers regularly refer to class rules, the message in the room is clear: We are striving to live up to the ideals we've set for ourselves in all areas of our school life together.

Logical Consequences

Now that the classroom rules are finalized and you're regularly connecting them to learning, it's time to introduce three types of logical consequences. Many upper grade students may have experienced consequences as heavy-handed and arbitrary punishments. Tell students that in this classroom, logical consequences are different; they're a set of tools to help students get back on track for learning, not punishments meant to force them to obey the will of the teacher.

The three types of logical consequences are:

- *Time-out*—This technique helps students regroup mentally and emotionally before they lose control, while enabling the rest of the class to continue their learning.
- *Loss of privilege*—If students are struggling to meet expectations during an activity, they lose a privilege connected to that activity. For example, if a student is being careless with a chemical during a science experiment, she might lose the privilege of doing hands-on experimenting and just observe for the rest of the period. The next day, after reviewing safety rules and showing that she understands them, she can regain the privilege.

- *Break it, fix it*—When a student breaks something, causes a spill, or hurts someone's feelings, even if unintentionally, he can learn to take responsibility for his behavior. For example, if a student rips a page from a book, the consequence might be that he carefully tapes it up.

When teaching logical consequences, the words and tone you use to explain them is key. (At this point in your teaching, it's not necessary to introduce students to the terms "loss of privilege" or "break it, fix it.") Consider the differences in approach in the following chart:

When Introducing Logical Consequences

Instead of talking about them as punishments . . .	Try talking about them as helpful tools . . .
"You should always follow the rules. You all signed the rules saying that you believed in them, so you'd better work toward them. If you make a mistake, I'm going to give you a consequence so you will do better."	"We all have times when we break rules. We might be having a bad day or we might be so wrapped up in what we're doing that we zone out a little. Logical consequences will help us get back on track when we need some help."

Giving some everyday examples can help students better understand logical consequences and how they'll work, strengthening the sense of trust and safety in the classroom. By using common examples that every student can relate to, we further reinforce the idea that logical consequences apply to all students and that everyone will experience them at one time or another. Here are a few examples that might work well with your students:

Everyday Example	Applicable Rule(s)	Logical Consequence
A student bumps into a shelf and knocks books onto the floor.	Take care of our classroom.	*Break it, fix it:* Put the books back on the shelf.
Two students are whispering and giggling while working together during math.	Do careful work.	*Loss of privilege:* Work separately or join other groups.
A student yells out ideas during a class discussion instead of raising his hand.	Be respectful.	*Time-out:* Take a break to regain self-control.

You might share these examples during a class discussion, have small groups of students discuss them together, or invite students to generate ideas for logical consequences and use those as a starting point. Make it clear that students won't be expected to come up with their own logical consequences during real rule-breaking situations.

Positive Time-Out

Because many students have experienced a punitive form of time-out, it's especially important to introduce this logical consequence very purposefully. You want to make it clear that in this classroom, time-out (what many teachers call "take-a-break") is used as a way to regain self-control, not as a punishment.

I've found that using a sports analogy like the one below to introduce time-out helps students see this practice more positively. After all, the coach and players are on the same team, and the coach is there to help the team achieve its goal, just like the teacher in the classroom.

> *Teacher:* "What does a basketball coach do if the team is starting to get out of sync? You know, players aren't passing, they're taking wild shots, people are confused about whom to guard…"
>
> *Student:* "The coach calls a time-out."
>
> *Teacher:* "Yup. The coach gathers the team for a short break and says something like, 'Okay everyone, let's get our heads back in the game. Remember to look for the open shooter and stick with the player you're guarding. Now, get back in there and play just like we've practiced!' That's how 'take-a-break' will work for us this year. When people are losing focus or control, take-a-break will be like a time-out in basketball. It's a chance to take a quick break, get refocused, and then get back into the game."

Next, use Interactive Modeling to show what going to the take-a-break spot should look like. Play the role of a student and ask a volunteer to say, "Mr. Anderson, take a break." Show how to move in a relaxed and direct way to the designated spot, sit there calmly for about twenty to thirty seconds, and then head back to your regular spot. Seeing the teacher modeling the take-a-break routine reinforces the idea that it's for everyone to use.

Over the course of the week, have students practice using the take-a-break spot, always during moments when they are in control and following the rules to make it clear that they're just practicing. It's helpful to keep a running log of who's practiced to make sure everyone tries it out at least once.

To further support the idea that time-out is positive and nonpunitive:

- *Let students know that if they feel themselves getting frustrated or upset,* they can use the take-a-break spot on their own to regain self-control or cool off.

- *Keep your tone neutral.* Sounding exasperated may cause students to focus on your mood rather than the rules.

- *For the next week or two,* consider signaling students when you think they're ready to leave the time-out spot. Later, teach students how to decide for themselves when they're ready to come back. This empowers them and helps them develop self-regulation skills.

In addition, teach the rest of the class to stay focused on their work when a classmate goes to the take-a-break spot. This will also help the student taking a break to regain control.

LAST THOUGHT

5–6

By the third week of school, we've achieved quite a bit of momentum as a class. In general students know how the classroom works, they're comfortable with academic routines, and they're starting to gel as a learning community. A good bit of effort is still required to keep students on track, but much less than in the first week. Soon, as we'll see in the next chapter, we'll be at the point where we can focus more of our energy on coaching, guiding, and stretching students so they can achieve even greater social and academic gains.

Weeks Four
to Six

Goals for Weeks Four to Six

During these next three weeks, we want to continue to build up the academic community and keep the positive momentum of the first three weeks of school going. Although much of our work now focuses on specific academic content and skills, we don't want to neglect the foundations of learning that make that work possible—effective classroom management, positive community, developmentally responsive teaching, and engaging academics. Our goals for weeks four, five, and six are for every student to be:

- *An active member of the learning community*—The classroom hums with productive activity; students are enjoying recess and lunch; and they're doing their best to be kind and respectful to everyone.

- *Fully engaged academically*—Students' stamina and capacity for working independently and collaboratively is growing; they're taking on more complex work; they're continually being appropriately challenged, both individually and as a class; and their successes, big and small, are reinforced.

- *More self-sufficient*—Like a true team, the class is trying hard to follow daily routines; the rules continue to serve as the anchor for discipline; and students genuinely encourage and support one another.

216

Overview for All Grades

In the first three weeks of school, we laid the groundwork for exciting academic work, especially in our teaching of academic routines and by modeling and practicing the foundational skills of listening, speaking, and collaborating. Lively activities gave students opportunities to move and interact with one another while engaging with meaningful academic content, and the first interactive learning structures were introduced and practiced, giving students formats for sharing and discussing work.

By the fourth week of school, we likely have a clearer sense of which things are working well and which are not. Perhaps students can focus well during quiet time but are more easily distracted during math. Or maybe recess generally goes smoothly but lunchtime has frequent bumps.

Wherever students are at this point in the school year, we must meet them there. By taking the time to step back a bit to gain some perspective and observe students individually and as a class, we can effectively reinforce what's going well and up the ante a bit while continuing to model, practice, remind, and redirect where students need more support.

Also, since we now have a handle on creating daily classroom schedules that balance academics with social skills learning, stillness with movement, and group collaboration with individual work, sample schedules are not provided in this chapter. However, if you notice students' energy flagging or their focus frazzling, consider whether the schedule might be a factor and compare it with the ones in the previous chapters to see what adjustments might help.

In weeks four, five, and six—to continue with our metaphor introduced in the previous chapter—we let go of the bicycle seat, stand aside (but still nearby), and continue to coach.

Kindergarten, First & Second Grades

At this point in the school year, the foundational work we've done setting these young students up for success with classroom routines, working as a learning community, and tackling academics begins to come together, enabling us to help students further develop essential social-emotional and academic skills and competencies in these next three weeks of school and beyond.

Flow of the Day

Morning Meeting

During these next three weeks, Morning Meetings continue to grow and shift with the class. As children develop more stamina, we can facilitate meetings that help them engage in a wider variety of activities while still fostering a sense of belonging, significance, and fun. We keep helping them connect positively with their classmates while also priming the academic pump and previewing the day's learning.

- *Greeting*—As students are ready, greetings can become a bit more complex. Greetings that we sing or chant, such as "Hello, Neighbor" are playful and help students practice essential skills such as concentration and cooperation. Still, a simple "Good morning" greeting will be ideal for most days, especially if we need more time for other Morning Meeting components. (See Appendix B for directions to the greetings, activities, learning structures, energizers, and songs mentioned in this chapter.)

- *Sharing*—Once children have mastered the basics, you can introduce, model, and practice new listening and speaking skills, such as using question words, and try different sharing topics and formats. On one day, children might engage in an around-the-circle sharing about favorite book characters; on another, they might engage in a partner chat about the upcoming weekend.

- *Group activity*—Students are likely ready for a wider variety of activities and more challenge. For example, Off My Back can help children preview or review academic content while practicing critical thinking skills such as asking purposeful questions and using deductive reasoning. If children will be working in small groups to practice readers' theater pieces (page 223) later that day, play a round of Group Charades in which they act out one of their scenes. This will give them practice collaborating and using communication skills while helping everyone rehearse for their upcoming skits.

- *Morning message*—Continue to keep messages for kindergartners and first graders simple these next few weeks. In second grade, you can vary the style and structure more, depending on students' reading abilities. For all children, include different ways to interact with the message. For example, by using tally marks to respond to questions like "What colors are you wearing today?" students gain math skills practice. And varying how children read the message each day builds fluency: you could invite all students to read chorally, ask just one student to read aloud, or write the message in two colors and have groups alternate reading by text color.

Recess, Lunch, and Quiet Time

Although we want to give children greater independence during these times, we need to continue to observe and make adjustments. For example, if children are slow to line up at recess or lunch, we might step in with a quick re-modeling. Most importantly, we want to use reinforcing language to highlight students' positive efforts and progress in meeting expectations during any routines that they still find challenging. Acknowledging students' progress will go a long way toward helping them solidify their positive behaviors into reliable habits.

Closing Circle and Dismissal Logistics

As the school year unfolds, it's tempting to go quickly through dismissal and closing circle in an attempt to squeeze in a few more minutes of instruction. But on days when it seems easier to skip a closing circle altogether, try to do at least a one-minute closing chant. Even something this simple can make all the difference in helping the day end peacefully rather than chaotically.

Teaching Academics

As we stretch students academically in these next three weeks and beyond, keep in mind that ideally children should spend most of their time in what psychologist Lev Vygotsky called the "zone of proximal development." Think of this as the "Goldilocks zone," where the work isn't too hard or too easy, but just right. That's where real growth takes place.

Academic Growth

Here are some examples of how we can support children as they encounter greater academic challenges so that they stay in the Goldilocks zone. These examples also show how we can continue to strengthen our learning community while increasing academic complexity.

- *Interactive learning structures*—To help children stay fully engaged academically, we continue to introduce new interactive learning structures throughout these three weeks and the entire year, choosing ones that best match our curricular objectives and the strengths and needs of our class. For example:

  - *Card Match*—Children each get a card that matches another card. Cards might be of animals, math equations, word parts, or any other academic content. Children find their match and then talk about it with their partner following a teacher prompt. For example: "Take turns telling one fact you know about the animal on your card."

- *Taking Sides*—The teacher states a yes-or-no question on an academic topic: "Do you admire the main character of the story we're reading?" Children then move to a side of the room—one side for "yes," the other for "no." Once they've moved, they chat with a partner about their choice. To begin a new round, the teacher asks another question.

- **Content-specific energizers**—Energizers are a great way to introduce new academic skills or help children practice ones you've already taught. For example, you can use Human Protractor to help build number sense and practice addition and subtraction, with a range from one to ten or even one to a hundred.

- *Academic Choice*—As children become more adept at managing supplies and choosing among various options, they'll be able to handle more complex Academic Choice assignments. For example, if first graders know the basic routines of reading and writing workshops, for a literacy block you might offer them the option to 1) write; 2) read independently or with a partner; 3) use sort cards to practice words on the word wall; or 4) find a new book in the school library. To learn more about Academic Choice, see Appendix A.

- *Guided Discovery*—To help children accomplish more complex academic work, we continue to use Guided Discovery so they can explore ways to work with supplies creatively and responsibly. A kindergarten teacher colleague of mine once had each of his students choose an animal from *The Mitten* by Jan Bret to study. As a part of their presentation to the class, students could use watercolor paints, clay, crayons, colored pencils, or bendable sticks or wire. But first he used a Guided Discovery session to help students explore each of these materials so they could make a good choice about which one would be best suited for their work. To learn more about Guided Discovery, see Appendix A.

A Whole-Class Project

There's nothing like a whole-class collaborative project to strengthen the learning community, help students hone new skills, and generate lots of excitement for learning. The key, of course, is choosing one that will be engaging, appropriately challenging, and manageable. If you're concerned that you won't have time for a class project because of curriculum requirements, look for ways to integrate those requirements into the learning objectives for the project. The following chart shows some of the academic skills students can strengthen through two sample project ideas.

Academic Skills Strengthened

Food Project: Making snacks from around the world	Readers' Theater: Performing favorite animal stories
Math • Knowing number names • Counting • Understanding relationships between numbers and quantities • Describing and comparing measurable attributes, including "more" and "less" **Social Studies** • Understanding the traditions and way of life of a group of people • Exploring the similarities and differences among various human cultures • Understanding how the physical world and natural resources influence people	**Language Arts** • Actively engaging in group reading activities with purpose and understanding • Understanding foundational print concept skills (following words left to right, top to bottom, and so on) • Recounting stories, including ones from diverse cultures, and determining their central message, lesson, or moral • When reading dialogue aloud, acknowledging differences in the points of view of characters by speaking in a different voice for each character • Reading with sufficient accuracy and fluency to support comprehension

Notice how each project is a great fit for this age range. Making snacks helps young children practice fine-motor skills while tapping into their interest in other people. Readers' theater helps them develop fluency and essential listening and speaking skills. Plus, a whole-class project enables children to feel more confident and capable as individual learners and as members of a team, knowing that they can achieve great things by working together. These kinds of projects also help set children up for success when taking on more challenging academic work throughout the year.

Teaching Discipline

In week three, we established rules with the class and introduced logical consequences. For the next three weeks, when we give logical consequences, we strive to connect them to the rules. We also look for opportunities to refer to the rules throughout the day, especially prior to situations that may be challenging, such as recess and lunch. This helps children see how the rules apply to all aspects of their day together.

We also keep referring back to the rules to teach children that choosing positive behavior is not about pleasing or obeying us, but about helping to make school a kind, welcoming place where everyone can reach their hopes and dreams. And we continue to watch for and reinforce small acts of kindness, cooperation, responsibility, and empathy, helping children strengthen their abilities to behave in positive ways and build their sense of community.

Using Logical Consequences

Teaching young children how to maintain self-control and other positive behavior skills requires a year-long effort. Reminders and redirections help keep them on track, and if those aren't enough for a child to shift gears, we may use one of the logical consequences described in the previous chapter: time-out, loss of privilege, or break it, fix it.

It's important to remember that logical consequences are not intended to punish children, but rather to help them connect their behavior to its effects and repair any damage their behavior may have caused. Effective logical consequences are respectful of children, realistic for them to carry out, and directly related to the behavior.

Positive Time-Out

Having set the stage in week three for using time-out to regain self-control, it's now time to teach students how to actually use it. We'll want to offer plenty of explicit modeling and practice.

- *Introducing*—Begin simply, in a matter-of-fact tone: "Everyone gets overexcited or upset sometimes and needs to cool down. Just this morning, I spilled my coffee and got frustrated, so I took some deep breaths to calm down." As a class, generate ideas for other ways to calm down, such as squeezing a soft ball or thinking about something pleasant, like a pet.

Then explain that time-out is another effective way to calm down and tell children how it will work. Emphasize that the time-out spot is where we can go when we need a break because we're losing focus or getting upset or overly excited. If some children have experienced time-out as punishment, you may want to call it "rest stop" or "take-a-break." Explain that you'll tell them to go to time-out if you notice them just beginning to go off track, so they can get back on track as quickly as possible.

■ *Modeling*—To help children learn how this procedure will work, model it several times over the course of a few days, using Interactive Modeling (see Appendix A). Be sure to model how to:

- Go directly to the time-out spot without talking.

- Sit quietly and refocus by taking deep breaths or trying one of the ideas the class brainstormed. (You may also want to keep some calming-down supplies such as a squeeze ball or soft toy at the time-out spot.)

- Rejoin the class quietly and matter-of-factly. For these younger children, it's best for you to decide when they return from time-out, at least for the first several months of school. Eventually, students may learn how to "read" their own feelings and decide when they're ready to return. You might teach and practice how to do this later in the year, once students have mastered the basics of time-out.

> **Teaching Time-Out Tip**
>
> The rest of the class also needs to know what to do when someone is going to time-out. Model and practice how children can stay focused on their own learning, which will also help the student in time-out regain self-control.

■ *Practicing*—Once you've modeled time-out a few times, tell students that everyone will get to practice it over the next few days. Explain that while they're practicing, a child will go to the time-out spot only when he or she *is* following the rules. This helps children become familiar with the time-out routine in a stress-free state of mind before they use it "for real." (If a child is actually misbehaving, use another technique to respond during this practice period.) Keep track of who goes to time-out for practice to ensure that all students get at least one chance to try.

Once everyone has had a chance to practice, announce that you're going to start using time-out for real. As you do, remember to use a calm, matter-of-fact tone when telling children to go to time-out. After a few days, check in with the class and talk briefly about how the use of time-out is going.

Loss of Privilege

Sometimes a child shows us by his behavior that he's not yet ready to meet the expectations a situation demands. When he does, we might decide that he loses the privilege of working with someone, doing an activity, or using a certain material for a time, depending on the situation. In essence, we're setting more limits for the child until we decide that he's ready to try again. Once the child shows us that readiness, we can restore the privilege.

Loss of Privilege in Action

- If a pair of children start telling jokes and getting silly instead of working on a math puzzle, we might say, "I'm giving you each a new partner" or "You need to work by yourselves. I'll give each of you your own puzzle."

- If a child is using scissors in an unsafe way, we might say, "Hand me the scissors. You can try using them tomorrow while I watch and help you use them safely."

Break It, Fix It

Breaking something or hurting someone, whether intentionally or unintentionally, gives a child an opportunity to learn how to take responsibility for their actions and repair any damage or hurt their actions have caused. When we use this logical consequence, it's important that the "fix it" part directly relates to and is in proportion to what the child did.

Break It, Fix It in Action

- If a child accidentally runs into someone on the playground and knocks her over, you might say, "Kylie, stop running. Help Aliyah up and see if she's hurt. Then report back to me." If Aliyah is hurt, you might have Kylie make sure Aliyah gets to the nurse.

- If a child is rushing around and knocks over another student's work, you might simply say, "Samuel, check with Donte to see if he wants your help putting his work back together."

To learn more about responding to misbehavior and logical consequences, see Appendix A.

LAST THOUGHT

K-2

During the first six weeks of school, we've seen individual children and the class as a whole grow in many ways. Although challenges still remain, children have made great gains socially, emotionally, and academically. We've built a solid foundation for their growth and learning during the rest of the year!

Third & Fourth Grades

Clearly, there's still much to focus on in these next three weeks of school. At the same time, it's useful to step back and reflect on how far individual students and the class as a whole have come since day one. This progress is what we can build on for weeks four through six.

Flow of the Day

Morning Meeting

In these next three weeks, you can adjust Morning Meetings to reflect students' changing needs and skills. On a day when students are going to work in teams, a small-group activity such as Group Charades can help prepare them for those collaborative efforts. If the class seems droopy on a rainy day, a lively song can help perk everyone up.

During this time, we also want to be informally assessing students' skills and continuing to help them grow in competencies such as cooperation, empathy, listening attentively, speaking effectively, and self-regulation—skills essential for meeting the more complex academic challenges they'll soon take on.

- *Greeting*—If students are ready, introduce and model a greeting that is more lively and involved, such as the Lumberjack Greeting or Fish Greeting. You might even invite students to invent their own greetings. However, if you need more time for other meeting components, a simple "Good morning, _____!" with a handshake is always a good choice. Regardless of the greeting used, remember to help students focus on being friendly and welcoming. (See Appendix B, for directions to the greetings, activities, learning structures, energizers, and songs mentioned in this chapter.)

- *Sharing*—In addition to practicing and strengthening the skills of dialogue sharing introduced in week three, you can also give students practice in more advanced speaking and listening skills to lay the groundwork for richer sharing and academic conversations. These skills include:

  - Sharing one main idea with a few supporting details
  - Remembering key information that was shared
  - Asking respectful questions
  - Answering questions thoughtfully
  - Making relevant comments (focused on the sharer)

  To add variety, practice these same skills using other sharing formats such as partner chats and around-the-circle sharing.

- *Group activity*—Once students are ready for more challenge, introduce activities that require greater cooperation and help prepare them for small-group work. Here's one that tends to work well at this point in the school year:

Group Juggling

The goal of this game is to see how many balls the group can toss to each other at the same time.

1. Before starting, talk about how to help each other be successful, such as by getting the person's attention before tossing him or her the ball.

2. Students take turns tossing the ball to a classmate, so that everyone receives it just once. This sets the pattern for the game.

3. The activity is then restarted, with the ball following the same initial pattern.

4. As the group is ready, the teacher adds another ball, which follows the same pattern, and then another, and so on.

To start building a repertoire of favorite activities, you can keep using previously taught activities that went well, changing them slightly from time to time to add variety.

■ *Morning message*—During these next three weeks, use your morning messages to help students practice and strengthen core reading and other academic skills, and continue to build a stronger community through shared reflection. For example:

> Good Morning, Cool Class!
>
> As we continue to write plenty of poetry today, we will explore amazing alliteration. It should be incredibly interesting and phenomenally fun!
>
> If the underlined words are examples of alliteration, what do you think "alliteration" means? Be ready to share your thinking!
>
> Your tenacious teacher,
>
> Ms. Oden

> Dear Mathematicians,
>
> We've been doing great work with equivalent fractions this week. Let's keep at it!
>
> In the box below, write a fraction that is equivalent to either ¾ or ⅔.
>
> Cheers!
>
> Mr. Johnson

You can also vary how students interact with the message to support their learning that day. For example, if students are learning to summarize and paraphrase, they could restate the message in their own words. Another day, they might read the message chorally using different voices (excited, grumpy, and so on) to help them prepare for a readers' theater later that day. And, of course, reading the message several times each morning helps all students practice fluency.

Recess, Lunch, and Quiet Time

By the fourth week, these times of day will be flowing smoothly for most students. For those who are struggling, provide some individual re-modeling and coaching as needed. If Cameron strongly overreacts on the playground when upset, for example, you might decide to work with him on taking a time-out on his own to cool off. We also want to continue to monitor how things are going during these times for the class as a whole. Periodically, take a little time during a brief class discussion to reflect with students on what went well during these times and how to improve on what did not.

Closing Circle and Dismissal Logistics

By week four, we may be tempted to drastically shorten the time we allot for the end-of-day routines or even skip the closing circle so we can devote more time to academics. However, some students may still need a fair amount of time to organize themselves at the end of school—and all students and the class as a learning community benefit from a closing circle each day, even a very brief one when time is tight.

One idea for this end-of-day time is to provide some choices, so those students who need more time packing up can have it while others can use the time to explore a personal interest, read, or work on a project. Providing extra time for those who need it also helps ensure that everyone gets to take part in the closing circle.

Teaching Academics

Looking back over the first three weeks of school, we can see where we've been, where we're going, and what adjustments we might need to make. In a short period of time, we've helped students develop more confidence and stamina and gradually started to increase the level of challenge, all while establishing a positive tone that helps students feel excited about learning and safe taking risks. For the next three weeks, we continue to build on these efforts—coaching students in overcoming obstacles and reinforcing successes as they engage in more rigorous work.

Academic Growth

As students encounter greater complexity in the coming weeks, here are some ways we can support their continued progress and sustain a positive learning community.

■ *Interactive learning structures*—Continue to introduce new interactive learning structures to help strengthen collaboration skills and more advanced speaking and listening skills. For example, as part of their literature circle or book club work, students might engage in a Museum Walk to discuss and analyze multiple short story characters.

■ *Content-specific energizers*—By introducing a few new energizers each week, while still repeating and adapting ones students already know, we can help students stay fully invested in their learning. For example, I taught The Fidget Family during Morning Meeting to help students practice listening skills and then used it as a movement break while reinforcing those listening skills later in the day. A third grade colleague also adapted this silly story into a narrative related to the social studies unit her class was studying. It was a fun way to help students solidify key skills and remember content.

■ *Academic Choice*—As we continue to help students master essential skills such as effective decision-making, we can also offer them more varied and complex choices. For example, to present what they've learned about a topic in science or social studies, they could choose to build a diorama, create a computer presentation, or write and perform a skit or song. To learn more about Academic Choice, see Appendix A.

■ *Guided Discovery*—When students explore how they might use supplies to enhance their learning, their daily classwork becomes richer. Consider setting a goal of introducing one new supply every week or so. You'll be gradually increasing students' repertoire of learning tools, which will enable them to more successfully tackle academic challenges. To learn more about Guided Discovery, see Appendix A.

Using Guided Discovery to Revisit Materials

It's also helpful to use Guided Discovery for materials students have used in earlier grades, such as markers and rulers. Their familiarity will boost students' confidence and creativity in coming up with new ways to use those materials this year.

Whole-Class Project

Another way to introduce variety and increase academic engagement is through a whole-class project. Working together as a team toward a common goal also strengthens the class's cohesion as a learning community and promotes academic growth.

One project that's particularly well suited to developing third and fourth graders' literacy skills is putting on a class play. Consider using a well-known fairy tale or picture book read-aloud as the anchor text for the play. Students then get to practice retelling and paraphrasing part of the text. Students this age also delight in acting, making scenery, and learning new literacy "rules," such as identifying the speaker, giving stage directions, and other essentials for writing a script. Here's a simple outline for this project:

- Create a script template or find one online.

- Have students work in small groups, each adapting one section of the story. Students choose their section or you can assign them. Depending on time and available materials, students could also create simple scenery for the section they adapt.

- Invite each group to rehearse and present their section of the play to the rest of the class, in sequence. You may even want to invite the class to perform their play for families and other classes.

The table below lists a few key language arts skills related to such a project.

Adapting a Story Into a Play: Language Arts Skills

- Understand the elements of a play
- Understand characters' different points of view
- Plan, draft, revise, and edit a piece of writing
- Write dialogue as a way to describe and understand characters
- Speak clearly

Whole-class projects, whether they last one day or one week, can take the learning community to a higher level. Students gain a sense of accomplishment that comes with succeeding at a task that no one person could do alone. They'll also feel more confident in tackling increasingly challenging academic work as the year progresses.

Teaching Discipline

During these next three weeks, we continue to make the classroom rules come alive, using them to help strengthen positive behaviors and provide a safe, supportive learning environment. Regularly referring to the rules keeps the rules—not us—at the center of discipline. Students learn to be responsible, kind, and caring not in order to please or obey us, but because we all agreed that we need these rules to help everyone achieve their hopes and dreams.

At the same time, students will inevitably forget rules and make mistakes. We're still responsible for helping everyone stay on track with their learning. We continue teaching and reinforcing positive behavior skills and help students meet expectations by giving appropriate logical consequences when they head off track.

Using Logical Consequences

We want to take a teaching stance whenever a student demonstrates that he or she is unable to meet the expectations a situation demands. When we approach misbehavior from this perspective, we're better able to stay calm and figure out an appropriate response. Students typically need our help connecting what they did to its hurtful effects. They also need our help in seeing how using the rules as guidelines can help them stay in control of themselves and get along better with everyone.

During these next few weeks, continue to build on the teaching of logical consequences (time-out; loss of privilege; break it, fix it) that you started in week three. Remind students that logical consequences are not a punishment, but rather a way for them to shift away from unproductive behavior and repair any damage their actions may have caused. Keep in mind that for logical consequences to function as a teaching tool for positive discipline, the consequence given should be respectful of students, realistic for them to carry out, and directly related to the behavior.

Positive Time-Out

During weeks four to six, I tend to use time-out frequently and for all students to continue reinforcing the message introduced in week three that time-out isn't a punishment, but rather a helpful technique we all can use to regain self-control. Here are some tips for using time-out effectively during these next few weeks:

- *Check in with students*—I like to regularly ask the class how well time-out is working. I might say, "Let's check in on how we're using the take-a-break chair. How well do you think it's working?" I also privately check in with individual students after they've returned to their work from a time-out, especially if they seem confused about what the class is doing or why they needed to take a break.

- *Teach self-regulation*—Time-out is a great technique for supporting students' development of self-regulation. As a class, you might brainstorm ideas for how to settle down when they're feeling angry or overly excited. Students will likely come up with lots of useful ideas, such as closing their eyes, taking deep breaths, and thinking about something calming.

You can use Interactive Modeling (see Appendix A) to teach students how to use one or more of these techniques while taking a break. Throughout the year, return to this discussion as needed, adding more ideas for self-regulation and practicing them together. Students will gradually develop a menu of calming strategies, giving them a greater sense of control when they go to time-out.

Another way to help students develop self-regulation is to teach them to monitor their own emotional gauge, and when you feel they're ready, encourage them to take themselves to time-out if they're beginning to feel upset or unable to focus. They'll still need to go to time-out when we direct them to do so, but they'll be steadily growing in their self-awareness and sense of responsibility for their own behavior.

Loss of Privilege

Depending on the situation, we might decide that a student loses a privilege related to a specific misbehavior. For example, a student who is distracting his partner might lose the privilege of working with that classmate for the day. A student who keeps forgetting to replace the caps on markers, causing them to dry out, might lose the privilege of using the markers until the next day after a review with you of the proper way to care for them.

Before we restore privileges, we may need to coach students or provide some ongoing support so they can be successful the next time. As soon as they demonstrate readiness to meet the expectations, we restore the privilege.

Loss of Privilege in Action

- If a student is tossing pattern blocks around when he should be using them to measure angles, we might say, "Put the blocks away. You can use one of the other two choices to practice measuring angles. We'll talk later about the proper way to use the pattern blocks."

- If a student doesn't play by the rules during a tag game at recess, we might say, "Come out of the game. For the rest of recess, you can swing or take a walk around the playground. Tomorrow before recess, we'll talk about what you need to do to join in the tag game."

Break It, Fix It

In using this logical consequence, we want to make sure the "fix it" part is directly related to and in proportion to what the student did. For example, if a student accidentally knocks over another student's tower of blocks, we might have him pick up the blocks and offer to help his classmate rebuild the tower. Having the student put away all the blocks would not be proportional to the behavior mistake. Think of these kinds of situations as teaching opportunities that allow students to learn how to acknowledge and repair any damage or hurt their actions have caused.

Break It, Fix It in Action

- A student is walking through the hall, running her hands along the walls. She knocks a poster off a bulletin board. You might say, "Carla, head back to our room. Get the stapler and reattach the poster. Then meet us in the gym when you're finished."

- If a student isn't paying attention and forgets to save her essay on the computer, you might say, "Anna, you can work on recreating your essay during quiet time today and morning arrival time tomorrow. Then we'll check in and see how you're doing."

To learn more about responding to misbehavior and logical consequences, see Appendix A.

LAST THOUGHT

3-4

As the first six weeks come to a close, it's a great time to take stock of just how far every individual student has progressed as well as the class as a whole. And don't forget to think about all that you did to make that happen. There are always things we want to improve upon, but just as we help students build on their successes, we can do the same for ourselves!

Fifth & Sixth Grades

After three weeks, the life of the classroom likely has a comfortable feel and flow for students. More importantly, the sense of trust and safety that's resulted from our building a learning community together makes it possible for students to achieve great things in the days ahead. With our steady and kind guidance, students can keep growing in significant ways as learners and as emerging young adolescents in these next three weeks—and throughout the rest of the year.

239

Flow of the Day

Morning Meeting

Do you sense that students still need more support in being friendly and respectful to everyone? If so, continue to focus these next three weeks on activities that help strengthen the classroom community. But if students are generally working pretty well together, they're probably ready for more complexity and challenges during Morning Meeting.

No matter where your students are, try to connect most Morning Meeting components to that day's or week's learning goals. This will help keep meetings feeling meaningful and continue to build community while preparing students for what's ahead. With a bit of planning, you can make these connections very natural and seamless. Here are some ideas to try during weeks four to six.

- *Greeting*—Greetings that involve new kinds of handshakes or saying "hello" in a foreign language continue to add fun and variety. You might even invite students to teach a greeting to the class. In one fifth grade class I taught, two students invented a complicated handshake that was based on those they saw baseball players do. It involved high-fiving, side-fiving, knuckle-bumping, and pointing to the sky. With guidance, the two students used Interactive Modeling (see see Appendix A) to teach the greeting to the class, and it instantly became a favorite.

  As greetings become more complex and playful, however, upper elementary students may lose sight of the essential elements for any greeting—helping one another feel welcomed and included. Remember to reinforce these values from time to time.

- *Sharing*—If you introduced dialogue sharing in week three, continue to model, practice, and reinforce the skills needed to speak clearly and concisely, listen closely, and ask relevant questions. Starting in week four, you can introduce and model how to make respectful comments. Keep checking in with students about their sharing topics, because upper elementary students often want to share things that aren't appropriate for school and need our help navigating this confusing territory.

  Continue to mix in other sharing structures that connect with the learning ahead. For example, if students will tackle a tough issue in social studies later, have them share their initial thoughts with a partner. Or use the same sharing structure, such as Four Corners, at Morning Meeting that you plan to use in a content area later that day.

- *Group activity*—Activities that build community while helping students develop curriculum-related critical thinking skills can give Morning Meetings even greater depth and power. Here are some activities that help support upper grade students in developing key skills in any content area this time of year:

  - *Five Questions and Three Clues*—Challenging and fun, this promotes deductive thinking, and allows students to take a risk when they feel ready to do so.

  - *Flub It!*—This involves focused concentration and sequencing skills. It also helps students learn to accept mistakes as a valuable part of learning.

  - *Hands Up!*—The class chants various items in a predetermined category, such as "fictional characters." Once students become capable at this activity, increase the complexity by using more challenging categories such as "multiples of twelve."

  See Appendix B for directions to the activities, learning structures, energizers, and songs mentioned in this chapter.

- *Morning message*—As you look at the day's schedule, what's a topic you want students to think about more deeply? Or a skill they need extra practice with? Asking yourself questions like these can help you write morning messages that students will find relevant, interesting, and purposeful.

> **Morning Message Tip**
>
> Keep checking in with students to make sure they're reading and responding to the morning message each day, and from time to time reflect together on how well this routine is working overall.

Recess, Lunch, and Quiet Time

At this point in the year, recess and lunch are likely going pretty smoothly. However, even if we don't hear of any problems, we can't assume that everything is going as well as we'd like. Because these times are so social, they can be especially challenging for this age group, so we still need to regularly observe recess and lunch for ourselves and talk as a class about what's going well and what isn't.

In particular, we want to be alert for any signs of bullying, exclusion, or other mean behaviors—and nip them in the bud. With older elementary students, we also need to check in privately from time to time, because some may not want to speak up in front of their peers.

Closing Circle and Dismissal Logistics

During these next three weeks, we want to continue to set students up for success in taking on more responsibility for end-of-day routines. We'll still need to reteach and remind, but our goal is for students to start relying more on each other for help with these routines.

Also, for these highly social students, ending the day together with a closing circle is particularly valuable. Avoid the temptation to skip it, if at all possible. Even a brief closing circle or group reflection while in line to leave the classroom reinforces the importance of community, teamwork, and collaboration.

Teaching Academics

As we reflect on the first three weeks, we're mindful of the challenges we've faced in getting here, but our most important focus is on successes, big and small. Our goal for the next three weeks is to consolidate gains made in the first three weeks and to help students continue to move forward with new learning. By the end of week six, we hope to have established a dynamic classroom community in which students feel excited, confident, and prepared to engage in all the learning that's ahead.

Academic Growth

Here are some ideas for helping students build academic skills and become more self-motivated learners in the next three weeks:

- *Interactive learning structures*—By week four, most students will be ready to try new and more challenging interactive learning structures that can support them in achieving specific learning goals. For example, Jigsaw (see next page) provides a fun and efficient way to help students analyze main ideas and supporting details from multiple texts in any content area.

- *Content-specific energizers*—Upper grade students often lack enough opportunities to move during their day, but as academics become more involved, movement breaks are even more important for these students. Taking a few minutes to do a lively activity, especially one that reinforces content-specific skills, can refresh students and help them refocus on their learning. For example, if you notice students getting restless during science, try a few rounds of Alphabet Aerobics with science terms as the focus.

Jigsaw Directions and Tips

1. Divide students into "research groups" (four to five students per group). Assign each group a letter and a corresponding text to read. For example, group A reads one text, group B reads another text, and so on.

2. After reading, the research groups discuss main ideas and supporting details from the text they just read.

3. Regroup students into "jigsaw groups" with at least one representative from each research group: Each jigsaw group would have one member from group A, one from group B, and so on.

4. Each jigsaw group member shares ideas and details from their original research group.

5. Continue forming new jigsaw groups as time (and number of students) allows.

- Explain the directions and model forming small groups as needed.

- Tell students how much time they'll have in research groups and in jigsaw groups. Provide one-minute warnings.

- Consider having students use note-taking sheets for both groups.

■ *Academic Choice*—To support students' accelerating academic growth, try offering them more choices about what and how they learn. For example, if students are taking on a genre study in language arts—where they can choose the genre according to their interests—we might give them a planning sheet that will help them set some learning goals for themselves. They might, for example, note some key questions they'd like to answer about the genre they've chosen. To learn more about Academic Choice, see Appendix A.

■ *Guided Discovery*—As upper elementary students take on more challenging work and do more projects, these explorations can be especially valuable. For example, as tablets, apps, and other technologies become more a part of the daily work of the classroom, Guided Discovery can help students explore and share various ideas for using these tools more effectively. To learn more about Guided Discovery, see Appendix A.

A Whole-Class Project

The first whole-class project, in which all students work together toward a common goal, gives them a chance to put into practice many of the academic and social-emotional skills they've been developing in these early weeks of school. It can also serve as a unifying event—something that further strengthens the classroom community.

A service-learning project is a great one for fifth and sixth graders because it taps into their growing awareness of the world and provides them with rich opportunities to tackle meaningful academic work. Here are a few examples to consider:

- *Fund-raiser*—Students could organize a yard sale to raise money for the school library, a local organization, or a struggling community farther from home. Curriculum connections include social studies (economics, social justice), math (working with money), and literacy (creating advertisements).

- *Tutoring*—Consider partnering with a younger-grade class to provide reading, writing, or math tutoring. Upper-grade students will gain a sense of greater responsibility toward the school as a whole while reinforcing their own math and literacy skills.

- *Awareness campaign*—Is there a cause students can connect with locally, such as helping to raise awareness about recycling or energy use? Students can gain science and social studies content knowledge and practice skills such as persuasive writing (op-ed pieces, blog posts) and public speaking (speeches, video blogs).

Teaching Discipline

Going forward, we're likely to notice growth in students' positive behaviors, stemming from the work we've done establishing rules, referring to them regularly, and building up a sense of community, safety, and trust. We want to continue to reinforce students' efforts at these positive behaviors. At the same time, their growing familiarity with you and each other means that they'll also feel comfortable exploring new behaviors and relationships. As a result, unkind behaviors, such as teasing and forming cliques, may pop up more now.

Continuing to observe students and check in with them as a class and individually can help us learn about potential problems and address them before they escalate. By taking a teaching stance when it comes to discipline, we can help students continue to stay on track with their learning and with developing social-emotional competencies, especially cooperation, positive self-assertion, responsibility, empathy, and self-control. We also better prepare ourselves to stay calm and figure out an appropriate response in the moment.

Using Logical Consequences

After introducing students to logical consequences as ways to fix mistakes rather than punishments, we want to continue this teaching during the next few weeks. Emphasize how logical consequences can help anyone who makes a behavior mistake connect what they did with its hurtful effects and learn how to take responsibility for their behavior. When we teach older students that logical consequences are about taking responsibility for their words and actions, we're framing these discipline tools in a way that meets students where they are developmentally and promotes their social and emotional growth.

Remind students that you may use a logical consequence if someone is acting in a way that falls short of the spirit and intent of the rules everyone has agreed to use as behavior guidelines. Point out that if a reminder or redirection isn't enough to help a student shift gears, you may decide to use a logical consequence (time-out; loss of privilege; break it, fix it). Remember that for logical consequences to function as a teaching tool, the consequence given should be respectful of students, realistic for them to carry out, and directly related to the behavior.

Positive Time-Out

Having learned about and practiced time-out during the third week of school, students should be ready to use it successfully starting in the fourth week. However, older students may feel more self-conscious about time-out than younger ones, so use time-out for many different students to keep it feeling safe and fair. Here are some tips:

- *Reinforce a positive tone*—Talk with students about how time-out is working so they'll continue to feel that this technique is being used as a supportive tool. You might ask, "How's take-a-break working for us?" or "Turn and talk with a neighbor—how do you think time-out is going so far?" Also, check in privately with individual students if they seem upset or confused when asked to take a break. It's important to make sure time-out is serving its purpose as a technique for calming down and regaining self-control.

- *Focus on self-regulation*—You can further strengthen students' self-regulation capabilities by introducing strategies for regaining composure while in time-out. You might ask the class, "When you're upset, what's something you do to calm yourself down?" After brainstorming and listing ideas, prompt students to more fully consider them: "Everyone turn and talk with a partner. Which of these strategies might help you calm yourself down next time you take a break?" Then post the list by the time-out spot for a handy reference. Teaching students to better regulate their own bodies and emotions—important in every grade—becomes even more critical for those just entering adolescence.

As the year progresses, you can also help students become more independent and develop their self-regulating skills by teaching them how to use time-out on their own. You can start by teaching them how to become more self-aware of when they're starting to lose focus or get upset, and then model and practice how to take themselves to the take-a-break spot to get recalibrated. Though some students will continue to need our help with time-out throughout the year, most can learn how to use time-out independently to regain self-control.

Loss of Privilege

As we give fifth and sixth graders more responsibilities throughout the year, they're bound to make mistakes—after all, it's part of the learning process—and loss of privilege will often be the appropriate consequence. To ensure that students understand why they're losing a privilege, refer to the rules the class agreed to follow.

For example, to a group of students who are arguing and disrupting the kickball game during recess, you might say, "Our rule says 'We treat everyone with respect.' For the rest of recess, you'll have to leave the kickball game and find a different activity to do." Later in the day, check in with these students and discuss how they can work together to resolve conflicts during recess.

Loss of Privilege in Action

- If one student tells another that he doesn't want to sit next to her during independent reading, we might respond, "Our rule says 'We treat everyone fairly.' For the rest of reading today and tomorrow, you've lost the privilege of choosing where you sit. Before you get this privilege back, we'll talk a bit about our rule and how you can do a better job of following it."

- If a student keeps distracting his work partner, we might say, "John, you'll have to work by yourself for the rest of this period. Tomorrow, I'll check in with you about how you can work productively with a partner."

Break It, Fix It

In using this consequence, it's important that we make sure it's directly related to and in proportion to what the student did. Students may also benefit from our preceding this consequence with a time-out, especially if they seem frustrated or angry.

For example, suppose one student got angry at another and called her names. You might tell this student to take a break and then follow up with a consequence: "Your words hurt Juanita. You can't take them back, but you can try to make amends to her. Are you ready to discuss some ideas for how to do that?" Also, encourage an apology, but don't force it. If the student who hurt someone's feelings isn't sincere, the student who was hurt won't find the apology meaningful. (See more examples on next page.)

Think of these kinds of situations as opportunities to help students learn to take responsibility for their actions—by acknowledging and making amends for any damage or hurt their words or deeds may have caused.

Break It, Fix It in Action

• If a student gets frustrated while working in a small group and messes up another student's work, you might say, "Donovan, take a break. When you return, check with Lin to see if she wants your help repairing her work."

• If a group of students refuses to let other students play basketball with them at recess, you might start with a loss of privilege ("No more basketball for today"). Then, you might follow up with "break it, fix it." For example: "When you exclude classmates, that hurts their feelings and goes against our rule, 'Be kind to everyone.' Inviting them to play tomorrow might help them feel better."

To learn more about responding to misbehavior and logical consequences, see Appendix A.

LAST THOUGHT

5–6

Take a moment to reflect on the first week of school and how far individual students and the class as a whole have come in just six weeks. Although we may recall opportunities lost or situations we wish we had handled differently, let's keep our focus on the progress students have made—the big leaps and the small steps—because it's this growth that will propel them forward for more great learning in the weeks ahead.

Primed for a Great Year

As I write this conclusion, my own two children are finishing up their sixth week of school. Their perspective gives me further insight into just how important these early weeks of school are to all of us. While they work on homework, my son declares, "I really like math this year. It's challenging and fun!" My daughter says, "Dad, I think I'm doing really well in school now. Can I share some of my writing with you?" It's a huge relief to learn that they both feel excited about school—and are primed for a great year of learning.

For us teachers, with the whirlwind of the first day long past and the first six weeks ending, this point in the school year is the perfect time for reflection. We know our work wasn't flawless, but we focus instead on all that we've accomplished during this time. Maybe students who barely sat still in the first week now read on their own for twenty-five minutes. New friendships are likely blossoming. Students are becoming more responsible and independent, taking more academic risks, and engaging more deeply with their learning.

In the coming weeks, we keep building on these successes. We continue to model new routines (and revisit old ones when they need a little attention). We keep academics fresh and engaging by using Academic Choice, interactive learning structures, and other practices that boost learning. From time to time, we reflect on how classroom rules are sustaining a safe, joyful, and challenging learning environment that enables everyone to reach for their goals.

During these first six weeks we've gotten to know students, and they've gotten to know us—and we've learned a lot about ourselves, too. Our hard work in laying a strong foundation for the year is paying off. Students and teachers alike are now primed for a successful year!

Key *Responsive Classroom®* Practices Discussed in This Book

All of the recommended practices in this book come from or are consistent with the *Responsive Classroom* approach to teaching—an evidence-based approach to education associated with greater teacher effectiveness, higher student achievement, and improved school climate. *Responsive Classroom* practices help educators build competencies in four interrelated areas: engaging academics, effective management, positive community, and developmentally appropriate teaching.

Following are summaries of the *Responsive Classroom* practices discussed throughout this book. To learn more about the *Responsive Classroom* approach to teaching, visit www.responsiveclassroom.org.

Academic Choice

When we build a safe and supportive community and then offer students guided choices about their academic learning, they frequently choose work that's neither too easy nor too difficult, but just challenging enough to be engaging and motivating. Academic Choice is a structured way of giving children these kinds of confidence- and competence-building experiences.

In an Academic Choice lesson, children have choices about content (what they learn), process (how they learn), or both. For example, students studying fractions might choose what to study (from three sets of eight fractions, choose one set) or how to study (whether to use fraction bars, work with pattern blocks, or draw).

Academic Choice lessons consist of three phases:

Planning. Students make thoughtful, learning-related choices; for example, if they generally work with pattern blocks, for today's Academic Choice math lesson they might decide to stretch themselves by choosing fraction bars.

251

Working. Students follow through on their plan as the teacher circulates, checks in, guides, and redirects as necessary.

Reflecting. Students think about their work, considering what went well, what they learned, and what they might do differently next time.

Many years of experience have demonstrated that Academic Choice yields impressive benefits: increased student motivation, stronger thinking and problem-solving skills, improved academic achievement, fewer problem behaviors, and more skillful social interactions.

For more information, see *The Joyful Classroom* from *Responsive Classroom* (2016).

Note: All the books listed as resources are published by Center for Responsive Schools, the developer of the *Responsive Classroom* approach to K–8 teaching. See page 287 for more information and visit www.responsiveclassroom.org.

Closing Circle

Just as Morning Meeting sets a tone of pleasant anticipation for the day's work, a classroom closing circle—a five- to ten-minute gathering that consists of a group activity or two—brings the school day to a peaceful end. A teacher might, for example, invite students to pair up to talk about something they learned during the past day or week and then finish with a group friendship song or cheer. Simple and brief, closing circles have a big impact on learning, behavior, and classroom climate.

No matter how the day went, a closing circle can help build trust and cooperation in the classroom—and this, in turn, sets the stage for students to do their best learning.

Closing circles benefit the adults in the classroom, too. A hectic dismissal can leave teachers feeling exhausted and unproductive, even if most of the day went smoothly. After using closing circles, many teachers report ending the day with a more positive attitude and increased energy.

For more on closing circles, see *Closing Circles: 50 Activities for Ending the Day in a Positive Way* by Dana Januszka and Kristen Vincent (2012).

Energizers

Energizers are quick, whole-group activities that can be done anytime in the school day. They can be lively or calming, have an academic component or not. They can be used to transition children between learning activities, as a pick-me-up during intensive lessons, or as a way to keep order during waiting times. Energizers can be done with students in a circle, at their desks or tables, or even while they're standing in line.

Although teachers use energizers for many reasons, their primary purposes are to provide:

- **Mental and physical breaks**—The mind and body breaks that energizers provide refresh students so that they're better prepared for learning.

- **Connections through play**—Energizers provide a safe and structured way for teachers to connect with their students and for students to connect with one another.

- **Focusing**—Energizers help gain students' attention when they may be distracted.

Essentially, energizers are a playful, purposeful way to incorporate physical exercise and mental stimulation into even the most tightly scheduled classroom days. Energizers don't take much time, but they can have a huge impact on learning.

For more information, see *Energizers! 88 Quick Movement Activities That Refresh and Refocus* by Susan Lattanzi Roser (2009). For sample energizers mentioned in this book, see Appendix B.

Guided Discovery

Guided Discovery is an inviting way to introduce students to materials, classroom or school areas, or activities. A teacher might use Guided Discovery to introduce a learning center, such as the library or computer area; a specific material, such as crayons or a compass; or an activity, such as journal writing or quiet time.

A Guided Discovery consists of five steps:

1. **Introduction**—The teacher names the material, area, or activity in a way that piques students' curiosity.

2. **Generating and modeling ideas**—The teacher asks for children's thoughts on how they might use a material or area or do an activity, and then models a few of their ideas.

3. **Exploration**—Children actively explore and try out various ideas while the teacher observes, reinforces, and redirects if necessary.

4. **Sharing**—Children share their explorations and observations in response to a focused question from the teacher.

5. **Cleanup and care of materials**—When the Guided Discovery is complete, the teacher asks children for ideas on how to put away materials and clean up work areas.

Working with the whole class, small groups, or individuals, teachers can use Guided Discovery both to introduce new materials, activities, and areas, and to help children explore new ways to work with those that are familiar. Offering a Guided Discovery for every material or activity is unnecessary; instead, teachers use it selectively in situations where they want to encourage creative exploration and elicit a wide variety of ideas from students about how to use a material or area or do an activity. Interactive Modeling, another *Responsive Classroom* practice (see opposite page) works better for routines and procedures that students need to do in just one way, such as completing end-of-day tasks or using scissors.

For more information, see *The Joyful Classroom* from *Responsive Classroom* (2016).

Interactive Learning Structures

Interactive learning structures promote maximum learning because they are both active ("hands-on," with opportunities for students to do things) and interactive (with opportunities for students to collaborate with partners or in small groups).

From simple partner chats to more involved small-group discussion formats, these learning structures support students in working together effectively and building up their knowledge base and skill sets. For example, Circle Map guides students first in brainstorming ideas around a topic or question, and then in using a graphic organizer to categorize and make sense of those ideas. Interactive learning structures give students practice in essential listening, speaking, and thinking skills and in key social skills such as cooperation.

The keys to success in using interactive learning structures are:

- Clearly setting out the expectations and learning goals
- Teaching and modeling the steps of the structure
- Teaching and modeling the key skills students need (such as taking turns speaking) so that they can successfully use the structure to reach the learning goal

For more information about the interactive learning structures in this book, see Appendix B.

Interactive Modeling

Interactive Modeling is a straightforward technique for teaching procedures and routines, such as lining up safely in the classroom, and social and academic skills, such as taking turns speaking and looking up a word in the dictionary. It's a great way to teach any routine or skill that needs to be done in one specific way (for safety, efficiency, or other reasons).

Instead of assuming that if we tell children how to do something enough times, they'll "get it," Interactive Modeling shows students exactly how to do what we expect and gives them a chance to practice meeting those expectations. It has built-in steps that help students notice for themselves the details of how a routine or skill looks and sounds in action, and it provides immediate teacher feedback. This powerful combination of noticing, practicing, and timely feedback enables students to engage more deeply in their learning and to remember more of what they've learned.

Interactive Modeling in Action:
How to Respond to the Signal for Quiet Attention

1. Say what you will model and why.	Teacher: "There will be times when I need to get your attention quickly. The way I'll signal for you to stop what you're doing and listen to me is by ringing this chime. I'm going to show you what to do when you hear it. I'm going to pretend to be a student, and Juan will be the teacher. Watch us and see what you notice."
2. Model the behavior.	The teacher pretends to be writing. Juan, a student she has prepped ahead of time to play the role of teacher, rings the chime. When the teacher hears the chime, she carefully puts down her pencil and looks at Juan.
3. Ask students what they noticed.	Teacher: "What did you see me do?" Juan: "You looked at me." Erika: "You put down your pencil." Teacher: "How did I put it down?" Erika: "You didn't slam it down." Teacher: "So what did I do?"

CONTINUED ▶

Interactive Modeling in Action, continued

3. Ask students what they noticed. (continued)	Erika: "You put it down gently." Teacher: "What else did you notice?" Kenye: "You were quiet." Teacher: "Did you notice anything else I did?" Devon: "You turned your body toward Juan." Teacher: "Why might that help?" Devon: "It means you're really ready to listen."
4. Invite one or more students to model.	Teacher: "Could someone else show us how to respond to the chime the same way I did?" Sara volunteers. The teacher directs Sara to start writing. After a moment, she rings the chime. Sara responds just as the teacher did.
5. Again, ask students what they noticed.	The teacher leads the class in a brief, focused discussion of what they noticed Sara do (as in step 3). (If you teach younger children, you may want to repeat steps 4 and 5 before moving on.)
6. Have all students practice.	Teacher: "Now everyone will practice. Your job is to respond to the chime just the way Sara and I did. This time, I'll do the watching and noticing." The children all start writing. When the teacher rings the chime, all the students put their pencils down, turn and look at her, and are quiet.
7. Provide feedback.	Teacher: "That was fast! You were very careful with your pencils, and your quiet faces looking at me told me that you were all ready to listen. Responding to the chime like this will help us be efficient with transitions this year. That will help us learn more!"

For more information, see *Interactive Modeling: A Powerful Technique for Teaching Children* by Margaret Berry Wilson (2012).

Morning Meeting

Morning Meeting is a twenty- to thirty-minute whole-class gathering at the beginning of each day. The purpose of these meetings is to set a tone for engaged learning in a climate of trust, to build and enhance connections among class members through meaningful interactions and lively activities, and to give students practice in academic and social-emotional skills. Morning Meeting addresses students' basic needs to feel a sense of belonging and significance and warms them up for the day of learning ahead.

Morning Meeting consists of four sequential components, each with its own purpose and structure:

- *Greeting*—Students greet each other by name and may also shake hands, sing or chant, and do fun movements.

- *Sharing*—Students share some news or information about themselves or their learning and respond to each other's sharing, articulating their thoughts, feelings, and ideas in a positive way.

- *Group activity*—The whole class does a short, inclusive group activity that can reinforce learning and build class cohesion through active participation.

- *Morning message*—Students practice academic skills and warm up for the day by reading and discussing a daily note to the class posted by their teacher.

Although the Morning Meeting format is intentionally predictable, there's plenty of room for variation within this format. Meetings vary from class to class, with each meeting reflecting the different styles and goals of individual teachers and classes.

The time teachers commit to Morning Meeting is an investment that's repaid many times over. The sense of belonging and the skills of attention, listening, speaking, and cooperative interaction developed each morning are a foundation for every lesson, transition, and aspect of the day. Morning Meeting is a microcosm of the way we wish school to be for children—a learning community that's safe, respectful, engaging, and appropriately challenging for all.

For more information, see *The Morning Meeting Book,* 3rd ed., by Roxann Kriete and Carol Davis (2014). For sample morning meeting ideas for the greetings, sharing structures, and group activities mentioned in this book, see Appendix B.

Quiet Time

In the middle of the day, children need a break from the rigors of academics and the demands of social interaction. Quiet time is a brief period—generally fifteen minutes or so—after recess and lunch when children work alone in their own space and the classroom is silent. Quiet time helps create a classroom atmosphere of calm and recalibration, and readies children for a productive and focused afternoon.

During quiet time, children might draw, write, work on a computer, or catch up on an assignment. In the silence, they are often consolidating their learning, reflecting on their morning, or preparing for the afternoon. It is also a restorative time for teachers.

For more information, visit www.responsiveclassroom.org and search on the key term "quiet time."

Responsive Classroom *Approach to Discipline*

This approach to discipline helps teachers in a wide range of school settings establish calm and safe classrooms while helping children develop self-discipline and responsibility. It reflects the beliefs that we can teach discipline just as we teach any content area and that children learn more and misbehave less when they're actively engaged in their learning.

The key goals of this approach to discipline are to:

- Establish a calm, orderly, predictable, and safe learning environment
- Teach children positive behavior skills so they develop self-control and self-discipline
- Guide children to become responsible, contributing members of their classrooms, schools, and communities
- Promote respectful, kind, and healthy teacher-to-student and student-to-student interactions

Rules

For teachers using this approach to discipline, classroom rules are connected to students' and teachers' goals for academic and social-emotional learning. Often, students and teachers create the rules collaboratively during the first few weeks of school. Or teachers may decide to use school rules or previously established classroom rules.

Rules Creation Process

Collaborating with students on the classroom rules typically involves these steps:

1. Articulate learning goals (often called "hopes and dreams")	The teacher has students share their learning goals for the school year, often beginning this conversation by sharing his or her own goals. Families can also be invited to share their goals for their children.
2. Brainstorm a list of rules	The teacher and children collaborate to brainstorm a list of rules that can help everyone achieve their goals.
3. Frame the rules in the positive	The teacher coaches students to rephrase any negatively stated rules into positive statements. For example, "Don't run in the halls" becomes "Walk in the halls."
4. Condense the list to three to five global rules	The teacher and students work together to consolidate their list of specific rules into a few global rules. These global rules capture all the specific ideas and cover three main areas of behavior: caring for ourselves; caring for others; caring for the classroom/school environment. The rules are then displayed along with visual representations of each child's individual goals.

Once ideas are shared and rules established, the teacher continually revisits children's goals to make concrete connections between individual goals and classroom rules. The teacher's emphasis on this connection provides a strong reference point for the teaching and reinforcing of positive behavior throughout the year.

Teaching and Promoting Positive Behavior

With the rules in place, the teacher deliberately instructs students how to use the rules as guidelines for behavior and proactively sets up conditions that enable students to succeed. Key steps include:

- Teaching what following the rules looks and sounds like in various situations throughout the school day
- Getting to know and appreciate each child individually, developmentally, and culturally

- Making sure children's basic needs are being met (water, food, movement, bathroom)
- Addressing children's social-emotional needs
- Setting students up for academic success
- Using positive teacher language

Responding to Misbehavior

When children misbehave, we need to respond quickly, effectively, and nonpunitively. The goals for responding to misbehavior are to:

- Stop the rule-breaking behavior
- Maintain a safe, orderly classroom so other students can continue to learn
- Help students recognize and repair any damage caused by their behavior mistake
- Help students develop internal control of their behavior
- Preserve the dignity of the child and group

Cues, Proximity, Teacher Language

To meet these goals for responding to misbehavior, the teacher can use nonverbal cues (such as a finger to the lips), move closer to the student (which is often enough to get them to stop and refocus), use positive teacher language (see facing page), or try a combination of these techniques.

Logical Consequences

Sometimes children need more than cues, proximity, and teacher language to help them get their behavior back on track. In these situations, teachers might choose to use a logical consequence. Unlike punishments, logical consequences are respectful of children, realistic for them to carry out, and relevant to the misbehavior. The three types to consider using are:

- ***Loss of Privilege***—When a child isn't following the classroom expectations for an activity or use of a material, a logical consequence might be that he temporarily loses the privilege of doing that activity or using that material. For example, if a child isn't working cooperatively with her small group, she may have to work on her own for the rest of the class period. The teacher reviews expectations for small-group behavior with the child before restoring the privilege.

- **Break It, Fix It**—Making amends gives children a chance to face up to and fix their mistakes. For example, if a child spills her lunch tray, the consequence is that she cleans up the mess.

- **Time-out**—The purpose of taking a short break is for the child to regroup mentally and emotionally as a way of regaining self-control. To be a logical consequence and not a punishment, time-out must be used in a matter-of-fact and respectful way. The teaching and setup of the time-out procedure are critical, as is the teacher's tone when using time-out.

  Note that a "buddy" teacher in a nearby classroom, who uses time-out in a similar way to you, might be an option for when a student is struggling to calm down and unable to regain self-control. Having a student take a break in another classroom can often provide the space and time needed to settle down so he or she can rejoin the class.

The goal of logical consequences is not to stop misbehaviors altogether, which is impossible. Instead, it's to help children learn how their behavior affects themselves and others and to give them dignified ways to repair any damage their behavior may have caused.

For more information, see *Teasing, Tattling, Defiance, and More: Positive Approaches to 10 Common Classroom Behaviors* by Margaret Berry Wilson (2013) and *Rules in School: Teaching Discipline in the Responsive Classroom*, 2nd ed., by Kathryn Brady, Mary Beth Forton, and Deborah Porter (2011).

Teacher Language

Teacher language is how we talk with and to students; in essence, it's our teaching voice—our professional use of words, phrases, tone, and pace that enables students to engage in active and interactive learning. Our language serves as a powerful tool that can positively influence how children think, act, and feel. Whether for direct instruction, discipline, or casual conversation, the words and tone we use throughout the day will have a lasting impact on how well children learn and grow as students and individuals.

Three essential types of teacher language are:

- **Reinforcing Language**—observing children and naming their specific strengths and positive actions. For example: "I noticed lots of careful listening and pausing before speaking today." This kind of language is enormously effective because it helps children recognize exactly what they're doing well and when they're on the right track, and this recognition in turn enables them to grow further.

- *Reminding Language*—helping children remember expectations. This language can be used to explicitly state the desired behavior ("Remember to walk on the right side of the hall on the way to the cafeteria") or to prompt students to recall it for themselves ("What will you be doing to listen respectfully when your partner shares?"). Reminding language supports children in pausing and visualizing what to say and do before they take action.

- *Redirecting Language*—giving clear instructions when children have gone off track. This language is direct and and specific, which helps students stop inappropriate behaviors and get back on track quickly. For example, if a child is waving scissors around, the teacher might tell her: "Macy, put the scissors down now."

In addition, two other types of teacher language can powerfully promote children's learning:

- *Envisioning Language*—giving children a vision of what's possible and helping them to picture themselves achieving success. For example: "Authors write about what excites them. I'm looking forward to reading the inspiring personal narratives you'll work on today." Envisioning language can be used to motivate students when they take on new learning or encounter challenging situations socially. When children have a meaningful vision in their heads of what's possible, they're better able to turn that vision into a reality.

- *Open-Ended Questions*—asking questions that have no single right or wrong answer. Open-ended questions, such as "What would you do differently if you did this activity again?" draw on students' own thoughts, feelings, skills, and experiences. They encourage children to be curious and seek answers to satisfy their wonderings. They prompt children to think more deeply, share their knowledge, analyze information, and make connections among ideas.

For more information, see *The Power of Our Words: Teacher Language That Helps Children Learn*, 2nd ed., by Paula Denton, EdD (2014).

Engaging Activities, Songs, and Chants

Activities

These include:

- Morning Meeting Ideas—for a greeting, sharing, or group activity

- Closing Circle Ideas—to help students end their day on a peaceful, happy note

- Energizers—to help students get reenergized and refocused for more learning

- Interactive Learning Structures—to make academics active and interactive, and thus more engaging for students

These activities will keep students engaged in productive learning all day and can easily be adapted for multiple purposes throughout the year. When you use these (or similar) activities during the first six weeks of school, students start to master how to do them and you'll be building a repertoire to choose from all year long. In addition, these activities can be "scaled up" for upper elementary students or simplified for students in lower grades.

Songs and Chants

Whether part of a Morning Meeting or closing circle or used as energizers during the day, songs and chants can be effective at bolstering learning. For example, students might sing a song during Morning Meeting and then later that day sing the same song with altered words to reflect the content being studied. Adding motions or movement to a song or chant also reinforces the learning and helps students recharge and refocus.

Activities

Alphabet Aerobics

Display the lowercase alphabet for reference. As you chant each letter, children strike a pose that corresponds to the shape of the letter. For letters that "stand tall" on the writing lines, such as b, d, f, and h, students can stand straight up and lift their arms in the air. For letters in the middle of the writing lines, such as a, c, e, and i, students can stand straight, bend their knees, and place arms straight ahead. For letters with "tails" that drop below the writing lines, such as g, j, p, and q, students can squat down and put hands on the floor. Students can also use these poses to practice spelling each other's names, high-frequency words, and content-specific vocabulary.

Around-the-Circle Greeting or Sharing

Standing or sitting together in a circle for this activity allows everyone to see and be seen, which helps fulfill children's needs for belonging and significance. Going one at a time, students greet the neighbor to their left (or right), with a simple "Good morning, _____." The neighbor who was greeted responds, "Good morning, _____" and then turns to greet the next neighbor; the greeting continues around the circle.

For an around-the-circle sharing, the process is similar. Students take turns responding to a question or topic the teacher poses by sharing one word or one sentence. Possible topics include Favorites (color, book, character, hobby) and Something I Learned ("I just learned _____").

Ball Toss Greeting

You or a student can begin by greeting another student and then gently tossing or bouncing a ball to him or her. That student returns the greeting while holding on to the ball. He or she then chooses a new classmate to greet and pass the ball to; this pattern continues until everyone has been greeted. (For younger students, you may want to have them roll the ball instead of tossing or bouncing it.) Students can give a thumbs-up sign or sit down once they've been greeted so it's easy to see who's still waiting for a greeting.

Captain's Coming!

This game gets everyone moving. The teacher (the captain) stands facing the class (the crew). The playing area, as you define it, is the ship. When the captain calls an order, the crew has to follow it as quickly as possible.

- *The First Command: "Captain's coming!"* When this command is called, the crew snaps to attention (feet together, shoulders back, right hand at a salute) and shouts out "Aye, aye, captain!" This command can also be used to get the crew back to attention whenever you need to teach a new command, give a new direction, and so on.

- *Other Commands.* Teach the following commands a few at a time, and keep increasing the speed at which you call them out so that students have to respond faster and faster. Encouraging students to invent new commands adds a whole new element of fun to this game, and once they know the commands well, invite a volunteer to be the captain.

Basic Commands	Student Response
Bow!	Move toward the front of the ship.
Stern!	Move toward the back of the ship.
Starboard!	Move to the right of the ship.
Port!	Move to the left of the ship.

Advanced Commands	Student Response
Sailor overboard!	Join in pairs, grab an imaginary life preserver, and after counting (loudly) to three, throw it into the water.
To the lifeboats!	Join in trios. One stands straight and tall in the middle (as the mast); the two on the outsides row furiously.
Hardtack for dinner!	Make a gagging sound as if throwing up on the deck.
Swab the deck!	Pretend to mop the deck.
Walk the plank!	Take three giant steps forward (counting loudly) and pretend to fall off the ship (screaming).

Category Challenge

The teacher chooses a category (favorite TV shows, favorite foods, states, capitols, multiples of seven, and so on). While the class passes an object (such as a stuffed animal or marker) around the circle, a student volunteer tries to name as many items in the category as possible before the object gets all the way around the circle. At the end, the class gives the volunteer a round of applause.

Clock Partners

Give everyone a paper with a blank clock (see example) with space for students to write names by the 12:00, 3:00, 6:00, and 9:00 hours. Throughout the day, you can use the clock partners structure to quickly and efficiently form new partnerships. For example: "For this next math activity, work with your three o'clock partner." "Talk about the read-aloud chapter with your six o'clock partner."

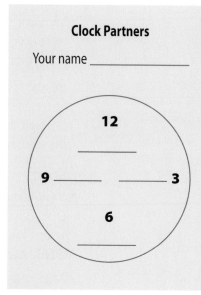

Clock Partners

Your name _____

Continuous Kickball

This variation of kickball uses the traditional two teams and several innings, but there's a lot more running. There's also no keeping track of the score or outs. After the ball is kicked to start the inning, the person runs the bases—and keeps going around—until the fielding team gets the ball to the catcher at home plate. Once the catcher touches home plate with the ball, the runner stops and stays on whatever base he or she is on or nearest. When the next player kicks, both players keep running around the bases until the ball again reaches home plate, and so on (multiple runners may end up occupying the same base). If a student needs to rest, he or she moves off to the side after crossing home plate. Everyone on the team gets to kick once, and then the teams switch sides.

Coseeki

In this variation of Follow the Leader, one student leaves the circle area and stands where he cannot see the rest of the group. The group chooses a leader who does a movement, such as touching her knee, which all the others follow. The leader changes the movement regularly and everyone follows her movement each time. The "hidden" student returns, stands in the middle of the circle, watches the movements, and tries to guess who the leader is. If he doesn't guess correctly in three tries, reveal the leader.

The Fidget Family

Before you read this fast-paced story aloud, assign each student a role. When students hear their part, they stand up, twirl around once, and sit back down. When you read the phrase "the Fidget Family," everyone stands up, twirls around once, and sits back down. Characters are: Ma, Pa, Billy, Tommy, Bridget, baby, Grandma, Grandpa, Old Mol, Old Dol, cat, dog, canary, gate, tree, road, house, wagon, and purse. You can add, delete, or change characters and names as needed and assign more than one character per student. You can also adjust the story to fit a current unit of study or invite students to write their own Fidget Family stories.

> Once upon a time, there was a family called the Fidget Family. There were lots of people in this family. There were Ma Fidget, Pa Fidget, Billy Fidget, Tommy Fidget, Bridget Fidget, and baby Fidget. They had several pets. They had a cat, a dog, a canary, and two horses named Old Mol and Old Dol. Through the gate, past a tree, and down the road to another house lived Grandma and Grandpa Fidget.
>
> One day, the whole Fidget Family decided to go visit Grandma and Grandpa Fidget at their house through the gate, past the tree, and down the road. Billy wanted to bring the cat, Tommy wanted to bring the dog, and Bridget wanted to bring the canary, but Pa Fidget said no. The baby cried.
>
> So they loaded up the wagon, hitched up Old Mol and Old Dol, and headed out through the gate, past the tree, and down the road to Grandma and Grandpa Fidget's house. They had just passed the tree when Ma Fidget realized she'd left her purse back at the house. Baby Fidget cried. So the whole Fidget Family turned the wagon around, and Old Mol and Old Dol pulled the wagon back up the road, past the tree, and through the gate. They finally found Ma Fidget's purse back at the house.
>
> Before they left, Billy asked if he could bring the cat, Tommy wanted to bring the dog, and Bridget wanted to bring the canary, but Pa Fidget said no. The baby started chewing on Ma Fidget's purse. Then the whole family got back into the wagon being pulled by Old Mol and Old Dol.
>
> They rode out through the gate, past the tree, and down the road to Grandma and Grandpa Fidget's house. They had a wonderful time, and the whole Fidget Family lived happily ever after!

Find Your Match

Students mix and mingle to find the student holding a matching card (prepared in advance). When everyone has found their match, they read, paraphrase, or summarize the information on their cards for the whole class. This activity is especially useful for reviewing content, building vocabulary, practicing spelling or math facts, and preparing for a test or quiz. It's also great as a greeting or combined greeting/activity in Morning Meeting.

Fish Greeting

Instead of shaking hands, students give a floppy fish greeting: heel of hand to partner's heel of hand, while gently flopping each other's forearms with the fingers.

Five Questions and Three Clues

This activity is a quicker variation of Twenty Questions. Choose one student to be the guesser and one to be the record keeper. Tape a card or slip of paper with a word or phrase related to what students are studying on the guesser's back. Have him turn slowly around so the rest of the class can see the word or phrase. The guesser then asks up to five yes-or-no questions to figure out what's on his back, and the class shows thumbs up for yes, thumbs down for no, or thumbs sideways for maybe. After five questions, the record keeper says, "Time to move on to clues." Students raise their hands if they want to offer the guesser a clue. He calls on up to three people for clues and can make up to three guesses. If he hasn't guessed correctly at that point, reveal the answer.

Flub It

This activity helps students learn that mistakes are part of the learning process. As students stand in a circle, have them count off starting with "one." Create a gap in the circle between the student who is one and the last-numbered student, so it's clear where the numbers begin and end. Then summarize the number order for students: "Our numbers go from one through twenty-six. Jack is one and Sasha is twenty-six." The student who is one goes first and says his number plus any other number in the circle (for example, "one and eleven"). Then the "eleven" student says her number and another number in the circle ("eleven and twenty-one"), and so on. If a student "flubs it" by forgetting their number or reversing the two numbers, he or she celebrates by saying "Yes!" while the rest of the class cheers. You can also have the student who flubbed it leave his or her spot and go to the highest-numbered spot while giving high fives to everyone along the way. The rest of the class then has to quickly figure out what their new number is, and the student who flubbed it (who is now the highest number) goes first to start the activity again.

Four Corners

In advance, prepare a set of four signs related to a main topic or question. Label each sign with one related subtopic or one answer to the question. For example, a main topic might be sea creatures, with the four subtopics being sharks, pelicans, dolphins, and starfish. You name the topic and then point out that each corner of the room represents one subtopic (or sea creature). Students go to the corner they are most curious about or most knowledge-able about and discuss that subtopic with others for a few minutes. On your signal, students can either rotate clockwise to the next corner or choose a new one to go to.

Group Charades

This traditional activity is a great way to practice vocabulary. Assign small groups of three or four students. Give each group an index card or slip of paper on which you've written a word or phrase related to something the class is studying. (Prepare these in advance.) Give groups a few minutes to figure out how they'll act out their word or phrase. Each group then acts out silently while the rest of the class guesses.

Human Protractor

Everyone stands in a circle, hands touching toes. Tell students that they're going to straighten up gradually, keeping their arms stretched out in front of their bodies. At the same time, they'll be counting from zero to an upper number you name. By the time their hands are reaching overhead, they should be at the upper number. Let students know that they need to remember where their hands are at different numbers, and set the range of numbers to suit the age and abilities in your classroom (0–10, 0–100, and so on).

Once students have moved through the range of numbers from toes to overhead, call out random numbers within the specified range. Students take the position for each number as you call it. When students are familiar with this activity, they can take turns being the number caller. For a variation, have students do multiplication, addition, or subtraction problems that lead to an answer within the designated range.

Inside-Outside Circles

Have students count off by twos. The ones form an inner circle and face out. The twos form an outer circle and face in, so pairs of students are facing each other. Give students a topic or question to discuss. Allow them one minute to share with their partners. Then, on your signal, the outside circle moves one person to the right while the inside circle stays in place, and everyone shares with a new partner. Repeat as time allows. Once everyone's comfortable with this structure, you can change topics or questions each time students change partners. You can also vary which circle moves and in which direction.

Just Like Me

This category game can help students make connections with each other. A category is named (by the teacher at first). For example, the teacher says, "I like to swim." Anyone who also likes to swim stands up and says, "Just like me!" and then sits back down. Another category is named and those who connect with it stand up. The goal is to find inclusive categories so that many people get to stand, as well as more personal categories that help students connect with others.

The Laughing Handkerchief

Hold a handkerchief high in the air. When you release the handkerchief, everyone laughs. When the handkerchief touches the floor, everyone stops laughing. The goal is to stop together, all at the same time. Once the game has been taught and practiced a few times, invite students to name other actions for when the handkerchief is falling (clapping hands, snapping fingers, stomping feet, etc.).

Lumberjack Greeting

As students stand in a circle, ask for a volunteer greeter. She walks over to another student of her choice to greet. The two students make a "thumb stack" with their four hands by alternating gripping each other's raised thumbs. Then the two students move their thumb stack back and forth as if they were sawing lumber while greeting each other. The original greeter returns to her seat and the student who was chosen picks another student to greet. Repeat until everyone has been greeted.

Mix and Mingle

To begin, students mix and mingle in the center of the circle. On your signal, they pause and pair up with a student near them. Once everyone has a partner, give them a question or topic to discuss. After a minute or two, give the signal and students once again mix and mingle until you signal that it's time to find a new partner; challenge students to pair up with classmates who are not their usual partners or best friends. Continue as time permits.

Museum Walk

Instead of looking at art in a museum, students view posters, charts, or other visual displays spread throughout the room on the walls or tables. In advance, display the items you want students to view as if setting up a museum. Assign partners and allow them to choose where in the museum to start their tour. As they view each display, they discuss it and add sticky notes with their questions or comments; they can also take notes in their notebooks. Give five-minute and one-minute warning signals to alert students to wrap up their tour. Then gather everyone for a whole-group discussion.

Off My Back

This activity is a twist on Twenty Questions. Choose a student to be the guesser. Write a number (or book character, science term, or anything related to classroom learning) on a sticky note and place it on the guesser's back, for example, "28." The guesser turns around so everyone can see the number on her back. Then she calls on classmates to answer yes-or-no questions about the number: "Is it odd or even?" "Is it less than fifty?" When the guesser thinks she knows the answer, she says a number and takes the sticky note off to see if her guess was correct. To prevent the questioning from going on too long, limit the number of questions or provide a hint.

Pica Fermé Nada

This is a "guess my number" game involving logical thinking and reasoning skills. When introducing this game, begin with a three-digit number. Write three blank spaces on the board and challenge students to guess the number. Take a guess from a volunteer and write it on the board. Then let students know how close the guess is by giving them the following clues for each digit in the guess:

- Pica: a digit is correct but in the wrong place

- Fermé: a digit is correct and in the correct place

- Nada: a digit is incorrect

Remember to give clues in the order of pica, fermé, nada, not in the order of the digits, or you'll give away which digits are fermés (correct). For example, if the number is 325 and the guess is 452, you'd say, "Pica, pica, nada." Using the clues, students guess another number. Again, give clues about this guess and keep going in this way until they correctly guess the number.

Once students have figured out the number, ask them open-ended questions about it, such as "What number is in the tens place?" "What is the place value of the three?" "Who can correctly say this number?" As students develop their math skills, use this game to practice working with larger numbers (five or six digits) or decimal places.

Pop-Up Number

Begin with everyone sitting in a circle or at their desks. Name a number from one through ten (for example, three) and explain that this is the "pop-up" number. Going around the circle or room, students count aloud from one to three, and every third student "pops" to their feet and remains standing. Children continue counting until everyone has popped up. For variation: Before choosing a number, ask: "Can anyone predict who will be the last one sitting?" or have the child who pops up say "pop" instead of the number. For older students, use multiples of seven, numbers divisible by twelve, and so on as the number to pop on.

Red Light, Green Light

One person serves as the traffic controller. Everyone else stands on the starting line. The traffic controller stands at the finish line, turns his or her back, and says "Green light." Everyone runs toward the finish line, but when the controller says "Red light" and turns around, they all have to stop. Anyone the controller sees who's still moving has to go back to the starting line. The first person across the finish line without being caught serves as the next traffic controller.

Scavenger Hunt

Use this to help students discover key information in a text, map, chart, or other resource, or new information about a classmate, character, or historical figure. In advance, decide on five to ten items you want students to search for. Use these items to create a Scavenger Hunt Checklist and give a copy to each student. So that everyone stays engaged, tell students they'll have just ten to fifteen minutes to complete the checklist. If students finish early, invite them to share responses with someone else who's finished or to name additional items or information they found interesting. Use the completed checklists to prompt whole-group or small-group discussions. Variation: Invite students to search for items in a category without using a checklist. For example: "Find parallelograms in our classroom."

Skip Counting

You can vary this game as students develop their math skills:

- For K–1 students, start with counting to ten by ones. When they're comfortable with that, practice skip counting by twos, fives, and tens.

- For second graders, start with counting to twenty by twos.

- For third and fourth graders, count by twos to start and then add threes, fours, fives, and tens.

- For fifth and sixth graders, practice counting by sixes, sevens, eights, nines, and so on as they master multiplication facts.

You can add movement to skip counting by having students alternately stand and sit as they count. For example: "Two!" (stand), "Four!" (sit), and so on. Invite students to brainstorm other movements to do as they count, such as jumping jacks or knee bends.

Spider Web Greeting

The student who begins the greeting holds a ball of yarn. He greets someone across the circle and gently rolls or tosses the ball to that person while firmly holding on to the end of the yarn. The person who receives the ball of yarn greets another student across the circle and sends the ball to that student, again making sure to hold on to the unraveling strand of yarn. Continue until everyone has been greeted and the yarn has created a web across the circle. To undo the web, students greet each other in reverse order until the ball of yarn is wound up again.

Swap Meet

Students form pairs and exchange one idea on a current study topic that you've named. Give students about two minutes to swap ideas, and then signal them to mingle and form new partnerships. Encourage students to "collect" as many new ideas as possible, but at least three, and to write them down. You can use this structure to wrap up a unit, prepare for a quiz or test, or brainstorm new ideas on any topic.

Tag Games

- *Blob Tag*—One person starts as the tagger. Once someone is tagged, he or she holds hands with the tagger, forming a blob. Once a fourth person is tagged, all four people can stay together or split up into two separate blobs. Blobs can split apart and rejoin throughout the game as long as everyone who has been tagged is holding hands with at least one other person. The last person tagged becomes the next tagger and starts a new round.

- *Category Tag*—In this variation of Freeze Tag, a category is called (geology terms, favorite books, animals of Asia, etc.). To avoid being tagged, runners shout out something in the chosen category and drop to one knee as the tagger approaches them. This gives runners a short break while the tagger quickly tries to find someone else.

- *Elbow Tag*—One student is the tagger and two or more students are the runners. All the other students link elbows with a partner. The tagger tries to tag a runner. To stay safe, a runner can join elbows with one of the pairs, forming a trio. The student on the opposite side of the trio then has to break off and become a runner. If a runner is tagged, they pause for five seconds and become another tagger.

- *Elves, Wizards, and Giants*—In this variation on rock-paper-scissors, students form two teams and set boundaries consisting of a center line and two opposite end lines (or safety zones). Each team meets in private and chooses one character for their team: elf, wizard, or giant. Teams return to the center line and face each other. When the teacher calls "Go!" each team reveals its character as follows: Giants stand tall with their arms over their heads. Wizards put arms out and wiggle fingers as if casting a spell. Elves kneel and pretend to draw back on a bow and arrow. (If both teams pick the same character, they regroup and choose again.)

On the count of three, one team chases the other, according to their characters: Giants chase wizards, wizards chase elves, and elves chase giants. For example, if Team A is wizards and Team B giants, Team B would chase Team A. Anyone on Team A who can make it back to their end line without being tagged is safe. Anyone on Team A who gets tagged joins Team B for the next round.

- *Excuse Me, Please*—Various bases or markers are spread throughout the playing area. When a player gets tagged, he or she immediately becomes the tagger. The new tagger has to count loudly to five before trying to tag anyone. The markers or bases serve as safety zones. When a player is touching a base or marker, he or she can't be tagged— but only one player at a time can occupy each base or marker. However, if another player comes up to a base or marker that's already occupied, he or she can say, "Excuse me, please," and the player on that base or marker has to leave right away and elude the tagger or find another base or marker.

- ***Fishy, Fishy, Cross My Ocean***—This is similar to Blob Tag. The first tagger stands in the middle of the playing area. Everyone else stands at a starting line, facing the tagger. When the tagger says "Fishy, fishy, cross my ocean," everyone tries to run to the finish line without being caught by the tagger. If they're caught, they immediately become a tagger but have to stay in one place, waving their arms like sea anemones and trying to tag anyone who comes too close as they try to get across the finish line. Keep repeating until only one person is left. He or she then becomes the starting tagger for a new game.

- ***Freeze Tag***—In this classic tag game, there is no safety zone. If a tagger tags you, you freeze in place. Anyone who is not frozen can unfreeze you by touching you. This game works best with a few taggers. When the taggers freeze everyone, a new game starts with new taggers.

- ***Stuck in the Mud***—In this Freeze Tag variation, when students are tagged, they stay stuck in place with their feet spread apart. They can be unstuck when a classmate crawls underneath them.

- ***Toilet Tag***—People who are tagged kneel or sit with an arm extended, to represent the handle. When someone who is free pushes their "handle" down, they make a flushing sound and are free to run again.

Uncommon Commonalities

As students sit in small groups their challenge is to see how many non-obvious commonalities they can discover. For example, although it might be obvious that all group members are in fifth grade, it might be surprising to discover that they all have at least one sister. Students record their "uncommon commonalities" on a piece of paper and share what they discovered with the class. You can also do this activity in content areas—for example, to find similarities between characters or historical figures.

A Warm Wind Blows

Bring enough chairs to the circle for everyone except one person, who will serve as the caller. The caller stands in the middle of the circle and says, "A warm wind blows for anyone who _____," filling in the blank with a category (for example, "knows the answer to ten times twenty" or "likes to play basketball"). Everyone for whom that statement is true comes to the center of the circle and then, along with the caller, quickly finds a new place to sit. The person who doesn't get a seat becomes the next caller and names a new category. Repeat as time allows.

What Are You Doing?

A student goes to the center of the circle and pantomimes a simple action, such as tying her shoes. The next student in the circle approaches her and asks, "What are you doing?" The student tying her shoes responds by saying something completely different, such as "I'm jumping rope," and then resumes her place in the circle. The student who asked now pretends that he's jumping rope. The next student in the circle approaches him and asks, "What are you doing?" This goes on until everyone has had a chance to pantomime an action.

What's the Change?

As a volunteer stands in front of the class, everyone observes him carefully. The student then moves to a place where the class can't see him and changes something subtle about his appearance. For example, he might switch his watch to the other wrist, untie a shoe, or undo a shirt button. He then returns and stands in front of the class. Students use their powers of observation and memory to guess the change.

Who Remembers?

Students share briefly about something: a favorite food or something they do to relax. The teacher takes notes to use in creating "Who remembers?" questions for the group after everyone has shared. For example, the teacher might ask, "Who remembers someone who said their favorite food is frozen yogurt?" "Who remembers someone who said they relax by being near water? Listening to music?"

Word Family Caterpillar

The class works together to collect words in a particular word family. For example, a class might collect words in the "ake" family such as bake, flake, mistake, and so on. Each word is added as a caterpillar segment on a wall display. As students think of new words or learn new words from the same word family, they add a new segment to the caterpillar display.

Songs and Chants

Black Socks

Sing or chant this as a whole group, emphasizing the bold words.

> *Black socks,*
> *They **never** get dirty.*
> *The longer I wear them,*
> *The stronger they get.*
> *Sometimes*
> *I think I should wash them*
> *But something inside me*
> *Keeps saying not yet,*
> *Not yet,*
> ***Not yet.***

Hands Up

This chanting activity helps students build critical-thinking skills. To begin, name a category (adjectives, adverbs, geometric shapes, etc.) to insert in the fourth line of the chant. Sitting in a circle, chant together:

Hands up	(put both hands up)
For 2015	(or current year)
Gonna name	(clap, clap)
Some [category]	(clap, clap)
One apiece	(clap, clap)
No repeats	(clap, clap)
No hesitation	(clap, clap)
No duplication	(clap, clap)
Starting with	(clap, clap)
[Child's name] _____	(child says something that fits in the category)
	(clap, clap)

Keep repeating the chant, each time naming the next person in the circle until everyone has had a turn. Or you can invite the person who just named a category item to choose someone to do the naming next. Do as many rounds as time permits.

Hello, My Name is Joe

This chant gets everyone moving from head to toe.

> *Hello. My name is Joe,*
> *And I work in a button factory.*
> *I have a wife, and a dog, and a family.*
> *One day, my boss said to me,*
> *"Hey, Joe. Are you busy?"*
> *I said, "No."*
> *He said, "Push that button with your right hand."*

On the last line, everyone begins pushing an imaginary button with his or her right hand. The chant then repeats as everyone keeps pushing the button with their right hand. This time, at the last line, the boss tells Joe to push the button with his left hand. Now everyone pushes buttons with both hands. The chant continues, adding in a right foot, left foot, chin, hip, elbow—and whatever other body parts you (or students) want to add, while continuing to keep all the previously named parts in motion. To end the chant, the boss asks, "Are you busy?" Everyone then exclaims, "Yes!"

Hello, Neighbor

Students form an inner and an outer circle and face each other to form pairs, who greet each other using this chant:

Hello, neighbor, what d'ya say?	(wave to partner)
It's gonna be a wonderful day.	(circle arms over head and move down to side)
So clap your hands and boogie on down.	(clap hands and wiggle down)
Give a little bump and turn around.	(gently bump hips and turn in place)

The inner circle then moves one person to the right so everyone has a new partner and repeats the chant. This continues until everyone is back in their original places. For a variation, instead of bumping hips, students can jump ("Give a little jump and turn around") or raise hands high ("Then raise your hands and turn around").

High Low Up & Down

The leader sings or chants:

>*High low*
>*Up and down*
>*Can your voice*
>*Make this sound?*

>Leader in a high voice: *La la la!*
>Group echoes.

>Leader in a low voice: *Ugh ugh ugh!*
>Group echoes.

The leader then repeats the "high-low" verse, offering more sounds for the group to echo (for example, meow, ruff; beep, boom; eep, oop; goo, ga).

Peanut Butter, Grape Jelly

Students get a kick out of this song.

>*Peanut butter, grape jelly*
>*Peanut butter, grape jelly, peanut butter, jam*
>*Peanut butter, grape jelly, peanut butter, jam*
>*Peanut butter, grape jelly, peanut butter, jam*
>*I like peanut butter, yes, yes ma'am*
>*My mother says one day she'll bet*
>*I'll turn to peanut butter so get set*
>*The biggest jar of peanut butter you've ever met*
>*But I haven't turned to peanut butter,*
>*Nope, not yet.*

Ram Sam Sam

Depending on students' energy level, you can have them do this one sitting down or standing up. Practice saying the words and doing the actions together slowly, with emphasis on the bold words. As students gain expertise, say the words faster, slower, softer, and so on.

*A **Ram** Sam **Sam**, A **Ram** Sam **Sam***
*Ghoolie **Ghoolie** Ghoolie **Ghoolie** Ghoolie*
Ram** Sam **Sam!

*A **Ram** Sam **Sam**, A **Ram** Sam **Sam***
*Ghoolie **Ghoolie** Ghoolie **Ghoolie** Ghoolie*
Ram** Sam **Sam!

*A **Raffi**! A **Raffi**,*
*Ghoolie **Ghoolie** Ghoolie **Ghoolie** Ghoolie*
Ram** Sam **Sam!

*A **Raffi**! A **Raffi**!*
*Ghoolie **Ghoolie** Ghoolie **Ghoolie** Ghoolie*
Ram** Sam **Sam!

Actions When Sitting Down

Ram Sam Sam: Make two fists and gently tap them together, alternating which fist is on top when you chant the next line beginning with "Ram."

Ghoolie Ghoolie: Hold arms bent at elbows in front of you and roll forearms around each other.

A Raffi: Lift arms high above you.

Actions When Standing Up

Ram Sam Sam: Stomp your feet, alternating to the beat.

Ghoolie Ghoolie: Twirl around.

A Raffi: Jump up, look up, and reach your hands up high.

We're All Back Together Again

A nice one to use after a weekend or a long holiday break.

1) The group echoes as a leader sings each line:
   Good morning!
   How are you?
   I'm so glad
   To see you!
   Let's sing and
   Be happy
   'Cause we're all back together again!

2) Then everyone chants together:

With a one and a two	(hold up one finger and then two)
And a how do you do?	(pantomime a handshake)
With a big hello	(give a big wave)
We're ready to go	(put fist up in the air with excitement)
We're all back together again!	(circle hand up and around, pointing to the group)

10 Sources for Read-Aloud Books

Reading aloud to students helps them build vocabulary, reading comprehension skills, and listening skills. It's also an opportunity to teach about character, setting, main ideas, and supporting details by asking open-ended questions after you read or at stopping points as you read. For a list of good read-aloud books for students in grades kindergarten through six, ask your school or local librarian, or check out organizations such as the following:

- American Booksellers Association Indies Choice Book Awards/E.B. White Read-Aloud Awards: www.bookweb.org/btw/awards/ICBA.html

- American Library Association (ALA) Book, Print, and Media Awards: www.ala.org/awardsgrants/awards/browse/bpma?showfilter=no

- Bank Street College Best Children's Books of the Year: http://bankstreet.edu/center-childrens-literature/childrens-book-committee/best-books-year

- International Literacy Association Choices Reading Lists: www.reading.org/resources/booklists.aspx

- National Education Association (NEA) Teachers' Top 100 Books for Children: www.nea.org/grants/teachers-top-100-books-for-children.html; Reading All Year Long: www.nea.org/grants/resources-to-get-reading.htm

- Read Aloud America: www.readaloudamerica.org

- Reading Is Fundamental: www.rif.org

- Storyline Online: www.storylineonline.net

- United Through Reading: www.unitedthroughreading.org/booklist/booktype/featured-books

- World Read Aloud Day: www.litworld.org

Planning for Special Situations

There's always some unpredictability to the school year—a new student appears one morning, we catch the flu or our child does, an opportunity suddenly arises for a great field trip, and so on. These types of events happen every year, and although we never know when they'll pop up, we do know they *will* pop up eventually!

Here are some general guidelines to help you prepare for the unexpected:

- *Keep name tags handy*—When a new student, guest teacher, or tour guide on a field trip can use students' names, everyone feels valued and is more likely to be cooperative and productive.

- *Discuss possible scenarios before they happen*—Of course, we can't always anticipate certain situations. But just as we practice fire drills so students know what to do should a real emergency occur, we can help prepare them for special events and times when we're absent. In advance, let students know what to expect for these times and discuss how to keep the learning going.

- *Connect to class rules*—When discussing expectations for a field trip, new student, or guest teacher, help students use the class rules. For example: "What are some ways we can follow our rules when a guest teacher is here?" "How might our rules help us welcome a new student?" Consider bringing a copy of the class rules on a field trip to help everyone remember that the rules apply whenever the class is together.

Guest (Substitute) Teacher

Few teachers make it through an entire year without missing a day. Having plans in place can help students be prepared for working with another teacher in our absence. Here are some tips:

- *Use the term "guest teacher"*—Unlike the more common "substitute teacher," this title conveys a sense of authority, welcome, and respect. After all, they are a teacher and a guest of the class. This simple change in terminology can help set everyone up for a better day.

- *Stick to a few key routines*—Which parts of the day can the class do fairly well independently? Make sure these are included in the plans. For example, consider a fifty-minute reading period instead of a thirty-five-minute one if that's a good time of day for the class. Try not to include parts of the day that are especially challenging for students or ones that require a lot of management by the guest teacher.

- *Provide plans for the guest teacher and a colleague*—Once plans are set, leave a copy for the guest teacher and also give one to a colleague. If possible, ask a colleague to introduce the guest teacher to the class to help begin the day on a positive, welcoming note.

New Student

It's not that unusual for a new student to suddenly appear at any point during the school year. With a little preparation, we can help the class welcome the new student so he or she feels included right from the start. Here are some tips:

- *Have a set of supplies ready*—Keep a set of basic supplies handy (writing journal, book bin, and so on) in case a new student arrives. He or she will feel taken care of and time won't be wasted scurrying around looking for supplies.

- *Designate two helpers*—Designate two students, ideally a boy and a girl, to help the new student get acclimated. They can help explain how to order lunch, use the bathroom sign-out system, and handle other important logistics. They can also invite the new student to play with them at recess and eat with them at lunch.

- *Have a seat ready*—If possible, have at least one open seat in the classroom in case a new student arrives. Also, have the two designated helpers sit with the new student so they can show him or her the classroom "ropes" throughout the day.

- *Have a Morning Meeting planned*—At the start of the year, design a Morning Meeting that will work well with a new student in the room. Keep it low-risk and welcoming. For example:

  • *Greeting:* Greet neighbors in the circle with a simple "Good morning" handshake.

- *Sharing:* Use an around-the-circle sharing, such as "One thing you like to do outside of school."

- *Group activity:* Try "A Warm Wind Blows" (page 275), using categories that will help the new student make connections with the class (hobbies, pets, favorite foods, and so on).

- *Morning message:* Use the same message as you would regularly.

Indoor Recess

Some students look forward to indoor recess; others do not. Here are some tips to help this time go more smoothly for everyone:

- **Scaffold**—Early in the year, consider offering just a few choices, such as drawing or playing previously learned games. As the year goes on, add in more choices and complexity, just as you would do in other areas when students are ready. For example, you might offer a variety of board games, computer games, or open free time. Also consider joining with another class and letting students move between classrooms.

- **Label materials for indoor recess**—Will you reserve certain materials such as jigsaw puzzles and board games exclusively for indoor recess? If so, have these labeled and stored separately. I had a storage shelf designated just for games. Anything with a red sticky dot meant it was available as a math game; a yellow dot was a literacy game; and a green dot was just for indoor recess.

- **Monitor**—Because indoor recess can be challenging for some students, move around the room and check in with them, making sure everyone is on track.

Field Trips

Students will be more successful with field trips if we start to prepare them early in the year. Here are some tips:

- **Scaffold**—Could the class walk to a place nearby for a short, simple first field trip? Younger grade students might walk to a neighborhood grocery store as they learn about their community. Older grade students might walk to a local park to make science observations. This allows us to model and students to practice routines so they're ready for more extended trips later in the year.

- ***Give concrete learning tasks***—One way to set an academic tone for any field trip is by assigning specific tasks for that trip: students might answer a list of questions, draw a map, compile notes, or take photos.

- ***Set chaperones up for success***—Whether chaperones are parent volunteers or other staff members, give them a specific list of responsibilities. Make sure that students who are likely to struggle with self-control stay with you or other school personnel who can best support them.

About the *Responsive Classroom*® Approach

All of the recommended practices in this book come from or are consistent with the *Responsive Classroom* approach to teaching—an evidence-based education approach associated with greater teacher effectiveness, higher student achievement, and improved school climate. *Responsive Classroom* practices help educators build competencies in four interrelated domains: engaging academics, positive community, effective management, and developmentally responsive teaching.

To learn more, see the following resources published by Center for Responsive Schools and available from www.responsiveclassroom.org • 800-360-6332.

Classroom Management: Set up and run a classroom in ways that enable the best possible teaching and learning.

> *Interactive Modeling: A Powerful Technique for Teaching Children* by Margaret Berry Wilson. 2012.

> *What Every Teacher Needs to Know*, K–5 series, by Margaret Berry Wilson and Mike Anderson. 2010–2011. (Includes one book at each grade level.)

> *Teaching Children to Care: Classroom Management for Ethical and Academic Growth K–8*, revised ed., by Ruth Sidney Charney. 2002.

Morning Meeting: Gather as a whole class each morning to greet each other, share news, and warm up for the day of learning ahead.

The Morning Meeting Book, 3rd ed., by Roxann Kriete and Carol Davis. 2014.

80 Morning Meeting Ideas for Grades K–2 by Susan Lattanzi Roser. 2012.

80 Morning Meeting Ideas for Grades 3–6 by Carol Davis. 2012.

Doing Language Arts in Morning Meeting: 150 Quick Activities That Connect to Your Curriculum by Jodie Luongo, Joan Riordan, and Kate Umstatter. 2015. (Includes a Common Core State Standards correlation guide.)

Doing Math in Morning Meeting: 150 Quick Activities That Connect to Your Curriculum by Andy Dousis and Margaret Berry Wilson. 2010. (Includes a Common Core State Standards correlation guide.)

Doing Science in Morning Meeting: 150 Quick Activities That Connect to Your Curriculum by Lara Webb and Margaret Berry Wilson. 2013. (Includes correlation guides to the Next Generation Science Standards and *A Framework for K–12 Science Education*, the basis for the standards.)

Doing Social Studies in Morning Meeting: 150 Quick Activities That Connect to Your Curriculum by Leah Carson and Jane Cofie. May 2017. (Includes correlation guides to the National Curriculum Standards for Social Studies—The Themes of Social Studies, the *College, Career, & Civic Life C3 Framework for Social Studies State Standards*, and the Common Core State Standards for English Language Arts.)

Morning Meeting Professional Development Kit. 2008.

Positive Teacher Language: Use words and tone as a tool to promote children's active learning, sense of community, and self-discipline.

The Power of Our Words: Teacher Language That Helps Children Learn, 2nd ed., by Paula Denton, EdD. 2014.

Teacher Language for Engaged Learning: 4 Video Study Sessions. 2013.

Teacher Language Professional Development Kit. 2010.

Engaging Academics: Learn tools for effective teaching and making lessons lively, appropriately challenging, and purposeful to help children develop higher levels of motivation, persistence, and mastery of skills and content.

The Joyful Classroom: Practical Ways to Engage and Challenge Students K–6. From *Responsive Classroom.* 2016.

The Language of Learning: Teaching Students Core Thinking, Speaking, and Listening Skills by Margaret Berry Wilson. 2014.

Teaching Discipline: Use practical strategies, such as rule creation and positive responses to misbehavior, to promote self-discipline in students and build a safe, calm, and respectful school climate.

Teasing, Tattling, Defiance and More: Positive Approaches to 10 Common Classroom Behaviors by Margaret Berry Wilson. 2013.

Rules in School: Teaching Discipline in the Responsive Classroom, 2nd ed., by Kathryn Brady, Mary Beth Forton, and Deborah Porter. 2011.

Responsive School Discipline: Essentials for Elementary School Leaders by Chip Wood and Babs Freeman-Loftis. 2011.

Teaching Discipline in the Classroom Professional Development Kit. 2011.

Movement, Games, Songs, and Chants: Sprinkle quick, lively activities throughout the school day to keep students energized, engaged, and alert.

Closing Circles: 50 Activities for Ending the Day in a Positive Way by Dana Januszka and Kristen Vincent. 2012.

Energizers! 88 Quick Movement Activities That Refresh and Refocus by Susan Lattanzi Roser. 2009.

99 Activities and Greetings: Great for Morning Meeting . . . and other meetings, too! by Melissa Correa-Connolly. 2004.

Special Area Educators: Explore key *Responsive Classroom* practices adapted for a wide variety of special areas.

Responsive Classroom for Music, Art, PE and Other Special Areas. From *Responsive Classroom.* 2016.

Preventing Bullying at School: Use practical strategies throughout the day to create a safe, kind environment in which bullying is far less likely to take root.

How to Bullyproof Your Classroom by Caltha Crowe. 2012. (Includes bullying prevention lessons.)

Solving Behavior Problems With Children: Engage children in solving their behavior problems so they feel safe, challenged, and invested in changing.

Sammy and His Behavior Problems: Stories and Strategies from a Teacher's Year by Caltha Crowe. 2010.

Solving Thorny Behavior Problems: How Teachers and Students Can Work Together by Caltha Crowe. 2009.

Teasing, Tattling, Defiance and More: Positive Approaches to 10 Common Classroom Behaviors by Margaret Berry Wilson. 2013.

Child Development: Understand children's common physical, social-emotional, cognitive, and language characteristics at each age, and adapt teaching to respond to children's developmental needs.

Yardsticks: Children in the Classroom Ages 4–14, 3rd ed., by Chip Wood. 2007.

Child Development Pamphlet Series, K–8 (based on *Yardsticks* by Chip Wood; in English or Spanish). 2005 and 2006.

Professional Development/Staff Meetings: Learn easy-to-use structures for getting the most out of your work with colleagues.

Energize Your Meetings! 35 Interactive Learning Structures for Educators. From *Responsive Classroom.* 2014.

Roxann Kriete taught at both the elementary and secondary levels during her thirty-five-year career in education. She began working at Center for Responsive Schools (then Northeast Foundation for Children) in 1985, retiring in 2011 after serving for ten years as the organization's executive director.

Paula Denton, EdD, began teaching children in 1982 and working as a *Responsive Classroom* consulting teacher in 1990. She later managed program development at Center for Responsive Schools.

Mike Anderson taught third, fourth, and fifth grades for fifteen years in Connecticut and New Hampshire. In 2004, Mike was the recipient of a Milken National Educator Award for excellence in teaching. He began presenting *Responsive Classroom* workshops in 1999 and later joined Center for Responsive Schools as a *Responsive Classroom* consultant and program developer.

ABOUT THE PUBLISHER

Center for Responsive Schools, Inc., a not-for-profit educational organization, is the developer of *Responsive Classroom*, an evidence-based education approach associated with greater teacher effectiveness, higher student achievement, and improved school climate. *Responsive Classroom* practices help educators build competencies in four interrelated domains: engaging academics, positive community, effective management, and developmentally responsive teaching. We offer the following resources for educators:

PROFESSIONAL DEVELOPMENT SERVICES

- Workshops for K–8 educators (locations around the country and internationally)
- On-site consulting services to support implementation
- Resources for site-based study
- Annual conferences for K–8 educators

PUBLICATIONS AND RESOURCES

- Books on a wide variety of *Responsive Classroom* topics
- Professional development kits for school-based study
- Free monthly newsletter
- Extensive library of free articles on our website

FOR DETAILS, CONTACT:

Responsive Classroom®

Center for Responsive Schools, Inc.
85 Avenue A, P.O. Box 718
Turners Falls, Massachusetts 01376-0718

800-360-6332 ■ www.responsiveclassroom.org
info@responsiveclassroom.org